Cape Breton
W O R K S

MORE LIVES FROM **CAPE BRETON'S MAGAZINE**
EDITED BY RONALD CAPLAN

D1590473

Breton Books
Wreck Cove, Cape Breton Island
1996

Unless otherwise noted, most photographs are by Ronald Caplan.

Photo of the Martell children on page 37 by Clara Dennis, courtesy photo collection, Public Archives of Nova Scotia. The photographs in Hattie Carmichael's chapter: milking on page 86 from Josie Matheson Bredbury; potatoes on page 87 and sheaves on page 91 courtesy *Canadian Geographic Magazine*; pile of hay on page 92 and bundles of wool on page 97 from Ruth Matheson, North Shore; woman with scythe on page 92 and shearing on page 96 from Malcolm MacDonald, Fourchu; niddy-noddy on page 97 from Beaton Institute, University College of Cape Breton. In Gordie MacDougall's story, most of the formal boxing pictures that did not come from the boxers themselves came from the collection of the late Art MacVicar, New Waterford. Most of the photographs of Joe Delaney's scarecrows are by Daniel Aucoin of Cheticamp.

Production Assistance: Bonnie Thompson
Darkroom Work: Grant Young and Carol Kennedy
Typesetting: Glenda Watt and Wendy Wishart

Canadian Cataloguing in Publication Data

Cape Breton works

(Canada's Atlantic folklore-folklife series)
ISBN 1-895415-24-1

1. Cape Breton (Nova Scotia) — Biography. I. Caplan, Ronald, 1942-
II. Series

FC2343.3A1C3 1995   971.6'9'00992   C95-950267-X
F1039.C2C3 1995

INCLUDED IN BREAKWATER BOOKS'
Canada's Atlantic Folklore-Folklife Series

Cape Breton Works is a mate to **Cape Breton Lives**, a book of selections from **Cape Breton's Magazine** published by Breakwater Books in 1988 as part of Breakwater Books' splendid Canada's Atlantic Folklore-Folklife Series. **Cape Breton Works** is being included in that series as well, despite that it has been published by Breton Books. Our thanks to Clyde Rose, Breakwater's publisher, for the honour of including two of our books in what is a major contribution to publishing in the Atlantic Region.

DEDICATION
This one belongs to Bonnie Thompson,
without whom....

Contents

Editor's Introduction

What seems to me to be of particular value is not so much what happened to people as what they made of what they had—and what, looking back, they find worth telling.

I continue to sit amazed at the generosity of time and the careful attention people offer in relating these stories—even that they bother at all. I sometimes see my role—recording stories in Cape Breton at the end of the 20th Century—as replacing a generation that has gone down the road or into television- or even cyber-space, leaving me with their elders at the kitchen table or on the back porch, interested and asking and being told, not in any hurry to get away, actually eager to go through an album or the old tools in the basement, photographing everything, taping, visiting the stones in a restored cemetery or the foundation of their family's first home. But that's not entirely fair. A lot of the generations who might be listening *are* listening—and I find that extraordinary as well.

This engagement—I've said it so often—my being there, is *not* the old way. First of all, there's my tape recorder. And the photographs and stories will probably end up in *Cape Breton's Magazine*, and I will sell what I collect back to the community from which the stories first came. An odd engagement. And still they take time with me, give careful attention to detail, give welcome and encouragement and thanks.

I think a lot about how people put their lives together, about whether or not they had choices, and how their lives fell into place. Over and over, I hear of some who had no opportunities except if they went away. And of others who could have been what they see as so much more, had they been able to stay away, had they not "got the call" to come home—and being the youngest or the oldest or the only one unmarried, came back to take over the farm, the fishing grounds, teach in the community, handle central for the ring-down telephone—and in addition care for the old people until they died.

I think of this in terms of myself.

I never forget that I came to Cape Breton at what felt to me as just about the end of the road. I fell in among a people who interested me and treated me well, perhaps out of habit, perhaps out of pity, perhaps because they saw value in me of which I had lost track. In any case, it sustained me long enough to focus on the place and my own possibilities in terms of the place, long enough to create *Cape Breton's Magazine*. That was in 1972.

Cape Breton WORKS is the fifth book of selections from the magazine that has been my work for almost 25 years.

I cannot think of my days in Cape Breton as anything other than an arena where I was given space to find what I could do, to hone whoever I am, bound by the freedom and bondage of the materials and the deadlines—and the permission to gather, and to give back.

I don't really know what desperate young people are doing to get their lives together today. I sometimes think of the losses here of everything from industries to the semi-independent fisherman-farms as the loss of a kind of sheltered holding tank for people without direction—the loss of arenas in which skills and attitude toward skills can be learned, while cutting wood for a season, working shifts in the General Yard at the Steel Plant, bringing in hay on a farm where the older people could no longer manage, hanging on the other end of a crosscut saw for strength and stories and three meals a day. For a time. For self worth. Even for entertainment. Some informed rock in the stream to cling to, some chance to be of value, something solid from which to step off, to leave or to stay, to make a life.

There seem to me to be fewer and fewer of these arenas that can absorb people when their only alternative is to run away, marry, or hang themselves—these arenas that put them alongside skilled people, in the home, on the water or in the woods.

I don't have much more to say about this. It comes to mind when I think about how Cape Breton works. I do not know what is to be done. I just don't know.

In my case, I continue to travel Cape Breton with a tape recorder and a camera and I listen to stories of what another has called "extraordinary ordinary people," which is my work, collecting a record of lives others have accomplished, and of the Cape Breton they achieved. I listen for evidence, testimony.

And I continue to walk that odd line between being a business person and being a researcher, being involved and detached. No one that I interview has any doubt but that our being together is aimed toward the next issue of *Cape Breton's Magazine*, and I am never entirely free of knowing that there are ads to be sold, stories to be edited, and the magazine itself delivered to the stores. These kinds of deadlines keep me going even when other kinds of urgency fail, and store sales and ad sales reflect on the fact that this isn't pure scholarship, but rather the longterm survival of a publication tested, issue by issue, in the community from which it has come. I like that risk and affirmation.

And I like this realization: that Cape Breton Island is an achievement. It is a day-to-day accomplishment. I know it in the the fierceness with which the home-and-school, the local hall, the church, the older ways, the respect for hospitality and conversation, good times, family—are still unashamedly defended here. I know it in the stories told out of Cape Breton lives.

Cape Breton WORKS is a book about love and boxing and sailing and accidents that didn't happen—it is centred on food and family and farming and fishing, coal and steel—on going away and coming back and dealing with possiblities and with what was thrown in their way. *Cape Breton WORKS* is a book about some of the strategies and techniques of survival in a tough, tough place—the voices of surviving remnants in a world under siege. The telling of stories is just one of those strategies, those accomplishments.

Ronald Caplan
Cape Breton's Magazine
Wreck Cove
Cape Breton Island

Margaret Neil James MacNeil:
A Love Story

I was born in Scotch Lake to Neil and Isabel Beaton. And there were
twelve children in the family. From what I've been told, when I was very,
very young, we were fairly well set. My father worked in the quarry. He
went to work in the quarry when he was only eleven years old, as a water
carrier. And my mother was a great worker, and they got along great.

Until 1939. My father got hurt in the quarry. He broke one hip and he
fractured the other one, and as a result of it, he got a piece of steel in his
eye, and he went blind.

There were twelve of us—four boys and eight girls. There was Kathe-
rine and Angus and Duncan and Annie and Martin and Mary Sarah and
Mary Florence. And then came myself. Then there was Mary, Elizabeth,
and Florence, and John David.

My most vivid memory is in 1939 when my father got hurt. I'll never
forget that evening. One of the neighbours came to the house and told us

1

that my father was hurt and they were taking him to North Sydney. And my mother always had a pair of clean socks when he came home from work because his feet would be always wet from sweating and working. She grabbed the socks off the clothesline that was hanging over the stove in the kitchen, and she took off. And we all stayed home and prayed.

And the next thing we heard was my father was in the hospital. And of course, this was a real tragedy as far as we were concerned, because Daddy was so precious to us, you know. He never came home from work in the quarry, that I can remember—now, I was only about eight years old at this time—but before that I can remember, the five younger girls would always go to meet him. And he'd always leave something in the lunch can. Today I'd get it and tomorrow another one would get it. But he always had some little thing to give us. And I can remember, every time we would meet him in the road, he'd open the lunch can for whatever was in there, and give it to us.

And he never ever treated one of us different to the other. We were his, and—he was great. He was a great person. Affectionate, very affectionate father.

And you could see the love between him and my mother so clearly. I still remember—one of the things he always did was brought my mother a cup of tea in bed in the morning, before she got up. And then went to the barn and did the barn chores. And my mother would have breakfast [ready] when he got [back]. And when he got hurt, that was one thing he asked us to continue doing for him. "See that your mother gets a cup of tea before she gets up in the morning." And we always did it. And even when it came to my brother Martin that was home the last with her, Martin always saw that she got her cup of tea.

And [the accident] wasn't bad enough. Two weeks [before my father got hurt]—it was on the 18th of April, the house burned, in 1939.

[The house was] completely destroyed. I'll never forget that day. Remember an old lady down home. At that time we used to call her Mrs. Hanson. She ended up to be a Mrs. MacDonald before she died, and she was over 100 before she died. And she was a great friend of ours, particularly my mother's. And she came to the school and told the boys to go home. But we didn't think anything of it, you know. She left the girls all in school. But it was that the house was burning, and the men from the quarry ran over with the trucks. So, when we got to the top of the hill where we could see the house—Ann and I and Sarah were the ones that were left in school. My oldest sister stayed home that day because Mum wasn't well. So she was home to take the smaller ones out of the house.

They said there was—you know, there used to be loose bricks in the attic, to [get in to] clean the chimney. And they figured that a spark must have got in the attic some-how. Because the fire started up there. And my sister went to the well to get some water. And when she was on her way back, she saw the smoke coming out around the eaves of the house. And she hurried back to the house. And my mother got the kids out. And sat up on the hill with the children to protect them from going back in the house. Because they wanted their new shoes and they wanted their stuff, their treasures, and she had to hang onto them. So she had to sit and watch the house burn.

Margaret's parents, Neil and Isabel Beaton, Scotch Lake, July 28, 1951

The only thing they saved was a table that my grandfather in North Sydney had made my mother. And that table is still down in Scotch Lake. And that's the only thing that they saved.

But anyway, the people were very good to help us out. As luck would have it, my father had enough money saved—and that was right after the Depression—that he was able to pay a carpenter to build the outside of the house—you know, build the shell of the house, and stud it. (*And there was no insurance?*) No such a thing.

Look—that's where I think I learned so much about being good to your neighbour, and doing for somebody else, instead of being selfish and wanting to do for yourself all the time. Because my mother was the kind of person, when anybody was sick, she went and helped them. And she got people ready when they died, prepared them for [death]—put them in their coffin. My father was one of those, if there was a baby born and it wasn't well, my father would quit work at the quarry and go to Bras d'Or to have that baby baptized, regardless if he lost time or not, it didn't mean a thing to him.

He was a very religious—oh, yes. The rosary was—well, if you didn't say the rosary, forget it. You were going to be given one hell of a tongue-lashing....

And I often heard my father say that the day that he got hurt—he often

3

thought about it after that. He had a sick cow that day. And he was down in the barn a lot longer than he intended to be. And he hurried back home to have his breakfast, to get off to work. And he always took his cap off, when he went outside of the house, when he was going to work. I remember seeing him doing that. No matter what weather there was, he took his cap off and he blessed himself, and he said some prayers. On his way to work. And he'd be walking, of course, all the time. And—it was only about a half mile to his work.

But that morning, he said, he didn't do it. And he always said, "Look what happened. So whatever you do, don't forget your prayers in the morning." So, prayer meant an awful lot to us all, because of him telling us that story.

My father went blind shortly after he got hurt, from the accident. He got a piece of steel in his eye.... But one eye affected the other. And I remember the first time I knew he was blind. See, on account of him being hurt, he hid it on my mother. Because he didn't go totally blind at one time. He got blind over a length of time. But see, he had crutches. And we'd be helping him. So, he didn't have to go too far, and he was quite familiar with everything. So, he could see out of the side of his eye first.

And then one day I was home—oh, several years after that—I was home with him and I was sick. And I said, "Daddy, I'd love to have a drink of water." And he said, "Well, there's no water in, dear, but it won't be long before there will be." And he took the bucket, and he went to the spring to get some water. And whatever happened—he used to count the steps, you know. And whatever happened to him, whether he was excited over the fact that I was sick and I wanted a drink of water and he was hurrying—he missed the gate. And he kept up the road. And he got astray. And he couldn't get himself back home.

So he was hollering. And I heard the hollering, and I went out. I went over and I told him to come back down, "You're too far up. Come back down." So I went to meet him at the gate and I took him home. And I said, "How come you did that, Daddy?" He said, "Well, I'm blind, dear. But don't tell your mother. As long as I can keep it from her, she's got enough worries on her shoulders without that."

So he was quite awhile before Mum realized that he was really totally blind. He didn't want to give her any more of a burden than she had.

I was very close to my father. Yeah.

But anyway, I went to work different places.... So from that, I used to go back home every once in awhile. I'd just have a day off and I'd go home. Usually when we went home we helped Mum, you know, house-clean or bake or do whatever had to be done.

When I grew up, I thought that I would like to be a Sister, because I

4

worked with the Sisters in the hospital in North Sydney, and then I worked in the orphanage in Bras d'Or for awhile. But even before that, I thought about being a Sister. And I used to talk to my father about it. My sisters went to be nuns. Sisters Mary and Elizabeth went in August 1952 and Sister Florence went in August 1953.

But anyway, I gathered some [information] and asked some questions and all. So then this day I went home. He'd be out at the woodpile. He was blind, you know. But he'd mark the stick of wood with his arm. And he'd saw the wood. So he was sitting out on the woodpile. And I went out and I said to him, "Daddy, you know what? I was thinking that there's something more I can do to save my soul than to lock myself up in a convent." And he said, "Well, dear, if that's what you think, you'd better not go for awhile yet. You think about it."

So I just didn't say anything more about it. Because I felt that there were my parents—and at that time if you went to the Sisters, you didn't dare think of coming home. Supposing people died, you might get home, but you might not, too. So I said there was no way I was going to leave my parents like that. And my older sisters were working, and one was married at that time, and the other one—I think Ann was married then, too. So I decided, "To heck with this. I'm going to keep on working as I am."

It so happened that my brother's wife got sick in Baddeck—Duncan's wife. So I stayed over there, and helped her. And then, once she got on her feet, I worked for a little while in the telephone office over there. And then I looked after an old lady who was 102 when I left there. I worked there for thirteen months. An old Mrs. Roberts.

And I left there the 1st of August, 1954. And decided that I was going to go to work in Sydney. I had a chance for a job in St. Rita's Hospital. I was twenty-two.

But anyway, this was when I saw the picture of the little children in the paper. This Neil James MacNeil was looking for someone to help him look after the three children. And it said in the newspaper—their picture was in there, and it said, "We are Francis 3 1/2, Mary 2 1/2, Michael 1 1/2. We would like someone to help Daddy take care of

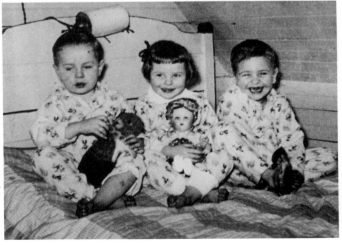

us." It was an advertisement in the *Victoria-Inverness Bulletin*. And it said, "You will get a good home and wages. Apply Neil James MacNeil, Gillis Point." And I didn't know where Gillis Point was, and I didn't know who the people were or anything.

But I had friends in Baddeck who I always went to church with. And we were going to confession that evening, and they picked me up. This was a Saturday evening. And I said, "Did you see the picture of the little ones in the paper?" And poor Tena MacLean, Lord rest her, said, "Yes." And I said, "Wouldn't I like to go tackle that job!" And I said, "But I don't know if I can do it or not. If he still needs anybody or if I can do it or not." So, she never said anything.

But she was related to Neil. She never said she knew him or anything. So, I guess when she went home that night she called over to her cousin over here, Mary Dan D., and asked Mary if Neil had got anybody. And—I laugh about it now, because, you know, the way things'll happen!

So anyway, I had a couple more days to finish at Roberts', and I had told that old Mrs. Roberts' grandson, Willie, that if he would get me paper, I would paper the living room and her bedroom upstairs, that needed papering, before I'd leave. So, I was upstairs this Monday morning, finishing papering this bedroom. And it was just around noontime. And the phone rang. So I went and answered the phone, and here was Tena. And she said, "I have a visitor up here for you." And I said, "Oh, what? Who's that?" And she said, "The father of those three children." "Oh, my Lord," I said, "don't let him come down here yet." And I said, "How did this happen?" And she said, "I phoned over, and he doesn't have anybody, any housekeeper, so he's wondering about you." So I said, "Well, keep him there, for goodness' sakes, until I get cleaned up." I was just finishing papering and I had the border to put up. So she said, "Okay."

So Tena went to give him the tea. But Neil James was anxious to get down to see me and get back, because he was driving the schoolbus. So I went upstairs and I put the border on the bedroom, and I came down and I got washed. So the knock came on the door. "Lo and behold," I said, "I lost this job, whatever'll happen." Because I looked like death warmed over, with a pair of overalls on me and a plastic apron, and my hair up. So I said, "Oh, heck with it, I'll give it a shot, anyway."

So, I opened the door, and there was Neil.

And I said, "You'll have to excuse the look of me because"—I told him what I was doing. He said, "Look, if I came here and saw you all dressed up, I wouldn't think too much of you." And I said, "Well that's okay then." I said, "You sure hit the jackpot then...."

So he said, "I won't take too much of your time. I just wondered if it was possible for you to come and help me."

6

See, he kept the three oldest. The baby was taken by the grandmother until he would get somebody to look after this. So he told me about the three children. But he didn't say anything about his parents and his aunt....

He came over to get me the 1st of September. He sent me a very nice letter after I said yes, I'd try it. He wanted to know if I wanted to come over to see the place before the 1st of September. So I wrote a letter back—no, that I wanted to do some things for my brother's wife—her housecleaning. And I wanted to take her children to Sydney and get clothes for the kids for school, and stuff for school for them. And I said, "I'll come the 1st of September...."

But anyway, John Elliott MacNeil down here—may the Lord rest him—went over to Baddeck with him, to get me. And we drove John Elliott home—he just lived down across from the schoolhouse. Neil James drove the schoolbus. And when he got down to the end of the road, he stopped the bus and

Margaret in Baddeck, before she went to work in Iona

he said, "I have something to tell you." And I said, "Oh"—to myself—"Lord, I hope you've got those kids you're talking about!" But I didn't say it to him, you know.

He said, "I have my mother and father with me." He said, "You know, when I got married," he said, "I promised to look after them. And," he said, "I have to try and do my best to look after them. But," he said, "they're a really big help to me." As far as he was concerned, he didn't think they were going to be any problem.

I said, "Well, that's all right." In fact, I thought that was kind of nice, you know, to have more adults in the house.

And then he said, "But there's something else."

I said to myself, "Good night, what else!" Here I was over here and I didn't know how to get out of here, no matter what. So I said, "What else?" And he said, "Aunt Lucy is with me. But," he said, "she won't stay too long. We'll likely have to put her in the Home." And I said, "Well, just don't jump the gun. We'll see how it—it can't be that bad. We'll see how we get along."

We came up to the house. I got out. And I can see the kids yet, coming to meet me. And I had bananas for them. They weren't one bit interested in the bananas. All they wanted to do was hold my hand. And as far as they were concerned, I was the one that they prayed for, that was going to keep

7

them together. Because Neil always used to tell them to pray that they'd get someone to help him look after them.

And he told me after that [before I came] Francis was in the barn one day with him, and Francis was sitting on the milk stool, and he was shaking straw. And he said, "Daddy." And his father didn't answer him. So he said, "Daddy," again. "Well," Neil said, "I guess I'd better answer him." He said, "What?" Francis said, "Suppose if I prayed hard enough, would God send us another Mommy?" So, Neil's answer was, "Children, pray hard that God will send us someone to look after you."

Because Neil at that time had no intentions of getting married again. That was out of the question, as far as he was concerned. And he always feared that he couldn't love anybody as much as he loved Kay. And I admired him an awful lot for that.

I got along great with the kids right from the very start. And with his parents, too. Neil took me to the house and he introduced me to his parents, and he had to hurry to do the barn work because Fr. Rankin was being waked at Iona that evening, and we were all going to go.

So, while he was at the barn, Grandma asked me where I was from. And I said, "I'm from a place called Scotch Lake. It's near Bras d'Or." I said, "I don't know if you ever heard of it before." She said, "Oh, yes, I did." She said, "There was a friend of mine that used to go out to Scotch Lake." And she said, "I'm sorry I can't tell you her right name. But they used to call her Flora Kimber because she worked for the Kimbers." And I said, "Well, her name was Flora Gillis, and she was my grand-aunt—my father's aunt. And my father was the nephew that she used to go and houseclean for." And she said, "Well, if you'll be half as good as her, you'll get along just fine!"

So that was my introduction to Gillis Point.

The next thing she said was, "Can you make biscuits?" And I said, "Well, I can make a good stab at it." And she said, "Well, we're short of bread, and I forgot to tell Neil to get some." So I said, "Okay." So she said, "I'll heat up the fire, and you make a pan of biscuits, and we'll have supper."

So when Neil came in there was a pan of biscuits in the oven and there was a bonnach on the end of the table. And Neil said in Gaelic to his mother, "What in the world did you do?" He thought that I was going to get discouraged right away. And she told him—in Gaelic, of course—that the bread was low, and she asked me if I could make a pan of biscuits. Her hands were quite crippled and she found it hard to bake. So, when I realized what he said, I said, "Oh, that's all right. I might as well start today as tomorrow...."

But anyway, we went to the wake and to the funeral [of Fr. Rankin].

8

And I found out after that Neil had sent a letter to Fr. Rankin telling him that Kay had died, and sent money for a Mass. And he said to him, "Before long"—in the letter back—he had got a letter about the middle of August from him—"before long, you'll have someone to look after your chil-

Margaret Beaton and Neil James MacNeil
at a school picnic in MacNeil's Vale

dren." And Neil also told him that if he didn't get somebody by the 1st of September, that he was going to have to consider giving the children up. And this was just killing him. But I didn't know that till after I came here. He was in a pretty bad position. Because he travelled, and he had everybody looking for somebody. But it was hard to get anybody to come. Especially when he had his parents and his aunt.

But I was in my glory. I thought it was just the best place I struck yet, you know. To me, the wash done, the baking done, and the meals made, was the most important things. And if anybody was sick. As far as polishing the floor, and all the rest of the fancy things, they were secondary. You know.

(*And how did you fit in first?*) Well, when Neil would go anywheres, they'd cry to go with him. He couldn't go anywheres, except on the schoolbus. When he went on the bus run, they'd stay home. But any other time, he was going to the store or he was going anywheres, they followed him all around the fields, everywheres. But after I came, the next time he was going somewhere, "Where're you going, Daddy?" And he'd say where he was going. "Well, 'bye!" And if they wanted to go to Iona— they used to call ice cream "peem." So Neil would say, "Do you want to come to Iona with me and I'll get you some peem?" And they wouldn't go unless I'd go. They wouldn't leave me home. They were like they were guarding me, you know, that I wouldn't go anywhere on them.

So I remember one Saturday I was half through scrubbing the kitchen floor. And they wanted to go to Iona so bad. And it was near time for the store to close. I had to go to Iona like I was, to let them get their ice cream and come back home, because they wouldn't go without me! But I'll never forget that day. I said, "For goodness' sakes, I hope nothing happens on the way." Because I wasn't very well dressed, going heading to Iona.

In November I went to South Cove to a dance, with the neighbours down here. And Mary woke up—she always slept in a single bed in her father's room. And Francis slept with his father, and Michael was in a cot, in a crib. But when Mary woke up at night, she came in across the hall, into the bed with me. And she started this night across the hall to go in bed with me. And Neil hollered at her to come back. And she said, "I'm going to bed with Margaret." And he said, "No, come back here." And she kept going. She pushed the door open and she saw I wasn't in the bed, and she started to cry. She said, "Margaret's gone!" And he said, "Oh, she's only down at Jimmy Allen's"—this was the house down below here. Which was where I went, but then I went from there to the dance. And she looked out and she saw that—"She's not—there's no lights on." And she said, "She's gone, just like Mommy, and she's not coming any more." And she started to cry and screech. And he did everything to try to keep her quiet.

Well, when I came home, he and her were sitting on the trunk in the hall. And I never saw a child in such a state in my life. And he was pretty upset. And he just said to me, "Go in your room, and I'll put her in with you when you're ready, when you get in bed."

So I thought to myself, "Well, what did I do?"—you know. But anyway, I went in, and she came in. Well, if she woke up once, she woke up a dozen times that night. And she'd hug me and say, "Oh, I'm glad you're here. I'm glad you didn't go away." And she was just petrified. And I said, "I have to go to some things. But I'll come back. I won't go and leave you. Look at—all my clothes are here." And I was trying to pacify her, you know, that I wouldn't go and leave my clothes.

So the next day, Neil went on the bus in the morning. And he really didn't talk too much to me before he left in the morning. He just got up and he did the barn chores, and he came home and he had something to eat, and he went on the bus. When he came home off the bus, he said, "We have to talk." And I said, "Okay." So we went upstairs and we talked.

He said, "I never want to see that child going through what she did last night, again." I said, "Well, what do you expect to do? What do you expect me to do?" He said, "Well, I don't know." He said, "I really don't know. I didn't sleep all night. And I was thinking about it this morning, and," he said, "the children are getting awful attached."

So, I said, "When you go to Iona this afternoon, why don't you...." See, my faith is pretty deep, and I depend a lot on priests, and always did. Or Sisters. Either one or the other. I have great faith in them. And if they let me down, it's a terrible letdown. But I've never had that experience, so I don't know really how I'd accept it. But I think it would be terrible.

But anyway, I asked Neil to go see Fr. Bernie Chisholm, and ask him if I could talk to him. So that evening—we put the kids to bed, and we told the old folks we were going up to Iona, that I wanted to see Fr. Chisholm.

10

So, we didn't tell them anything until we came home, other than that. We didn't even tell them about what Mary had gone through the night before. Because Neil tried to protect his parents from a lot of the extra anxieties that might be going on with the kids.

So I went to Iona. And of course, right brave, I went in, I told Fr. Chisholm who I was, and where I was working.... Oh yes, he knew, from seeing me in church, with the children and everything. And I told him what happened the night before. And he stood there. I said, "I would like to relieve Neil's mind and the children's too. I was wondering if you would make up an agreement for me that I would stay until the baby was fourteen. And then they'd be old enough to look after themselves. And then I could be on my way."

And he said, "Well, how old are you?" And I said, "Twenty-two." He said, "Now, how old are you going to be by the time this happens?" I said, "Well, that doesn't really matter. It's what I want to do." And he said, "Well, yes, it does matter. You're pretty fond of those kids." "Oh," I said, "I can't leave them. God," I said, "I'll die if I have to leave them."

So he asked about the old folks, how I got along with the old folks. I told him they were just wonderful, you know. And he said, "And what do you think of Neil James?" And I said, "I admire him for the effort that he's putting in to try and raise those children after losing his wife." And I said, "I'd like to help him as much as I could." And I said, "I can't leave those kids," I said, "no matter what. I'm after getting too fond of them myself."

So he said, "Well, you go out to the kitchen and tell Neil to come in." So, Neil went in and talked to him. Then he talked to the two of us. I guess he asked Neil about marrying me—did he ever think of it? And Neil said no. That he loved Kay and he couldn't love anybody else. Didn't think he could do justice to anybody else. And Fr. Chisholm told him that she was dead. And that she couldn't do what he wanted done. And that if he was realistic about it, he'd have to do some considering.

So, we came home. [Fr. Chisholm] wanted to see us in a week's time. So we came home. And on the way home we stopped at Gillis's Point, and he said, "Well, what do you think? What kind of a mess are we in now?" And I said, "Well, I don't know." I said, "We'll have to see what your father and mother say and what my father and mother say. We just can't jump into something like this."

(*And Neil was a very religious person, too.*) Yes. He never came by the graveyard at Iona but he went to pray to Kay for help. And I still, to this day, now—my father's dead—I stopped at her grave and prayed before I went over to his grave. I stopped at his father's grave and his mother's grave and Aunt Lucy. I never knew [Kay] in person, but I know her so well. Because of all that he told me about her. And as far as I'm con-

11

cerned, she's somebody real special. Because she brought those four children into the world, that I have.

I never forget an Anniversary Mass for her. And I think an awful lot of her brothers and sisters. They were all very, very good to me when Neil was sick at the last and died. They couldn't have been better. My own brothers and sisters weren't any better, and that's saying some, because my own brothers and sisters were—are—some terrific people. So, when Neil was sick in Ontario, they were really, really good to me, and I'll never forget that. I made them all a MacNeil tartan luncheon cloth in memory of Neil.... Because I really wanted to do something in some way to say, "Thank you. What you've done was appreciated."

(*When you stopped at Gillis's Point, what were you talking about?*) The gist of the conversation was what the priest had to say, and where we could go from there. Neil's biggest worry was that he couldn't love me. And he wondered if I was willing to accept a situation like that. (*Were you in love with him then?*) No. No. (*There was no thought of this between you.*) No. No. Never even—you know, I've often worked where there were men in the house, and it didn't ever bother me—never jarred me one way or the other.

(*How long was it, Margaret, from the time you first came here until the night that you stopped at Gillis's Point?*) I came September the 1st, and that was near the end of November, around the 17th or 18th of November, I think that was, that we went to see Fr. Chisholm.

So, anyway, I came home. We came home, we talked to his parents. And then I said, "I have to go home and talk to my parents." So I went down to see my parents, and took the kids down with me. Went down on the train one night. Father met me with a taxi. And went home. And I told them what my mission was. And I asked them what they thought of it. And my father said, "Well, Margaret, do you remember the day at the woodpile, you said there was something more you could do to save your soul than lock yourself up in a convent." He said, "My dear girl, if you take on that responsibility," he said, "there's no other way that you'll save your soul. And if that's the way you feel, that's what you should do. You have my blessing. But remember this: the day you marry that man, you're the mother of those children, and don't you ever forget it."

I said, "What about you, Ma?" And she said, "The only thing I ask you, Margaret, is that you come home to be married in your own parish church. And we'll have a dinner here for you." And she said, "Do you have any plans yourself?" And I said, "No. I just came home to ask you if you thought it would be okay." And Dad said, "Well, you're old enough to make up your own mind. But," he said, "I think a lot of you for coming home to tell us about it."

So I came home and I told Neil that as far as they were concerned we could go ahead. So we went and we told Fr. Chisholm. We thought we were going to get married in June. But Fr. Chisholm said, "That little girl is not going to know June from January." He looked at his calendar on the desk and he said, "You'll get married the 4th of January." So it was Fr. Chis-

Mary, Michael, and Francis, with Margaret at their mother's grave

holm who really proposed the marriage bit. Neil and I had no intentions of that when we went to Iona. I wanted an agreement.

But anyway, Neil went to town the next Saturday—that's only a couple of days after that. And he brought home a diamond ring for me. And I said, "What in the world did you go spending money to buy that for?" "Well," he said, "I gave Kay a ring, and if I'm going to marry you, you're not going to be treated any less."

So he gave me the ring that night. And the next day at dinnertime, I was making dinner and, like, I used to prepare the plates for the kids. And Mary spotted the ring, and she said, "Oh, you've got a new ring, Margaret." And I said, "Daddy gave me this." And she said, "How come you gave her a ring and you didn't got me one?" [Margaret chuckled.] I said, "Well, Mary, this ring means I'm going to be your Mommy." Well, she was kind of happy about that, but she still would like the ring, you know!

(*What about the other children?*) Francis called me in the pantry and closed the door. He was the oldest—he was four at that time. See, I came in September and he was four the end of October. He'd call me in the pantry and close the door, and he'd hug me and kiss me and he'd say, "I love you, but don't tell anybody." But Michael was the kind that he was always up in your arms, and hugging you and kissing you. You know, he was only—he wasn't two until after I married his father. I got married on the 4th of January, and he was two on the 18th.

I got married in Bras d'Or. Went home to my own parish.... But anyway, we didn't say too much in the community. Neil, I think, said to a few of his relatives around here—he told them, but we didn't say too much in the community about it. But his father and mother were the first to know. And they were quite happy. [But] I said, you know, "The only thing I'm afraid of is people are going to start talking." The fact that his wife was only dead eleven months. Well, you know, they had the old thing about that it should be at least a year before you'd even start thinking about looking for somebody else. But you know, there was no consideration of the fact that he had the children and he had to have somebody to look after them.

But I didn't feel a bit funny about it because I lived here five months. And if you went with somebody for five years, I wouldn't have spent more time with them than I did with him. Because I was here twenty-four hours a day all the time, you know. And I helped him with his bookwork and I helped him with everything, from Day One, trying to get him straightened out. Because he had a lot of debts, and he had a lot of hard times. And the house needed a lot of repairs. We didn't even have the water in the house when I came here. I helped dig the waterline the fall I came here.

So anyway, Grandma said to me, "Don't worry a bit about that. Because," she said, "you know, Papa only just drove up to Jamesville and asked me to marry him. And we met at the glebe house and we put in our calls and we got married. And look at us! So," she said, "you needn't worry about anything like that, if that's all you're worrying about."

I was a little concerned that their people would feel that I came in the area and, you know, snatched onto Neil right quick. I was a little concerned about that. But I knew the situation myself. But it was hard to make people see that. But the ones that were close to us really knew what was happening and really knew what was going on.

And we got along great. Like I said, you know, we never had what they'd call a honeymoon. We were too busy looking after the children and the old folks and doing things at home. But Neil always—he said to me one day, "If you ever wanted to go on a honeymoon, where would you like to go?" And I said, "Well, I'd like to go to—P. E. I. or Annapolis Valley." So he said, "Well, some day, when the kids get big enough, I'll take you."

So when Michael was fourteen—when I said that that's when I'd be leaving, when Michael was fourteen—that year, he took me to Prince Edward Island for a weekend—all weekend. We left on Friday morning. We were supposed to come back on Monday, but we came back Sunday night because I was a little concerned about how the kids were making out, because we had never left them alone.

But his parents lived with us, and they both died here. Both died in the house with us. And they were really attached to me and I was attached to them. I'm telling you, when I lost them, I don't think I felt any worse when I lost my own parents.

Aunt Lucy stayed with us for several years. But she got sick, and she

14

went to the Home in North Sydney. And she'd stay there in the winter-time. She'd come [back] in June, around the first of June, and she'd stay until September. Around the end of September, it'd start getting cold, she'd go back to the Home. Because she could always go to Mass there in the wintertime, and she couldn't go here because she minded the cold. But she was here a couple of years, in bed, and I looked after her.

The poor thing died in North Sydney. And we waked her here. And gave her the same kind of a wake and funeral as her sister and her husband, who were Neil's parents, had.

(*You referred to Neil as "Daddy."*) From the day I came here, I hardly ever called him anything but Daddy, because of the children. Right up until the day he died.

And the children called me Margaret until I married their father. Francis asked me one day, "How are we going to know when you're our Mommy?" And I said, "I'll have a round ring on my finger. And when you wake up in the morning, I'll be in bed with Daddy. I won't be over in my own bed." And that's the only way I could tell them, you know. Because how were they going to understand anything else?

So they were waiting for this day, and they'd be counting the days, and how many more days. Usually, if we were going to go anywheres, we had to take them with us because they'd cry and cry. But this time, they stayed, and Mrs. Hughie MacNeil from down in Gillis Point there, she came and she stayed while we went away to get married.

So, the next morning they woke up and they saw I was in bed with Daddy. Francis woke up first, and he spotted me over on the bed, and he realized where himself was, you know. And he jumped over on the bed, and he dug down and he found my finger, and he found the round ring on my finger. And he hollered to Mary and Michael, "Hurry up, Mary and Michael—she's our Mommy now!" And he hugged me to no end. And kissed me and everything. Was he ever glad. And they'd say, "Mommy!" And they'd laugh, you know. They thought it was the funniest thing.

But you know, I don't remember of those children making the mistake of calling me Margaret after that. And Grandma and Grandpa had to call me Mama, too.

(*This is a personal thing. You don't have to get into it if you don't want. You got married. There was no love—it wasn't a love....*) No, it wasn't a love marriage.

It developed—it came gradually. I'll never forget my marriage—my wedding day. Because there were several things that were so different to me. One of the things was, when I walked down the aisle—and my father was standing at the back of the church with a candle—and he couldn't see me. And I started to cry. And the first thing Neil said was, "Oh, Lord,

15

you're not sorry already." And I said, "No." I said, "It's Daddy's candle that's taking the heart out of me." He wanted to be the first one to congratulate us. So he was standing at the last pew, with a candle....

And then—we came home. Then it was just like, "Oh, Lord, you know. I guess—I went through with the marriage, so I guess I'll have to go through with everything else." So it was kind of just a bit of an ordeal for me. And I could tell it wasn't his cup of tea, either. (*How do you mean an ordeal?*) That we would—you know it was like—hard for me to explain it. You know, even, like—you know, the idea that I had to go in bed with him. You know. It wasn't that I minded, in a sense, because I knew it was part of the deal. But it was, like, you know, I could really leave that out. You know?

We were pretty serious about the whole thing. And then, the attraction that I had for the kids sort of revolved into an attraction for him. I respected him very much. But I, you know, somehow or another I thought that that's all there was supposed to be to it. But it wasn't. Because I got to really care.

Then I noticed myself—now, not so long after I married him, he was driving the school bus, and he got stuck on the road, and he came home and he was all soaking wet. And his clothes were frozen on him. And I was trying to thaw them off of him, so that he could take them off. And I found myself really concerned. And it was then that I really thought, Well, you know, I really care. I really cared, in a sense, but it was then that I really knew that I really, really did care.

Then when I got sick—a year after, I got sick. I got hurt out here—I got squeezed between the horse and cart and the henhouse. And it was then that I knew that he really cared. Because he was so concerned over it. And I think that's when the real bond got—so that we really knew we cared about what happened to each other and what happened to the children.

Because I went that year—about a year and a half after I was married—and I had a cystic tumour removed. I got pregnant, just about a year after I was married. But I was only about two months pregnant, and I had a miscarriage. But the reason for the miscarriage was, I had a cystic tumour. So, as a result of operations and tests, the specialists decided that I couldn't have any children, unless I had another operation. And if I did, my chances of having a healthy pregnancy were very slight.

So I was very disappointed that—I always thought, you know, I would love to have had a child. But Neil came in that night to the hospital, after I had the operation and had the cystic tumour removed. And I was going to have this other operation. So he came down that night. And he came in. And he said, "I talked to Fr. Danny"—Fr. MacDonald. "And as far as I'm concerned, I'd like you to come home." He said, "I think you have enough responsibility." He said, "You have four children. How many more do

16

you need? And they're yours as well as mine." And it was then that I really felt that I really—we really had a close bond.

Because he said—one of the things he said to me up on the road that night [at Gillis Point] was, "Don't expect me to love you like I loved Kay."

The night he gave me the ring, upstairs in the hall—now, that was the first time he kissed me. And I said, "Oh, get out!" You know? I kind of didn't want him to kiss me. Because I was always standoffish with the people that I worked for. Make sure that they knew where they stood right from the start, you know. He said, "Oh, come on now, if we're going to make this work, both of us will have to cooperate a little bit." So that's the first time he showed me that he really wanted to try to make it a good marriage. So I said to him, you know, why did he spend so much money, and he said, "I'm not going to give you any the less than I gave Kay."

And he didn't. He was very good to her. Like he often told me about how good she was and how happy she was, and how good they got along when they worked together and everything. How well she was. You know, he still talked about his love for her thirty years after she was dead. And it didn't bother me one bit. But when I went in to have one of the operations that I had, I asked a priest in there to have a Mass said for her. I said, "She will intercede for me to get over this and get home to look after those children." And that priest said, "I've been long a priest, and I've never heard of a request like that. You bet you'll get better! And you'll be home, and you'll look after your children...."

So I had a close attachment to her, too. But in the letter that Neil wrote to me in Baddeck, before I ever left there, he said in the letter, "If I'm not being too bold, would you pray to Kay to help you to not go back on your decision to come and help me look after the children." So, you know, he was pushing her to help him—he was so sure she was in Heaven. I am, too. Because Neil always talked that anyone that died in childbirth went straight to Heaven. I know she's in Heaven, because I've prayed to her and I've got what I prayed for. And there's no way that anybody that's not in Heaven can help anybody. And I feel she's in Heaven, and I go up to her grave and I pray to her and that. I never saw the woman, but I just love her.

I laugh once a day when I see people getting married, and they have to have this and they have to have that and they have to have everything. And they don't leave anything to get after they get married. And I think they blow the whole thing at the one shot. And then they do nothing but fight over it. And that's one thing we didn't do—we didn't fight. If I said I wanted something, we talked about it and decided how we could arrange to get it, and when we could get it. It was the same with Neil.

Everything that I did was appreciated by Neil and by the kids, and by his parents. And I often remember Grandma—like, the kids would sleep every afternoon. So, after I had been sick, Grandma would say to me, "Now, Mama, you go upstairs and lay down with them. And I'll do the dishes. And then when you get up, I'll go and lay down." So that's the way we got along.

And Grandma got sick on the Saturday before Easter. And we had to have the priest, and she was anointed, and we had the doctor three times within a week. And they couldn't do anything for her. And the doctor said she wasn't going to live very long. But there wasn't anything they could do for her in the hospital that I wasn't doing here. That's the only thing she asked when we said we were going to send for the doctor was, "Now, Mama, don't let them take me to the hospital." I said, "No, I won't, Grandma. You won't go if I have anything to say about it." And the doctor said there was nothing they could do that we couldn't do here.

She lived twenty-eight days. But three days before she died—my back was quite sore. And I used to have to straighten it up by putting my hands on my hips, back hips, you know, to force myself to straighten up. So she said to me that day, "You're suffering a lot with your back, aren't you?" And I said, "Nothing more than I can stand, Grandma. When you get better, I'll go and have it looked after." And she said, "I'm not going to get better, dear. I'm going to Heaven.... I'm going to die. But when I get to Heaven, you'll be all right." And I said, "Well, that's good. When you get to Heaven, you tell God that I'm down here struggling. And I have to look after Grandpa and the kids and Daddy and me, so, see if I'll get better."

The wake was held here at the house, and the funeral. About a week after, Neil said to me, "You don't seem to be having much trouble with your back." And I said, "My back is good." He said, "Well, I think you'd better call that doctor again."

I went down, and the specialist in Sydney couldn't find the weak spot in my back. It seemed to have been corrected, whatever—he couldn't understand it. Neither could I. And I didn't ask any questions about it. But he said, "If it comes back at you, come down, and then we'll look after it." I never went back. That was thirty-three years ago.

And it's only this spring that I really started having an awful lot of trouble with my back.... But I attribute it to Grandma's prayers, and Grandma interceding for me, that I got well enough. So that'll tell you what kind of a person she was.

(*You have a very strong religious belief.*) Yeah. (*And Neil himself....*) Well, [the rosary]—it was more said [on the road] than said in the house. When we went anywhere, as soon as we got on the road, he said the rosary. And then when we got on the road to come back home, he said the rosary.

But it wasn't unusual for us—and particularly since Neil and I were alone, once we got alone. We'd say the rosary—one decade was for ourselves and one for the children and one for the grandchildren and one for the souls—his parents and my parents. And Sr. Florence, my youngest sister, died with multiple sclerosis when she was only forty. And we always prayed for her and to her, because she was considered a little saint. So it wasn't unusual for us to say maybe three or four rosaries on the way home. On the way going and on the way coming back. If we'd get tired talking about something, and we didn't have anything to say, you know, we'd say, "Oh, well, let's do the rosary." And we'd say the rosary. It was a joy for us. We enjoyed saying the rosary. It wasn't a labour, forced or anything. It wasn't anything we had to do.

I had a feeling that [Neil] wasn't going to make it [when he had a heart attack in Ontario]. I was very much afraid of it. And that's the first time I was ever afraid. Because he was very sick in 1981; in fact, four doctors in Halifax told me that he wasn't going to make it. And I told them they weren't God. Do what they could, and the Fellow up above was making the decision. And I just prayed and prayed and prayed. And when he found out that he had a heart attack in Brantford, he said to the nurse, "Don't worry. When Mama comes, we'll tell her and she'll pray, and I'll be all right." Now, that was asking an awful lot.

But anyway, I did pray, as I always do. But I prayed that God's will be done. I didn't want him to suffer. I knew he would be very unhappy if he had to stay in Ontario, away from Cape Breton, because his heart and soul was out here in Iona. But, as God saw fit, he didn't get out of the hospital.

(*Did Neil's parents live very long after you came?*) I came here in 1954. Grandma died in 1958—April the 28th, 1958. And Grandpa died on June the 16th, 1960. And Aunt Lucy died the 17th of March, 1971.

One day Grandpa was sitting in the dining room, and he was very down because—because of his health condition, he was making a lot of wash. He started crying—and I said, "What are you crying for, Grandpa?" And he said, "Oh, I'm making so much work." And I said, "Well, don't you worry. You just pray that washing machine keeps going, and I'll do the work!" And the washing machine—you could hear that washing machine to the main road, because it had been going for a good many years.

And Grandpa never really got sick. He went to bed one afternoon, to lie down. And later on that evening, he sat on the side of his bed to have supper. And he was ninety-four at that time. Sat on the side of the bed and had his supper. And he only went to lay down, and he was dead at six o'clock the next morning.

But, getting back to the washing machine. I washed after the funeral.

19

The next time I washed, the motor caught fire! So, the washing machine finished with Grandpa.

And one of the things Grandma liked—and because she liked it, she felt I liked it too—and do you know, she trained me to like it—was the crust of bread. The crust of the homemade bread. So every time I'd make bread, and when you'd go to break the loaf of bread to use it, she'd take the crust off both ends and she'd put it under a pot. You know, turn the pot upside down on the shelf in the pantry. And then, come teatime in the afternoon, she'd say, "I have our lunch." And she'd come out with the crust of bread for me and for her. And we'd have the crust of the bread—the heel of the bread, like we used to call it.

So, little things like that, that she thought about me as well as herself.

(*What was it that you told me you felt that the children should know that they did not know...?*) They should know why we got married so soon after I came to Gillis Point. Like, I came in September and we were married in January. You know, that's five months. So normally, if you do that, there's always the fear that people will say, "Oh, well, heavens. She came in and she took over, and she just married the man on the rebound, and before he could get time to think."

He certainly did get time to think. And it was well thought out. And there was no reason, no other reason for us to get married, such as having to get married or anything like that.

But I always was afraid that someone would say to the children, you know, that something wrong had happened, that would smear their father or me. And I wouldn't want them to have to live with that, because there wasn't. (*So you suggested to Neil, while he lived....*) That we should tell [the children]. And he said no, he didn't want to get into that. They were all grown up. (*But he didn't feel they should be told....*) He said, "No, they should be able to figure that out. And they never asked us, so why should you tell them?"

It was like something hanging over me, and I wanted to tell them. So, I told them. The day their father was buried, we all sat around the dining room table to discuss what was going to happen to the expenses of the funeral, and the property, and me.

So then I told them that I wanted to tell them about when I came to Gillis Point first. I always felt there was a cloud over that, and I wanted them to know the right story. So that's when I told them about it.

Well, the youngest girl cried. Because a lot of it she never heard, and she's very soft, and it's easy for her to cry. I said, "Don't cry, dear—this is something to be happy about." But the oldest fellow stayed at the table. Neighbours came in, so the rest of them went to the kitchen. And he said,

20

"I always thought the world of you, Mom. And that you were one in a million. And I really do now." And he cried his heart out. And I took him in my arms. Cried. I said, "It's good to get it out." Because he really didn't cry a lot. And I guess I surprised them all, because I was always a kind of a softy. And when Neil was sick—like, if he was half an hour late coming home—I'd be just in an awful state, worrying about him.

But then, when he died, I seemed to have got a second hold on things and I went through it and got along fine. With the kids' support—they were very good. But they were very, very concerned about me, too, because they knew that I was terribly, terribly attached to Dad. And they were very much afraid for what was going to happen to me when anything happened to him....

I wouldn't erase a day of it. No, wouldn't erase a day of it. I'm very proud of our children. And the one that'll tell me they weren't mine, they'd better be on their way. And I'm sure that's the way with the children.

I just wish that everybody that ever got married would have as happy a life as I had, and they would love one another as much as we did. For someone who, you know, we started out as a marriage of convenience, and turned into a marriage of real, true love. I just wish...some of it would shed off onto others.

Edited from Margaret's conversations with Ed Binns and *Cape Breton's Magazine*.

21

With Wilfred Poirier, Lobster Buyer

Wilfred M. Poirier, D'Escousse: I was born in 1885. I could say I was born probably eight or ten years younger—I don't look ninety-eight, do I? I still go to dances, you know. I had ten dances here two weeks ago. I was born in Poirierville, and I'm the only one left in that generation. I grew up in Poirierville. There was hardly any school in my days. We had a teacher—an old Scotchman, you know—as good as I am. But he loved his drink, and didn't give us any learning. What I learned, I learned at school in the United States at night. Not too much, but enough that I could do my business as a fish buyer.

My first job, when I was about thirteen years of age, I worked hard as a fisherman and on a farm—six dollars a month. That was in Pondville. The old man was a farmer, and he was a butcher. And I used to get up at half past four in the morning, go out fishing with one of his sons. When I'd get back, I'd have to clean the barn. I'd work till five o'clock at night. I wouldn't say they were my worst days. They were happy days. During that time—this is the best of all—I saved nine dollars and twenty-five cents in those two years.

I went to Boston. I paid $9.25 for my fare—steerage, you know—I didn't have any money to buy a room or anything. I had an old suitcase, with two eggs—this is the God's truth—and a couple of molasses cookies. And I happened to be talking to somebody from Cheticamp, a Frenchman, same as I was—and the steward came along, all dressed up in uniform. He heard us talking French. He asked me if I was French. I said, "You heard me." He said, "Where're you from?" I said, "Little town they call Poirierville." He said, "I've got an aunt living in Poirierville." So I told him my mother's name. He said, "We're first cousins." And he asked me where my bunk was—I showed him. If I had anything to eat—I told him. He said, "You're going to eat with me from now on till you get to Boston."

Two weeks after, I got a job on a hospital boat—twenty-five dollars a month and my board and bunk—that was taking the sick people for a sail down Boston Harbour for four or five hours a day. It lasted three months. After they tied up, I went to a fish plant. Thirteen dollars a week, ten hours a day—well, it was better than the six dollars I was getting in Pondville. So I worked there till November. Then I went back to Cape Breton, to Marble Mountain—where they used to get marble for Sydney, the steel work—and I finished up till late in December.

And in the spring—I had just passed sixteen—I went to New York, Long Island, as a fisherman. My brother got me the job. Forty dollars a month—I thought I had struck a gold mine! Promised Land, they called it. Fishing the Atlantic Ocean from Delaware to Boston, all along the seacoast, and out at sea, you know. They called them pogies. Menhaden was the right name. They run in schools—sometimes you get a thousand barrel, 500 barrel—big school of fish. We'd land them. Portuguese used to take them out, clean them out; and they'd make oil and this scrap guano—fertilizer. I fished on George's Bank in the winter. I was only seventeen. Trawling. In my days, there was only the cable and the anchor and sail—that's all. If you got caught in a storm, it was, "Stay up or go down!" I made trips sometime in 1902 or 1903. One of them was a broker. Coming in there with 75-, 80-, or 100,000, all haddock. "Sorry—it's a broker," captain would tell you. Means "No Sale." But there was a sale for them, don't worry. The captain and the dealer were working together to give us nothing but our board. All you got out of that trip was your bunk and grub. You had no money.

There was lots of robbery then. The fishermen that went out on George's or elsewhere had no education. They had to do something for a living. We never had a chance, you know. There were very few in my day were educated. Very few. But I learned a lot. I think I was fishing for about four years.

Then I got married, in Boston. She was a Poirier, and she was born a few roads from me in Poirierville. She was working in a curtain factory. She was a stitcher.

I made, I'd say, about fifteen different kind of work in my life. I even worked in a coal mine right in Glace Bay, seam No. 4. They were on strike that time, and I was practically broke. I didn't want to go and work. But I was down and out, I had to get enough money for a couple of months to go back to the States. I worked in a shoe shop—that was my best job. I made seventy-five, eighty dollars a week then. I was a laster— he just shapes the shoe and passes it to the finisher. And I worked optical work, as an inspector on lens. Then I went back again as a fisherman.

And then I got the job as a buyer, a lobster buyer. (*How did it happen?*) Well, every time I'd make a fishing trip, I'd stop at this place to buy a couple of lobsters. And one trip I made—it was a full trip—this woman was in there. She said, "Frenchie, how did you make out this trip?" I said, "Not too good." I said, "If I could get a job ashore, I think I'd work ashore." She said, "I can't pay you much money. But," she said, "I'll give you thirty-eight dollars a week to start with." She was the head boss. So, I worked there. I was just splitting lobsters. After awhile, she asked me if I'd take a job, to go down in Nova Scotia. She had me call on her husband who was in the office. He said, "There's a meeting in Gloucester tomorrow. You've got two languages—you've got a chance."

There were about ten or twelve looking for the same job, you know, college students, supposed to be people knew their business. However, they picked me out. Because I had two languages, you know. And I came from a place where the lobsters were plentiful.

So, they sent me down. Fishermen had just started fishing in this section here, on the Eastern Shore. And the first year I went down, I had to work with most of the clergymen, tried to organize the fishermen. We had a meeting, and they decided they'd ship through me, on consignment. (*Were the fishermen here shipping lobsters before that?*) No, they were just selling locally to the lobster canning factory. The first month I was buying, from about the 2nd of May to the last of May, I got 800 crates of lobsters. I knocked the nail right on the head. They went crazy up there in Boston. They didn't know how I was getting them, that I would get that much. That was a lot of lobster. And I only had this section—the Eastern Shore and Isle Madame—that's all. Some of those fishermen down at Grand River were big fishermen. Oh, they used to get a lot of lobster. I was the first agent down here. I kept buying from eastern Maine, New Brunswick, Nova Scotia, Prince Edward Island—and then Newfoundland. And in 1932, I think it was, I broke the record—when I took over Newfoundland. I cleared all the southern shore, down the Bay of Islands, up north, down to near St. George's Bay, Cape St. George. Buying on consignment.

24

The clergy were working with me on my side. I'll tell you why. See, I'm Catholic, and they were working with me, and I was working with them. We were trying to promote a better business, and give the fishermen a square deal. When I came here, they were getting about four to seven cents a pound for lobster. I started the price up, buying—if I bought—fourteen cents a pound. But the most of it was on consignment. Consignment means it was shipped to the market at a higher price—the fishermen would get a little more on consignment than selling outright here. But some of them would rather get the cash right away.

I glutted the market at our place two or three times. In 1935, I think it was, I glutted the market, I think, with about 14 million pounds of lobsters. I had about six or seven boats that were always loaded. We had a well-smack boat and we had trucks. We had the railroad. And we had the Nova Scotia Shipping Company. My best spot was in Cape Breton here, from Point Michaud to Scatari Island. And when I glutted the market, the company called me to tell me not to ship any more—"We can't handle them." "Well," I said, "I can stop buying, but you can't stop them from consigning. If you do, we're licked. They'll ship somewhere else." (*And I guess the price goes down when you glut the market.*) Oh, yes. Well, the price sometimes wasn't too darn high, but they never got below 18¢ up.

(*Starting off, you would go to a town....*) We'd hold meetings with the fishermen. At Grand River, Canso, Petit-de-Grat, L'Ardoise, Little Bras d'Or. Meeting in Newfoundland. Meeting around Halifax—all along the shore, wherever I'd be called. When I was called, from the clergymen or somebody at the head—a kind of a union they had, you know—they'd call me. But there was no real union. They'd group, in other words, they'd group and they'd work together. (*Would fishermen's organizations help your business?*) Oh, that was good. I liked it. I told them to organize. My company didn't mind that.

(*And the Antigonish Movement?...*) I used to work with one of them there in Antigonish. He was always after me to go to Newfoundland. Till they arranged among the clergymen to send me there. Oh, that was good, the Antigonish Movement. They were working with me, too. I had a clergyman tell the audience in a church in West Arichat to ship through me. At the sermon, see. Fr. Barrie was the same thing. He was more of a watchman—see that the lobsters were kept anchored, you know, nobody'd steal them. Even Fr. Boyd, who is now a bishop—he was a great friend of mine. Way up near Halifax, Canso—Fr. Boudreau was 100% with me. He made nine trips to Boston with me in the years I was in business. I slept in the glebe house. They all knew me. Fr. Poirier, of course, we didn't get along too well, because he didn't think we were paying enough. But he wasn't against me, in one way. I had no trouble. Lots of

25

times I didn't care whether I got them or not. I was afraid of glutting the market. I'd rather somebody else got a share of it.

(*Up to that point, was someone local buying their lobsters?*) Oh, yeah—for nothing. Lobster factories. Used to buy them for three to seven cents a pound. Of course, they weren't against me. Whoever was buying didn't like me, that was a sure thing—but they never hurt me. (*But they would have to pay a higher price after you started.*) That's right. But there was nobody against me. They were in business [they were merchants], and the more the fishermen made, the better it was for them. Some of them were against me in the beginning, then I put them to buy for our company when I was away somewhere else. (*The local merchants?*) Yeah. I'd give them so much money, and they'd have to give me a record of it when they bought. I shipped them out.

(*But it couldn't have been easy at first.*) It was kind of hard to meet the people. Certain fishermen sometimes, if they were cranky or drinking, you know, I had a little trouble at first. But there were no fights. I wasn't afraid of one of them, anyway, none of them.

(*Sometimes the fishermen shipping on consignment did not trust what happened to their lobsters when they got to Boston.*) Oh, that I know. When you ship on consignment, those lobsters arrive there in Boston, and they've got cullers to separate the lobsters, to select the small and the large. Then they are weighed out. And whatever weight you had, you got the price on that date—if it was 24¢ or 30¢ a pound, or 50¢—you got that. And if you had any weak ones, you got a little less. And the dead ones, the inspector'd throw them overboard. Sometimes a fisherman might ship a crate of lobster, but he wouldn't take care of them, and half of them would arrive weak or dead. He'd be the loser. But some of the fishermen would never lose one.

(*But a lot of them thought the culling was not....*) Was not legal, you mean, that it wasn't fair. But some of those fishermen had their own brothers working at the plant up there. We had them from Canso, and we had somebody from eastern L'Ardoise there. They were culling their brothers' lobsters, in Boston. And on the other hand, the inspector there—there's always two or three inspectors—how many little lobsters they took out of the crate and they fired in Boston Harbour—below the measure. (*And then when the returns would come back?*) The fishermen'd say they got robbed—short weight. The average was about 140 pounds to a crate. And sometimes they'd be ten pounds or eight pounds short, you know. (*And I'm sure they thought you were getting that.*) Oh yes, I wouldn't doubt that. But I was only getting paid my salary and commission.

I had a lot of fishermen trusted me. And I'm sure, when I did business, may the Lord kill me now, I never took a cent off them. Instead, I helped

them. If a fellow broke a crate or lost them, I'd find a way in the fall to help him. I'd come back with $1000 or $800, the company'd give me. Who wasn't satisfied, you know, I'd give them fifty or a hundred dollars. Rather than lose them, we'd pay them a little money. I'd always grant them so much. Because sometimes, some of them didn't deserve it, but they'd tell me, "I was short." Didn't always tell the truth, you know. I knew the fellow that was complaining. I'd pass him $200 or $300. And I'd get him back the next year. I'd say, "Now next year, if you don't take care of your lobster, don't ship them through me—ship them somewhere else." They wouldn't get sore at me. I'd tell them right away.

There's the time I had an argument with Fr. Poirier—he's my cousin. He and I didn't get along. He said we weren't paying enough—12¢ to 16¢ a pound. "Well, I'll see if the fishermen want to sell. I'm not going to give them more than they ask. I'm doing business for a company. They've got to live, and I've got to live. If they don't want to ship them, or sell them, let them go somewhere else." (*If the fishermen had organized and asked for one cent more, would they have gotten it?*) Oh, yeah. Yeah, they'd have got a couple of cents more yet. (*But they never did?*) No. There might have been a couple here and there, you know, they wanted their own way. So I told them, "You've got so many buyers, dealers in Boston. Ship there." Didn't bother me. If I lost one man, that didn't bother me.

(*Did you have an easier time in the Catholic districts than in the Protestant districts?*) I had a Protestant district down the Eastern Shore were my best fishermen. They didn't look at religion. Ah well, there, sometimes somebody died—I went to church, to the funeral with them.

(*It sounds like you did an enormous job. Did you physically handle the lobsters?*) No, no. What we'd do, we'd weigh the crate, I'd look at the lobsters, see what condition they were in. Then we'd weigh them, then I'd pay him. On consignment I didn't have to do that. (*Were you taking the lobsters to the train yourself?*) No, no. I'd tell them the train would be down and pick up your lobster. (*And the fishermen took them to the train?*) Right. I'd tell them the day they've got to ship. And I wasn't there; I'd be somewhere else. But they were shipping. I'd have a fellow was my buyer. He was a buyer from the fishermen. I used to give him so much to take care of the lobsters. And he'd ship them all by rail. Canso by boat, all along the Eastern Shore—all by boat. I might have shipped two truckloads, I remember. We had one well-smack, used to go down Main-a-Dieu and along the Eastern Shore there. They'd buy them, see. The lobsters alive in the pool of water in mid-ship. They'd stay alive all the way to Boston.

(*How could you be in all those places?*) I covered it. I started way up in Richibucto, Baie Chaleur, New Brunswick—in the fall, that was. That was August and September, till the 28th of September. And in the spring, the 1st of March. In the winter was from Yarmouth to Sambro—that was starting in December. First of December, and it lasted till the last of March—they had a long season there. Here, it was the 1st of May. Same in Newfoundland. (*So you were in different sections for different seasons?*) That's right. (*You would not be there every day, I guess. You would pick up the lobsters how often, in one place?*) Well, sometimes it would be, in one place, once a week. But Newfoundland, sometimes twice a week.

I think that I used more cars than anybody else. Company's cars. And I had about ten or twelve of my own. I must have used sixty-odd cars, I know, in my life. It wasn't paved from Portland, Maine, to North Sydney, covered with dust. The company gave me a car every year. I ruined two cars in one year one time. I think it was 1940. I made in my life, I'm sure, oh, five or six hundred trips. I was working out of Shediac in August and September, and I used to sometimes make two trips in one week to Gloucester at night.

I was busy all the time. I was on the road sometimes at night, all or part of the night, and the early morning I was out in my car—I had so many places to call in in one day. I wasn't tired, though. I had to be on the road. I could be in Canso, now, like today—by tomorrow morning I'd be down the Eastern Shore, or on this island. (*You were away from your wife an awful lot, to do your work.*) I was away from her about four months at a stretch sometimes. Then I'd see her for a week. But most of the winter, like January, February, I was partly with her. Come down in March, till December, I'd be busy. I know I've been away from home some Christmases. Couldn't get back.

(*And you had people who worked for you?*) Yes, I had a watchman in, oh, probably ten different places in Nova Scotia, and I had a bookkeeper, a little office in Petit-de-Grat. (*What would the watchman do?*) He'd take care of the lobsters I bought, see that they were always in clear water, the crate not overloaded. And he'd cull them out. If there was a dead one, he'd throw it out. One dead lobster can kill a full crate of 150 pounds overnight—that's what you've got to watch. Cull the lobsters, take the dead ones and the weak ones out. I'd pay the watchmen so much a month, you know. (*Would anybody ever have to watch the fishermen, to be sure the fishermen stayed with you?*) No, you can't tell the fishermen. You let him have his own way. Be nice to him, whether he likes you or not. Always try to be friendly with him. I could have had a dozen fights. I wasn't afraid of anyone. I'm not a boxer. When I was young, I wasn't afraid of anyone. And if they got sarcastic, I'd tell them off. "Ship somewhere else." But they'd always come back. I wouldn't insult them or anything.

(*Did you ever have a bad year?*) The bad year was in 1950. The lobsters were scarce. That's when my company sold out. There were no lobsters that year at all. Something like we have now. They sold out to a man in New York. He wanted me to live in Newfoundland, and I refused. You know, I was getting then past sixty-five. I said, "You've got younger men, send them there. I intend to get my pension. I'm through." (*Was there never a bad year before 1950?*) No. I never had a bad year. Must have been thirty-eight or forty years, I guess. Good years all the time—they were for me. Except 1950, when it was bad for everybody. The lobsters were very scarce. A little wharf down in Poirierville, where I was born, we had twenty-two boats for a time. Everybody was fishing. Lobster got scarce. Lobster got scarce. There's no more lobsters. The ground has been fished out. And what made the trouble is the drag from the beam trawlers has destroyed the bed of the ocean. It's the damn drag now, and the foreign ships come off 100 or 200 miles off of our land, and they drag the bottom, too. The lobsters spawn on the bottom between rocks, they pass thousands of little seeds—the female does—and they generally spawn around May. And in June and July they start shelling. Well, you imagine when there's thousands and thousands of little lobsters on the female, and a dragger comes along and rips the bottom. He kills everything. Kills the mother and the seeds—that's what happens. (*The dragger isn't going after lobster?*) No, he's going after fish, going after haddock, codfish, halibut, redfish—whatever he can get. And this goes on now. Now we have—sometimes I feel, if I could see well—I would write a nice letter. But we haven't got any representative of the fishermen. They take a farmer, a plumber—that doesn't know a squid from a frog—to represent the fish industry. I know that. I was a fisherman practically most of my life. From when I was a youngster, as I told you, thirteen years of age. I sometimes wonder why they're appointed, given these jobs of 30-, 40-, 50,000 dollars a year. And the fishermen making probably $1000, some of them. No, they take a shoemaker or anybody—they pick them out—or a farmer, and put him as a representative of the fish industry—the minister.

You can go somewhere, there might be a couple—two or three—would run me down. They didn't like me. They thought I was making too much money. I never got rich. I made a good living, and that was all. The company didn't throw their money away, because I was a buyer. I was getting a salary and a commission. That was a good living. I didn't have to work very hard. Didn't have to make a paper at night. The company trusted me. If I wanted $20,000—I had money in the bank—every bank manager knew me from Yarmouth to Cape St. George in Newfoundland. I had the bishop, his brother, as a purser in Newfoundland in the spring, because I couldn't cover it all. And if I wanted money—$20,000 or $30,000—we had money in every bank, you know. But supposing I ran short. I was short one night buying swordfish. And I had called the company for $10,000 for that day. And the bank manager came down at two o'clock in the morning with $10,000. I paid it. They wouldn't take a cheque. This would have to be the real money—cash. I remember that night. I don't know if it was 70 or 100 swordfish I bought.

(*Would you say that what you did improved the lives of the fishermen here?*) Very much. I can brag and say that. There was poverty, and more than poverty. I well remember when people were getting three to seven cents a pound. When I came, it started at fourteen cents up—it was a big difference. And in American money, there was a small premium on the American dollar.

Now, in the spring of the year—I am telling you the truth—I remember a place, an old woman had come and grabbed me—she was old—she kissed me. She said, "You brought us bread." This is the truth. I was bringing the money in. During the Great Depression, they had nothing to eat. I helped them. Sometimes—do you know how I feel sometimes?—I don't know if you do, but see on the wall there—I believe in Him. And I believe in helping, if you're poor. I send money to a monastery in New Jersey every second month. And in my mind, when I sleep at night, or I lay down— that He puts me to live, at the age of ninety-eight.

The Martells
of Flint Island Light

Margaret Martell MacQueen, Port Morien: My mother came to Cape Breton. She was eight years old. Amy Ethel Frances—that was her name. And then the Shepards adopted her. But that was her name. She got her birth certificate and everything from England—Birmingham, England. (*She was one of the Home Children.*) Immigrant. I guess they didn't call them immigrants at that time, they called them orphans or something. But there were boatloads and boatloads came over at one time....

Dad's home was in Black Brook. (*And how was he making his living before he went to the island?*) Fishing, I guess. And working in the pit. And he also used to [run] silent movies. I just remember vaguely. Tom MacInnes, who is long past gone, he used to bring them in, and Dad used to run the projectors. And he had a sawmill. He was a jack-of-all-trades, my father, what you call a handyman. He was a carpenter, a mason— masonry, you know, chimneys—mechanic, you name it.

I was five years old when he got the position of lightkeeper out in Flint Island. He was out there for eighteen years. So in that eighteen years, there were a lot of things happened.

(*How many children did they have at that time?*) We'll start from the older one and work down. There were fourteen in our family altogether. There was Billy, Raymond, Kenny, Loren, Ethel, myself, Audrey, and Murray—eight—when we went out to Flint Island. Johnny was born in 1933, and that's when my brother [Raymond] was drowned. He was the first one. We've had quite a few tragedies out there.

(*How was your brother drowned?*) Just a freak accident, really. I wasn't very old, but I remember they used to talk about getting seals, seal pelts. I remember this night at the table, they were talking, and [years later] Mum often referred to it. Raymond said, "We'll have a seal pelt for your room, Mum." And they went out—it was still early evening—it wasn't dark or anything. Then, they weren't coming home, and we could remember all the things that were happening. All of a sudden we saw Dad running for the boat.

Apparently, they saw the seals. At that time the ice, when it used to come in—this was the 23rd of March, 1933—there used to be big seals on the ice clampers. The ice at that time sort of used to come in, and it would pack. It would form a barricade around the island.

But anyway, they didn't come back, and they weren't coming back. You know what kids are like: you're in the house, and you're worrying about them, and wondering. So finally we saw Dad running for the boat. We knew something happened, but we didn't know what. But it was a beautiful evening: it was calm, and the water was beautiful. But there were just three big seas came. And it just capsized the boat that Billy— that's my oldest brother—and Raymond were in. And Raymond took a cramp, apparently, in his leg. He could swim, but Billy couldn't. And Billy clung to the boat. And Dad got this little canvas boat, and he got Billy. But by the time he got there, Raymond was gone.

(*How do they know Raymond took a cramp in his leg?*) Apparently, when they were both clinging to the boat, he told Billy that he had a cramp in his leg. Then he tried to swim ashore. And I suppose he couldn't make it. Mind you, they weren't that far from the shore. But it was just something that happened. He was fifteen at the time, and Billy was seventeen.

They couldn't find him that night, anyway. They searched. They couldn't find him. And the next day, on the shore—it was like on the northeast part of the island—there's a bank, and you go down on the shore. And there's a drop from the shore down to the water. I don't know if you've noticed, in the winter the water is clear, and you can see the bottom of the ocean. And you could see him down at the bottom of the ocean. (*Who found him?*) The family—Dad, and the boys.

[Port Morien] was our stopping place. When we'd come in any time, this was where we came in. We had a code. I don't know if you're famil-

32

iar with lighthouses, but the light flashes so many times this way and so many times that way—like, west, east, north and south. And there's so many flashes each way. That's regular. Until—see, what [Dad] did, he stopped the light. And when the light is stopped, people on the mainland would know that there was something wrong.

He did, he stopped it. To let them know there was something. And the *Montcalm* was the icebreaker at that time. And they finally came out. But it must have been a couple of days, anyway. And in the meantime, Dad had to pack the body in ice, and make a rough box.

So it was a terrible few days, anyway. (*When the light would be stopped like that, what could the people at Morien do?*) Well then, see, we had no communication whatsoever to the mainland. We had just an ordinary radio, and it was run by battery. But we just used to save it for certain programs, or we'd turn it on for the news of something.

[Dad] would listen to the weather, and if it was a fine day, he'd come in. He had a boat. And he'd come in and get the mail. And we used to get six months' supply of food. And we'd usually get it in, I suppose, October—we'll say October. And then whenever the ice would leave, that's when he could come in and get supplies and mail. (*But other than that, your mother and father and several children were out there on the island, and no connection. Is that correct?*) No communication. That was the only way that you'd have to know: he'd stop the light to let them know there was something wrong.

Any time Mum used to leave the island, and when Dad was going back and forth—they had a signal [light] they used, that he used to hook up [to] a battery. And four flashes were, "Everything was okay." And if there was something wrong, they used to flash three times.

But as far as the tragedy, see, he had to stop the light. And that was to let the people know in Morien that there was something wrong. (*Was it*

On Flint Island, left to right: fog station, lighthouse, old lighthouse (used for storage), and double dwelling house.

possible for people from Morien to get to the island?) Oh no, no, no. Not with the ice. They contacted the Department of Transport. They would send the boat out to find out what was wrong. And the government boat at that time was the *Montcalm*.

[My father] made a rough box, and he packed the body in ice, and kept it in the boathouse until [the *Montcalm* came]. Then they had the funeral. And he's buried at Homeville, in that cemetery up there. (*Were your parents able to come in for the funeral?*) No. Just Dad. (*Your mother didn't go. Did she ever talk about that?*) Oh, later years, you know, because it was—she hated the island, at times.

You know, there were times that she liked it. Once the tragedies were over, and things got back to normal, it was fine.

I guess it was after Ethel was drowned. We had three tragedies out there. Now when Raymond was drowned, that was 1933. But it was 1935 when Ethel was drowned. (*How old would she be in 1935?*) Thirteen.

This was one of the times that they were taking provisions out to the island, and something happened to the boat. The coil of the engine—they always carried spare parts—the coil burnt out, I guess. Anyway, when they went to get the coil, their spare one, it wasn't there. Somebody had taken it out of the boat. And they drifted up to Catalone—you know the turn up to the beach there at Catalone Beach. And in the boat that time there was Billy, and Edna, his wife—they were just married, in fact, in July of that year—and Kenny, and Ethel.

So they drifted. And it was the funniest thing: seals followed them all the way, the whole time that they were drifting. And they drifted out around like what we call the Southern Head into Catalone, Mira Bay there, that area. And the seals followed them all the way. Even when the boat capsized, and during the seas, because the seas were quite high—it started to storm that evening.

(*I heard that Ethel was swept from the boat several times.*) Yes. And [my brother] saved her. From what we understand, when she'd be swept out of the boat, he'd grab her and put her back in. Because she couldn't swim. Now, I'm not clear if the boat upset, or if it was just tossing on the waves. Because it was a very, very stormy night, and the winds were very bad, and the seas were very bad.

My brother [Kenny] was the only one that could swim there. And he took the rope of the boat...and he got ashore. But before that, he was hit on the head with the engine box cover and he was knocked unconscious for a few minutes. I suppose—when you're knocked out, you float. It was just a matter, he said, of minutes. And then when he came to, Ethel was gone. And Billy and Edna were clinging to the boat.

So he managed to get ashore. He had a rope in his teeth, and he swam

34

ashore. He was a good swimmer. And he rescued Billy and Edna. But they searched for days along the shoreline and everything, and they could never find Ethel.

But you know, as often as I think about it, it still bothers me. (*I guess it should.*) The fact, too, that she was never found. October 15th, 1935. And it's the strangest thing, looking back now, and you think about it. Lillian was born in March of that year, and this happened. And it seemed like, when one was taken, there was always somebody born. If you want to think in terms of fate or whatever. Lillian was born in 1935. March the 14th. Johnny was born in May of '33, and this was just after Raymond was drowned. You know, it just seemed to be a coincidence.

I have a picture of my little brother. He was only two years and five months. (What was his name?) Harold. Every once in awhile Mum used to come in. She used to stay with a family in Morien here that were friends of theirs. We did have a house in here, but it was rented.

It was in January. And Harold was two years and five months. And he had been in—and you know, we didn't have ice cream that much, or anything like that. And he had a pain in his tummy. And Mum thought it was just because he was eating ice cream when he was in Morien. This was just a day or so after they went back out to the island. Anyway, the pain got worse. So Dad [went]—I forget who was with Dad. The ice was quite broken up—you could get through the clampers and everything. But he had to take the little fellow to Glace Bay. He got him there. He got him in the hospital and everything, but it was too late. He had peritonitis. And it poisoned him, all gone through his system.

(*What did your father tell you about that trip?*) Well, he couldn't say very much, I guess, at the time, because we all knew the situation. We knew that he was lucky to get off at all. We knew that he was lucky to get in. It was just that—if you wanted to get off of there at all, you got in the boat and you went. You had to get through the clampers the best way you knew how. And you couldn't go in fifteen minutes—it's about five miles from here to the island. You just had to take your chances. And when an emergency came up, you got there the best way you knew how. And that was the best way.

But anyway, he didn't survive. (*And again, your mother wasn't there. She was deprived of that, too. And he's buried, I guess, at Homeville.*) Yes.

There's some humorous things too! But like I said, you have to really—I didn't know if you wanted this part of it, or—I'll get these sad things out of my way, and then I can tell you some other things.

I was thinking today [of Billy]. He was only nineteen when this happened. Here again. This was the 22nd of January. I have those dates in my mind because, you know, there are things that happen that are sort of outstanding in our lives, and you sort of remember them.

This was one of the times, again, when the weather was fairly decent. He came in for mail, mostly, or things that we might have run out of. And he was on his way back. And the boat—something happened to the engine. And he drifted. He tied himself, the boat, to the bell buoy, as long as he could—and then he drifted. It was one of the boats from Morien here. And Dad had to use the same signals again, you know—he had stopped the light to let them know there was definitely something wrong. It was one of the Murrants came out, anyway, and got the boat. And Billy's hands were frozen, his feet were frozen, he was in an awful mess.

He used grease [to protect himself]—what they used for the engines— this heavy grease. He rubbed himself with that. I guess it was the only thing that saved him, really. His hands and his feet were frozen. It's just a wonder that he didn't lose his fingers or his feet or anything. But he didn't.

(*You say that your father stopped the light. How did your father know that there was any problem?*) Well, we could see. When the boats would go—we'd just sort of have an idea what time they'd be coming back. And we used to watch for them. And we had what we called spyglasses. And we used to take our [turn]—we used to watch, and we always—I don't know—I'm not saying that Dad did, but for us young ones, we always had sort of a dread. Every time the boat left. It was the strangest—I suppose because of the things that had happened previously. But we always had a sort of a dread of things that were happening.

Many's the time when Dad would go in, and he'd say, "I'll be home in a couple of hours," or something. And we'd watch, and we'd watch, and we'd watch. And it would probably be a couple of hours later, maybe sometimes just before dark, he'd arrive. And Mum would say, "Where in the name of Ned were you?" That was her favourite expression. And he'd say, "Oh so-and-so, there was something wrong with their engine, and they wanted me to fix it before"—and this would be his excuse, why he wouldn't be coming. And it's true. He spent half his time at the wharf, fixing somebody's boat.

(*When this happened to Billy—I'm trying to understand—he got somehow to the bell buoy.*) He drifted close enough to—I guess—I'm just assuming that he got the rope around it somehow. And it lasted for awhile. But here again, I suppose that the rope cut after awhile. Lots of ice around.

He drifted out back of the island. It was out there that the men— whoever came from Morien and picked him up, and took him in. There was a period of time before Dad would get in to see how he was. And another thing, if there were messages to us, they would put them over the radio. (*You mean on regular radio, CJCB?*) Yes. Like, you know, if they had a message for Flint Island, they could send a message and let you know if everybody was all right. Things like that. It didn't happen often, but if it was an emergency, or something like that, they would do it for you.

(*Did you feel cut off from the rest of the world?*) No. When we were kids we thought it was great. We didn't think anything of it. I suppose there were so many of us there. We played ball, we learned how to skate. Every once in awhile you'd

Martell children on Flint Island. Left to right: Billy, Kenny, Ethel, Johnny, Loren, Audrey, with Margaret in front of her, and Murray.

see a great big sheet of ice, which would be an ice clamper. And we used to go off and we'd skate on that. Then eventually they made a rink on the island, and we skated. We had snowbanks outside of the house that we used to coast. And we used to jump over the bank in the snow—anything imaginable we used to do for recreation. We had lots of fun.

One year [Dad] made a washer for [Mum]. But we could only use it when it was foggy. Because the machines were in the fog station. He had like a bar, [and] like a puncheon, I suppose, a wooden puncheon—cut it off, and he made a washer for her. Hooked it up—it was electrical, of course—as long as the engines were running. (*Why could you only use it when it was foggy?*) Because you were using the engine for the foghorn, and it was government property. Everything out there was government property. If it was foggy, Mum would wash. The rest, she'd do in the tub on the washboard. And another time, he hooked up the house with electricity, and it was run off the same engines that were in the fog station. (*So any time you wanted light....*) We'd wish it was foggy.

(*Was there ever a shipwreck?*) Yes. A boat, yes. In fact it was a fisherman from Glace Bay. They were out, and it was a storm, I guess, and they drifted out to the island. And they were just washing on the shore, but yet, washing out past the island, when they got a rope to them somehow, and they pulled them in. And they were with us for, I guess, three or four days before they got ashore. A Mr. Pink, and John Turner, and Mr. Pink's son—they were from Water Street in Glace Bay.

The way when it's stormy, the seas are quite far off. And when they get into those seas, it's almost useless to try to do anything, because you go along with them. And it just so happened that they were washed to the island. But if they hadn't gotten them at the time they did, they would have washed right past the island and probably capsized in the seas, out further. I don't know if they lost the boat completely or if Dad had to take them in when it was fine.

(*Is this an island where it's difficult to get from the boat to the shore?*) It used to be, but Dad built a slip. And he had an engine that they used to pull the boat up on the slip. In high tides you could jump from the boat to the shore. But he was a handyman, he was a jack-of-all-trades. And if you'd mention it, he'd do it. If he was fixing your engine, and if he didn't have a part, he'd make it. So he could do anything.

(*What was your mother's daily work, for instance?*) The usual chores. And then when we'd finish, we'd quilt or we'd hook mats or things like that. The girls. There just always seemed to be something to do. The boys always had their chores outside. But like, you say, what would Mama's work be? But you're looking at twelve and fourteen kids! By the time you would wash for them. And, like I said, when she wasn't washing in the washer, she was washing in the tub.

(*What was your Dad's job?*) First of all, you'd have to get up in the morning, and you'd put the light out. Don't forget, this light is going all night. Then you had to make sure that it was clean, and your mantles—you'd have to make sure that it was ready for the next night. Then you'd have to make sure that the engines were in perfect condition, because you had to use them through the day, if necessary. In the fog station. (*Was there an engine for the lighthouse?*) No. In the lighthouse, you had to go up three flights of stairs. The lighthouse was ninety feet high. And each level—there was a weight—in each one of the ceilings there were three holes. You had to wind up those weights. You had to go to the top of the light; you'd wind those weights up. And when they'd start, this is what would make your light go around. And when it revolves—it has those big magnifying glasses—and as they turn each way, when it revolves, this is where you get your flashes on each side. (*So is it the magnifying glass that's actually turning?*) Yes. Around the mantle. And as the weights come down, this is what's making it turn around.

And you had to go up in the lighthouse—if it was dark, you'd light it at four o'clock [in the afternoon], okay? So you'd have to go up at eight o'clock, and twelve o'clock, and four o'clock in the morning. And you'd have to wind those weights up. (*Through the night. So the thing only ran for four hours.*) Yes. And if that weight went to the bottom, if you overslept or something and that weight went to the bottom, the light would stop. So therefore they would have to go up those three shifts a night. And the boys used to take their turn. When I was out on the island with Dad [after most of the family had left], I used to take one of them. And I hated it. Especially twelve o'clock at night, going out in that spooky lighthouse. It was just—if you dropped anything down, you'd get this awful noise. Well, you can just picture, a hollow place, and you drop something in it, how the sound would carry.

So this is what they had to do every night. That was like a ritual that they had to do. (*And this was seven days a week.*) This was seven days a week. You're not talking about just once in awhile. And see, and if they didn't do that, the light would stop. And therefore people would think there was something wrong, or else they weren't getting the message, if there were ships out in the water. It was all for a purpose.

John James and Amy Ethel Frances Martell; son Johnny

It had its good points and it had its bad. But we didn't think we missed anything when we were out there. (*And coming in, did you think you'd missed anything?*) Once we started to see how the other half lived. We missed plenty. (*What did they have that you didn't have, in the '30s?*) Well, I guess, communication with other people. (*There wasn't any way in which you felt on top because you had been out there?*) No. We felt sort of down under.

When we were out there, we didn't think we were missing anything. But then when we came in, we always felt like we were a couple of hicks from the sticks. You know, like, when you come in, and when you were mingling with the other socialites of the community.

(*In later years, when your mother would talk about*

Raymond's death, did she feel that they should have left the island after that?) I think, yes. But then, it's just like everything else. When it's stormy, everything is black. And then when you get sunshine, everything is beautiful, and you forget about storms. In other words, you think of the good times and forget the bad. (*I don't agree.... I don't think your mother forgot for one minute.*) She didn't forget, no, no. But like I said, you put it to the back of your mind. (*But then she lost another child. That was her oldest daughter?*) Yes.

(*So what do you think? Do you still think she didn't want to come off?*) I'm sure she did. I'm sure that—poor Mum was one of those persons that—if she had an ache or a pain, she was sure she had cancer....

(*We talked some years ago with a man who'd been thirteen years on St. Paul's Island. He said they were wasted years.*) As far as I'm concerned, now that's how I feel about it. It was years of my life that were wasted. And once we came off, for good, and we started realizing it, I never ever wanted to go back. Never, to this day, I've never gone back. Once we left that island for good, that was it. I said, it's a good place to visit, but you don't want to live there. That's about the size of it.

When Raymond was drowned, we were sent to bed. And somebody said something about Raymond, and [my sister] said, "He's behind the door there, hiding on us." He wasn't there, because he had drowned. But she thought she saw him behind the door. It was just sort of an apprehension, is it? Just something that you think has happened, that he's there and yet he's not there. (*Was this before she knew that he had been drowned?*) Before she knew. (*She said she saw him behind the door.*) Saw him behind the door....

And we always had a fear of bats. Because it always seemed that before something happened in the family, bats came in the house. This is superstition, of course. But it always seemed to happen, if a bat came in the house, we could always look for bad luck, you know, and something happened within the family. It always seemed to happen. (*Did a bat come in?*) Yes. Before each time. (*When you say each time, you mean before....*) An accident, something happened, yeah. Before Raymond died, before Ethel was drowned, before Harold. It always seemed—a bat did come in the house beforehand.... A bat came in the house before Mama died.... I'm not superstitious, but only of bats, because I associate them with things that have happened.

When Ethel drowned—the year Ethel drowned—that night, Mama heard her calling. We heard the next day that she had died. But it was during the night. We knew the boat drifted, and Mum knew the boat drifted, and I know she was upset and everything—concerned, worried—because we didn't know if they were going to make it or not. And she said that she heard her calling her that night. She told us when she got up in the morning that she heard Ethel calling her.

(*I think there's a lot more to your mother than we're able to say.*) Oh, I'm sure there was. (*Apparently she didn't speak of it all that much.*) Oh, she kept it to herself a lot. But a lot of times she did talk about things, but I suppose we didn't pay much attention. We probably talked with her, and we discussed it probably with her, but it maybe didn't register. It was things that happened, and we just talked about them, and that was it.

(*How did they actually get your brother Raymond?*) They got him with a grappling—that's a thing with a hook on it that they use in boats. They had to have a rope on it to reach, and put it down, and they hooked to his clothing and got it up. I wasn't very old, but down through the years, I can still remember when they got him and everything.

I don't care how young you are, I think things like this—it sort of stays with you. You probably forget a lot of it, but the main thing stays with you. I remember even, like, talking. I will say yes, that Mum did talk to us, different times, but it used to upset her when we'd talk about it. I remember when Dad had to pack him [Raymond] on ice. And he made the rough box. And he had to keep him in the cold—like, cold storage—but the coldest place was the boathouse, until—I guess it was four or five days, anyway, he had to stay there, until the boat came.

Looking back, it's a terrible existence. At the time we faced it, and we all faced it. But it's different, I suppose, for your parents, because they've lost somebody.

But with younger ones, children, you sort of forget it. You don't forget that they've gone. But you forget the actual thing that happened, and the way it happened. But with parents, I think, and especially there with Dad, it must have stayed with him the rest of his life. Because he had to do the actual work, he had to do the actual thing. He had to go get him, and he had to do all this, terrible things, in order to keep him. Just knowing that he was out there in the boathouse, and when we were home in the house....

(*Is there anything out there today, any mark, that says the Martells were on Flint Island?*) No. Nothing. Even the house was torn down.... I think even the light is not the same.

Harry Albert Bulley: Accidents Averted

Harry Albert Bulley is my name. I was born in the States—Washington. I was born in 1897. My father was working there. My father was born be-tween North Sydney and Sydney Mines, a place they call Centreville. He was a contractor; he used to build homes and stuff up there. But I never took his job. I came to Sydney when I was a very young fellow. I'd say I was about five years old. I went on the C.N.R. [Canadian National Railway] in 1915.

I always liked railroading. When I was a young fellow, I used to get engines [toys]—light them up, you know, stuff like that. I got a great kick out of it. I always liked railroading.

I worked at the round-house for quite awhile. I got my experience there, the first year. That was in 1915. We had to work, lighting the fires, getting the engines ready, express engines. We'd have to call those drivers that time. No telephone calls after a certain hour. We'd have to go give them two hours, and we'd have to go up where they were, their homes. We'd go, and we'd tap on the door, and we'd be sure he'd get up and answer us, eh? Then we'd come back and report that we'd given the call. We'd have to be sure that he'd hear the call. Because all kinds of nights, you know, all hours of the morning. They were pretty sleepy sometimes, the fellows. One week we'd have to clean the engines. Oh, we had to clean it good. They gave us the oil, and the waste. And even the wheels. We'd have to go underneath to clean all, you know, anything that was in there. They had very particular fellows, the drivers. We'd always polish her. And the next week we'd be on the turntable.

I worked in the roundhouse pretty near two years. I got out when I was twenty-one years old—firing on the road. This fireman took sick, and they got me out of the roundhouse, and I went on the engine. And I made a good run out on them. And I got my turn from that time on. (*What do you mean you made a good run?*) That means you kept her hot for the driver, stuff like that. You kept the steam up. You knew your work hand-firing, see. You had a shovel there. And when you put a fire in the engine, you turned your shovel upside down. That would fan the flames, and that would show you where to put your coal. That would show you where the holes were in your firebox. And then, if you wouldn't get the right smoke out of your stack, you didn't have the right fire in her. There's something wrong. You would have to get nice black smoke out of her stack, to have a good fire. Because you had different kinds of coal. This Sydney coal, it was very easy to fire. It clinkered a lot.

And I'll tell you: I was called a first-class fireman. I was no better than the others. But I'll tell you how. We'd leave before supper with this Inverness coal, and go to Grand Narrows. And half the way, it'd be clinkered. When I'd get to Iona, I'd go to work and clean my fire. They used to transfer mail at Iona. Well, I had time then to shake my grates; I'd clean my fire. And going over to the Grand Narrows bridge, I'd get my engine pretty hot. When I'd get to Grand Narrows, I'd go to work. I'd get up on top of the tender and fill my tender full of water. And the driver'd empty out the ashes out of the ash pan. I'd have a real good fire in there. And they'd wonder how I was always making up my time. The others that'd come to work, they wouldn't bother cleaning their fire at Iona. They'd come to Grand Narrows, they'd lost time. That was my secret. I had my fire all clean, all ready. Lose no time there at all.

I'm the only guy living today, in our own division, that fired that big engine by hand. I couldn't tell you how much coal was on, but we often cleaned off that tender. On the run. My run then was from here [Sydney] to Point Tupper, 102 miles. (*Would you be shoveling all the way?*) If you were a pretty good fireman, you wouldn't have to kill yourself. But if you were careless, you didn't know how to fire right, you'd have a hard job. And then you'd have to fight with the driver. The driver would want steam.

I fired quite awhile. Promotion was very slow then. I'd say I fired about ten years, anyhow. They had the S & L engine. There used to be a pit where they used to haul stone, off of Jefferson's. Anyhow, I got that train one time. John Willie MacDonald was the boss. And I made such a good record on her, they wanted to keep me on her. So I agreed, if they'd give me steady work on her, I'd take the engine. So, I took the engine, anyhow, and I made a good success of her. First I'd go in that quarry in the morning. We'd bring the load of stone in first. And then the afternoon, we'd go over after a load of coal. And lots of those fellows, when they had the load of coal, they'd have trouble coming over the hill at Jefferson's. Especially in rainy weather.

When I came in in the daytime with the load of stone, I'd go down to the roundhouse. That'd be in the morning. I'd have my lunch down there. Then I'd go to work. I'd get hot sand in the sandbox [of the engine]. And when I'd come over from Sydney Mines with the load of coal—they used to load up pretty heavy, you know—instead of pulling her out at Leitches Creek like the other fellows did, I'd take my time with the nice hot sand. And the hot sand would grab the wheels. They wouldn't slip. (*You had a way of throwing the sand?*) Yeah. Little valve there in the cab. And I wouldn't give her too much, now, just enough. The sand pipes were out under the wheel. And then I wouldn't have to pull her out, like the other fellows used to do. (*What does "pull her out" mean?*) That's the throttle. They were giving her too much steam, and she'd lose her feet. And that's a trick I had. Even the superintendent came over, John Willie MacDonald, wondering how I was getting over that road. Mostly, they had a lot of trouble getting over the hills. They used to stall there; they had trouble a lot. They'd have to flag out the flagman, and get the other train coming, stop the other fellow, see. And that was my only trick—the sand.

(*I saw the list that you wrote up of all the accidents that you were able to stop, that weren't accidents. Were you ever involved in an accident?*) No, I had pretty good luck. I never had one, my own cause, nothing at all. I always had pretty good luck. I always avoided them. I never got any demerits. There were accidents on the line. And a lot of those accidents were caused—well, I kind of explain it—by not being careful enough.

I was shunting at Big Brook, on the pickup. And the brakeman was standing on a pile of ties, see. I was shunting back like that. And I had a Johnson bar. That's not an air reverse, you know. A Johnson bar is the old-time lever. You could stop it pretty quick. And if I had the air reverse on that time, I couldn't stop her as quick as I did. So this fellow was standing on a pile of ties. Whatever happened to him, I don't know—he went headfirst between two cars. So anyhow, I told the fireman, "By golly, that fireman fell between two cars."

So we went down. The fall had knocked him out. He was underneath the car. Kind of dark then. So I told my brakeman, "You crawl under the cars and see how he's lying. Let me know." He came back and told me about it. I said, "Go back the second time and make sure. Because I'm going to move the engine a little bit ahead to get the wheel off his leg." So I moved the engine ahead a little bit and I got the wheel off his leg. Went back and got him out of there, and we put a binder on his leg, stop the bleeding.

We left. We reported all that at River Denys. And this operator wanted to know how long I'd take to take him to the hospital. I said, "I'm not going to try unless they give me a clear road. But if you give me a clear road, I'll do it in such-and-such a time." And I had an engine on there, 2412 was her number. She had high wheels. And I made a very fast run on her, on that train, very fast run. I made it faster than what I said I'd make it. And the ambulance was waiting for him when I got there. Well, that fellow lived. He only died here the other day. And I saved his life. And I got a nice card from his wife, congratulating me for what I did.

(*You were able to keep a lot of accidents from happening?*) Oh yes, dear man, yes, I saved an awful lot. And another thing, dear fellow, I wasn't sneaky about it, you know what I mean. But nobody got in trouble. Nobody was sacked over it, see. I saved them. For the sake of their family and stuff like that. I was keeping in mind, if they were sacked out of work, their family might be in want. And of course, if there was a liquor charge, or something like that, it'd be different. In an accident, if you had liquor—that'll do. Even the head man there, if he came up talking to you, and smelled liquor off you, he'd take you right out of the service. And he'd get a doctor at the next station to examine you, to prove his word, if you had liquor on you. You wouldn't have to be drunk. There you go.

I came into Orangedale. And nobody wanted to fire for this fellow. He was kind of a cranky fellow, you know, the old fellow, nobody wanted to fire for him. So they got me that day—they couldn't get a fireman. So I had my mileage in—you'd make so many miles, then you'd be cut off, by the end of the month. So they called me up; they asked me would I go with him. I said, "Yes. He's not paying me." I said, "The C.N.R.'s paying me. I'll go with him, certainly." So I went out with him, anyhow. It was all right going up. But we were coming down Orangedale, there was a fellow jumped on the engine, around Christmas time. And he had a bottle of something. I said something to him: "Don't give him that." But he took a drink before I knew it. And the first thing I know, he fell on the floor—whatever was in that bottle, I don't know.

Anyhow, I went to work, and I said to the brakeman, "Now listen, you'll have to help me. Because I've got to report this," I said, "if you don't help me." So the brakeman went to work, and he helped me out. And it was a hand-fired engine.

So anyhow, I took her, and I made the stops, and everything went well. I went down to the C.N.R. I got him on the ash pit. I got the fellow in the oil house to come out and give me a hand in with him. He was that drunk. So we took him in the roundhouse. "Let him sleep there. And I'm going

45

home for my supper, but I'll be back again." So I came back, and I went in the oil house and woke him up. He said, "Where am I? Who put me here?" I said, "Now listen. You get up. I'm going to take you home. And I'm going out with you in the morning. And don't you stay off. I'm going to call for you."

And so I went in the house in the morning. And he came with me. Nothing happened. I could have reported that, and I could have got, maybe, merit marks or something. That's what they gave you for good work like that. But the family'd be in want. That time gave him a good lesson.

[Here is a list Mr. Bulley prepared some time ago of accidents that didn't happen, while he was on the C.N.R. from 1917 to 1962:]

1. In 1917 firing on No. 5 train, coming from Point Tupper to Sydney, after shoveling fire in engine and then looking out the window, I saw the switch ahead turned for spur. I called out to the Engineer, Matheson, that the switch was not right. This was at Long Island. Thus a wreck was averted.

2. I was Engineer on Extra leaving Sydney for Point Tupper on a double-header. We got orders at Sydney for our meets. They were all changed at North Sydney, except our meet at George's River on 691 train. It was forgotten by the Engineer on the leading engine and the crew. I was the only one who did not forget. I sent my fireman to flag and saved a bad wreck.

3. I was engineer on passenger train No. 5 going west, running 10 minutes late trying to pick up this time. When I got over the grade at McArthurs I saw a train in the siding around the curve. I called out the foreman to look to see if the train was clear. The train's end was fouled, and there was no Flagman to flag me. Another accident averted.

4. Coming down as Engineer on Way-Freight one late stormy night in the winter. After shunting at North Sydney, orders were given to me with only the Green clearance. When I had a meet on Extra 71 at Gibbons, the order was not given to me. But I saw the other train coming and averted another wreck.

5. Coming down on No. 7 train as Engineer one morning in 1950, with 9 passenger cars. Looking ahead, I saw that the switch was not in the right position. I stopped the train and found that the switch was run through. I spiked the switch and reported it, thus saving another wreck. This happened at Tupper Junction and would have been a bad wreck as a derailer is at the other end of the switch.

6. Coming down on Way-Freight one morning for Hastings. We left early that morning from Havre Boucher, and there was a crew welding the tracks. They had five or six tanks on the trolley, and they did not flag me

as they were not thinking. I was almost on top of them when I stopped the train. Another accident averted.

7. Coming to Sydney on S & L Engine 70 with a full load of coal, 25 cars of coal and two loads of scrap at rear end. I got a High Ball from the train ahead that everything was all right. But I saw an engine on the track fouled ahead of me so I kept my brake on, saving a wreck.

8. Coming down as Engineer on 602 Railiner one evening late March in 1960. I had a lot of passengers. I left Stellarton late, and by making this time, I saved the passengers and Railiner from going over a steep cliff, about 50 feet deep and into the water. A train going west with two diesel engines struck the mud slide and went over the bank. Another accident averted by making up this time.

9. Engineer on Extra one night on double-header. I looked back going around Gillis Cove and I saw fire coming from the wheel of a car. I stopped the train and found a car off the track. I got replacers and put the car back on the track with nothing tied up. Another accident averted.

10. Engineer on No. 8 train after leaving West Bay station. I looked back at the cars and saw a light under a car. I stopped the train to examine this and discovered the journal of the wheel cracked. I had it set off and averted an accident.

11. Engineer on Railiner 602 coming into Sydney west of Townsend Street. There was a man asleep and drunk on the track. I stopped the train and got him off the track. Another accident averted.

12. Engineer on Railiner 601. On stormy winter morning at Sydney River Bridge, I saw a woman on the middle of the bridge. When she saw the train she got excited and did not know which way to go. I stopped the Railiner to get her off the track. Another accident averted.

13. Engineer on 601 going west, coming into Little Bras d'Or. An oil truck went in front of the Railiner at the crossing. I stopped the train in time to avert an accident.

14. Engineer on shunter in Yard. I missed the brakeman at the front of the engine. I stopped the engine, and found the brakeman's leg under the foot board of the engine. I save an accident and maybe the man's life.

15. Engineer on Shunter in yard backing up on train to couple on cars. The brakeman was going through the cars at the same time and the coupling only touched his stomach by my slight move in the coupling on cars. Accident averted.

16. Engineer on No. 7 train one morning. An oil truck full of gasoline crossed in front of me and stalled on the track, at Sydney River. I stopped the train just in time by using the Emergency Brake, saved a bad accident.

17. Engineer on 601 Railiner going to Hastings Junction one winter morning in 1962. A section man came out of van and jumped into the

47

snow in front of the railiner, and he got stuck there. I stopped the train just in time to get him clear. Accident averted.

18. Engineer on Railiner 601 one morning after leaving King's Road crossing, transportation truck backed right in front of me. I had to put on the Emergency Brake to stop. Accident averted.

19. Coming down on Second 7 as Engineer in 1943, I had a very important parcel for the hospital at North Sydney. I had a Freight Engine No. 3214 and made it in two hours flat, faster than they expected me.

20. Engineer on 602 one year, 1961 Christmas Night. There was a man very sick in the hospital waiting for medicine. I had two diesels and made the Railiner time 30 minutes faster than they expected me. Getting the medicine there in time to save the man's life.

I'll tell you—she'll tell you about me. I never missed one trip. Tell him about the time I went out and I slipped.

Margaret Bulley: We had two big trees in the front here. A gale took them down. Now they're not there. But he was going to work and he had his lunch box, and he got out there and slipped and fell against a tree and put his arm out of place. And he came in—I was going to call a doctor. "Don't call a doctor," he said, "I'll be all right." He said, "Give me a drink of water." And I did. Gave him a glass of water. And whatever he did—he went like that with his arm, put it back in place, took his lunch box, and went.

Harry: I'll tell you this one, too, you know, not bragging about myself. But I was a pretty hard man in my days. I took up wrestling, I took up boxing, and I was in good shape. Sometime around Christmas time, there'd be those fellows drinking. Anyhow, we left this Christmas time. So the conductor came up to me where I was. He seemed kind of nervous. I said, "What's wrong?" "Fellow back there gave me a lot of trouble." I said, "Is he drinking?" "No, he's not drinking. He's cursing and swearing—interrupting the passengers." I said, "Why didn't you put him off at Hawkesbury, where the cops were?" "Well, he promised to be quiet." So anyhow, we stopped there. I went back, anyhow—this other fellow with me, too. I said, "Listen, you're tying up the railiner here. What are you going to do, behave yourself or what? If you don't behave yourself, you're going off. And I'm that man that will put you off." He looked at me. I turned my back. He started. He went off like a paper bag.

I was sorry to leave my job in a way, but I was happy with the experience I had, that nothing happened. I was happy. And I didn't have a bad record. I was happy that everything went good for me, and I got along with them all. I never had any demerit marks, see, no demerit marks. I had wonderful luck on the railroad. Sure, wonderful luck, couldn't be any better.

A Visit with Janie Nicholson, Midwife in Baddeck

I was about seventeen when I went in [for nursing]. In 1904, I think it was. My father's people were in Boston. (*Did you feel you could get training there easier than in Nova Scotia?*) Well, I don't know. I liked the States, you know, I liked to stay there and live there. And then I took sick when I went in training, after a few months. I got the measles some way or another, I don't know how. And I was so anxious to work, you know. I was homesick for a little while at my aunt's. And I guess I got up too soon, and it was in the wintertime. And had quite a ways to go, you see, to work. And I got the relapse. Then I had to quit. (*You were working as a nurse at this point?*) Yes, at that time. I just got a few months in. But that few months was really good for me.

So then I got the relapse and I got a pain—pleurisy—and then I had to stay home. Oh, I felt so bad. And then the doctor said that the climate didn't agree with me there. Boston is a very damp place; it's low. And he said that he thought I'd have to come back home to my own country.

When I was in the States, I worked with a doctor there for a little bit, my aunt's doctor. I did a little work with him. Just to please me, he'd take me. I was so anxious. I thought, Well now, if I become a nurse—this was my ambition—if I become a nurse, and graduate, then I'd make enough money, and I'd go take up medicine. I wanted to be a surgeon. I wanted to operate. I wanted to see what is inside of a person. And every doctor I ever worked with, they always said they'd rather me than a graduate nurse, an R.N., working with them. That's what they all told me. One doctor told me, he said, "You missed your calling. You should have been a doctor." (*You just never had enough money to go?*) Well, no.

So then I was determined to carry on and do what I could about nursing. I got books, and I took a course that way. And then I went out working with the doctors, and doing midwife. (*This was back in Cape Breton, in Baddeck?*) Yeah. When I was at my aunt's [in Boston], her son's wife was having a baby, and oh boy, I had to have my finger in the pie, too. I was bound I was going to find out. So I was helping my aunt along with the doctor, and I was only about seventeen. So I got some training there, see. Everything I saw the doctor do, you know, I just put it right down in my head. (*It was a home birth, I guess.*) Oh yes. Those days, you never took anybody to a hospital to deliver a baby. The doctor came to help deliver the baby, and then we looked after the baby after that. I kept washing it for her and looking after it, and helping her, and everything. Oh, I just loved that work.

(*When did you come back to Baddeck?*) I'd say 1907. My mother got sick, and I had to come home. I didn't want to come home. Even if the doctor told me I'd have to come back to my own country, I said I wouldn't come. But then my mother sent for me, and had to come home. (*What was it that you preferred about the States?*) Well, I don't know. This was only a very small, little town at that time. (*Very isolated, too, I guess.*) Yeah, it was at that time. And I kind of liked that city life, you know, in a certain way. But not crazy about it at all. I wouldn't want to live in New York or any of those places, oh no. Halifax itself is city enough. (*How did you get back to Baddeck?*) Oh, I came by boat as far as Hawkesbury, then came on the train from there. And then we came from Iona on a boat. And when I landed on the wharf down here, well, I thought Baddeck looked so funny to me. Oh, it was at that time. There were only a few buildings here and there, you know. But anyway, I stayed home and looked after my mother.

Then I got married. He was a good-looking chap. I guess that's what got my goat. But anyway, I guess it must have been something I had to do. (*When you married him, did he say that you couldn't work?*) No, he didn't mind it too much. 'Course, then, I couldn't very well go out to work as much as I did later on. Well, I was having children, you know, and one thing and another. That'd keep you home.

But I'd always go, wherever they'd call for me, you know, or if there was any place I could go to help. Wherever there was a baby born, I'd always be there. Sometimes the doctor'd call me, and sometimes the women, you know, when they knew they were pregnant or something—they'd call me up and ask me. Or they'd write me a letter—there were very few telephones. And then, of course, I'd give them all the information that they should have about how to carry their baby and how to watch their diet, and all that. (*You were doing even that?*) Oh, yes. Well, land sake, you'd have to explain to, say, a young woman—she didn't know anything about it. You'd have to tell her what to do, how to take care of herself, how to watch her baby, that she didn't do anything that would hurt her baby. All that.

(*There was no prenatal care then either, was there?*) Well, not too much, no. Oh, of course, women those days, they worked hard and it didn't bother them any. No. Oh, I had to get a few babies alone, you know. If everything was coming all right, it was all right. But if not, of course, I couldn't.... (*You wouldn't have any tools?*) No, I had no instruments, you know. Only I had my own bag with all the stuff that I needed for myself. I carried a little of everything. Oh, I carried a thermometer, different articles that you'd need around. When you'd go into a house, well, there wasn't anything to work with. I'd have scissors and I'd have lots of sterilized cottons and things, old cottons in the bag, you know, if I needed it. Or probably I'd go to a house and there wouldn't be anything. I've been to a house where there wasn't even a basin. I'd go to the neighbour's, if there was a neighbour near, and I'd borrow a basin, or if it's in the town here, I'd come home and I'd take my own stuff up to the house.

I'd tell the woman, if I knew she was going to have a baby, I'd say, "Save all the newspapers you can." And I'd tell her how to make a pad, too. You see, you lay them together, you know, and then you take an old sheet and you cover them all over. You make a pad that would cover the whole bed. And that's the only protection that I had. The last few years, of course, they got rubber sheets. Before my time, I've heard my mother say, the mother, the woman that was going to have the baby, she'd make a little mattress out of straw, clean straw. The men thrashed the straw, you know, the oats and the barley, and then they'd have this clean straw for putting under the cows and horses for bedding. So she'd make a little mattress, see, out of that, and put it on the floor. And she'd deliver her baby on that.

(*Did they deliver in the same position—were they on their backs?*) Well, whichever way the woman was most comfortable. That's the way we did. But today in the hospitals, they have a delivery room, and they put you on a thing—it's much wider than that. Probably you've seen it. And that's where they deliver their babies now. Well, the way I delivered the babies those days was—well, whichever way she was most comfortable in

51

her pains. Sometimes women have pains all in the back and none in the front. And that's terrible hard, that's an awful hard birth. The pains were all coming from the back instead of where they should come, to press down. And then you'd have to take and rub that woman's back, or press against her back. You'd have to get in the bed—if the doctor was with you, or if you had another woman to help you—you'd have to get behind her in the bed and hold right onto her back and press all you could. So that's the way the poor children were born those days.

(*If it was a long labour, what would you do?*) We'd just have to wait. Well, you could find out that the baby's head was coming. A midwife was allowed that. The nurses are allowed that, too. You can examine with your hand, a rubber glove on. If you find the baby's head up there, well, you'd know that it's coming all right. But a breech birth, that's a hard birth.

(*Would you arrive generally just when labour was beginning?*) Well, just whenever the woman would have the first pain, she'd send for the doctor, and then the doctor'd call me. (*Would you usually get there before the doctor?*) Oh well, I'd go with the doctor. I wouldn't need to take my own car. One year Dr. MacMillan had one of those great big snowmobiles, you know, like a tractor. Oh well, that was an awful winter. That'd be almost forty years ago, I suppose. And it was an awful winter, that one. All the snow. That's why he got that snowmobile, see, so he could go way out in the country.

So he called me about midnight, and I was having my period at the time. And I was so warm in bed, and oh, my gosh. He said, "Janie, be ready in ten minutes. I'll be down after you." Jack [Jack Nicholson, Janie's second husband] said, "Oh, ain't you foolish, going out tonight." "Oh well," I said, "I couldn't refuse"—in a case like that. So I got up and I got dressed and I got my little bag with what I wanted in it. He came down, and I was waiting for him. "My gosh," he said, "you got dressed quick!" And away we started, way out in the glen. And the house was up on a hill. And down below the house was a big river. "Oh," I said, "you're not going to take this thing up to the house, are you, doctor?" "Well, how we going to get there? That's the only way we can. You going to crawl on your hands and feet," he said, "and your belly?" "Well," I said, "gee, I'm afraid the thing will upset going up that hill. We'll land down in the river." "Well," he said, "we'll both go together then. We'll all die together." "Well," I said, "I don't know, we may freeze to death before we die!"

So I got out of the thing, and oh, it was high up. I started jumping, and I went up to there in the snow. Hooo! I got out of there and I crawled up to the house, to the back door, and I got in. And there was a girl having a baby—she wasn't married. The mother was in the kitchen with a big fire on—a wood stove—nursing one of the other babies that this girl had. And the one that was having the baby was in the bedroom off from the kitchen. I went in to see what was to be done.

First, you see, I'd have to prepare them for birth. If they weren't right near their time, you see, I'd have to give them an enema and shave them and get them all ready for birth, for delivery. And I had lots of time—she wasn't too far advanced. I got her ready, and she started crying. "What a thing to do," she said, "my poor mother." "Well," I said, "it's too late crying for that now. Never mind. Think of what you're going through, and get this over. Then you can cry. And don't let it happen again." I got the bed all fixed up. I think I had rubber sheets then. So I got her all fixed up in the bed, and she wasn't too long before she had her baby. Oh, I think we

Dr. C. L. MacMillan
and a sketch of his snowmobile

were there about three hours or so. A lovely baby. But she was in the same pickle not too long afterwards.

Oh, I went in some funny places. I think of them sometimes and I wonder, my gosh, how'd I ever struggle through it. And I never charged one cent. I imagine Dr. MacMillan could tell you that if he wanted to. He could tell you that I did it all voluntary. (*You didn't take any money at all?*) No, well, you couldn't. Some places, of course, they could pay—but I wouldn't take it. But when you see a lot of little children around, you couldn't have the heart. I didn't really need it, you know. I had plenty home myself. Because I thought it'd be an awful sin for

me to go and take anything from those people. 'Course, I suppose if I really needed it, and that was the way I was making my living, probably I'd have to get something, some little thing, a dollar or so. A dollar went a long ways then.

What I'd have to do when I'd go to confinement cases, I'd have to get the woman ready—the doctor wouldn't have to do a thing. He'd just come and see how she was progressing. Then he'd go away and leave it all with me. And I'd have to wait till I knew the baby was just coming, then I'd call him. So he didn't have much to do. And when the baby was born and everything was over, well, he left it all with me. (*So he cut the cord?*) Yes, or I could cut it if I wished. (*And then he'd wait for the afterbirth?*) Oh yes, we'd have to wait. You'd have to let her rest a little while. Then she starts with pain again. But you've got to be very careful with the afterbirth.

Uterus is here, and keep holding up like that, and let her have her pain, but just ease it off a little bit. Then she'd probably have some more pains. And then, if the doctor wasn't there, you'd have to take ahold of the cord and pull it easy, while she was having her pain. To take it down. So you wouldn't pull everything with it. You'd have to be very careful about getting the afterbirth. (*That was almost the most dangerous part, sometimes.*) Yes, sometimes it is. Sometimes it's awful hard to get it. The only times I ever got the babies alone, I didn't have much trouble with the afterbirth. It seemed to come quite well.

Dr. MacMillan and I were talking together one day not too long ago down on the street there. I was at the bank, and he came out. We were talking about the days and the nights that we'd be out. Poor fellow. That night that he called me, and we had to go out in the country on the snowmobile: "Do you know," he said, "that I only went to bed about ten minutes before the phone rang. And," he said, "this is the third night that I've been out, and I haven't had any sleep yet." "Well," I said, "if things are slow when we get there, you can have a sleep." So things were slow, not very fast, and I got the old lady in the house, the grandmother—"Can you get a nice place for Dr. MacMillan to lie down?" I said, "Tuck some nice blankets around him." "Yes," she said. "Well," I said, "I'll wake you if I have to. You go ahead and sleep." So he did, he had a nice little sleep.

Dr. MacMillan—the first night he came to Baddeck here, I was with him that night. That same night, I was going to get supper. A knock came to the door. And it was Morrison. He said, "Can you come up to the house?" His wife was expecting a baby. I said, "Is she very sick now?" He said, "No, she's not very sick. She's just started, and I guess she has an idea that her baby's going to be born now." I said, "Would I have time to make supper?" He said, "Yes, I think so." So I did, I had my supper, and I got ready, and I went up to the house. I got in there. And she said,

"There's no doctor in town." "Well," I said, "perhaps we can get along without the doctor." And I thought, after a long time—I got her all ready, you know, for her delivery and all that—Jack came home that day, he'd said, "There's a new doctor in Baddeck." And she was getting pretty near delivering her baby. And I thought, Well now, I'd love to deliver this alone, you know, but then, I'd better not. I said, "There's a new doctor came to Baddeck today, and he's over in the hotel. You'd better run over and get him."

So, he was only here a few hours, you know, and he was pretty nervous. On his first case. So he came, boy, and he came up the stairs, and he almost went headfirst at the top of the stairs, he was in such a hurry. And he was nervous. And I introduced myself. I knew his name. I knew that Dr. MacMillan was coming—that's all I knew about him. And I took him in the room. "Oh," he said, "you've got everything all ready." They didn't have a bathroom, you know—a basin in the bedroom. So I got some water for him, and put a blue pill in the water, and towels and everything. And he put his sleeves up to here, scrubbed his hands and his fingernails with the brush, cleaned himself. And I thought, Gee, this is going to be a good doctor, all right.

So he went to work and he examined her, and boy, the baby was well on its way. I could have got the baby myself, for that matter. But anyway, she complained a lot, she made a big fuss. So, I'd have to give the chloroform, you know, for the doctor. (*How did you give it?*) Oh, form a little mask on her face, and sprinkle a little on. I'd stop giving it to her when the pain would stop, you see. And then when the pain would start to come, I'd give her another little whiff of it, see. Finally, she dozed off into this sleep, all right enough. So we got her baby all right—didn't have to use instruments or anything. It came very nicely.

(*Did doctors tend to use instruments, or did they tend to wait?*) Well, if he finds that the baby won't come without instruments, he'll have to. Oh, I've been with a woman—two women—that we didn't think we could save her. I was there two nights and two days, labour. And pains were no good. And the doctor said to me, "What'll I do, Janie?" I said, "I don't know, doctor, I'm afraid it's too late to take her to the hospital for a caesarean." Had to take them to Sydney to have a caesarean birth. "Yes," he said, "I think you're right there." I said, "It's too bad she didn't go to Sydney the first." It was her first baby, and she wasn't young.

So he said, "I guess we have to try and save the mother if we can." "Well," I said, "I'm getting tired, doctor, and I know you're getting tired. I haven't had any sleep for two nights now, and no rest all day." So, "Well," he said, "I think we'll just have to try and get this baby, that's all." He said, "But we'll have to have help."

So, the sisters were out in the kitchen—this is a farm, in a country house. So I went out to the door of the kitchen and I opened the door, and I said, "Would you girls come in and help me?" They went out the back door that quick, and into the woods they went. And I never saw a sign of them any more. Well, I went back and I told the doctor, "The women are gone to the woods." I said, "How about taking the man in—the sister's husband?" "Yes," the doctor said, "anybody that'll give us a help. If he'd come." I said to him, "Would you mind coming in and helping us? You won't see anything"—I had her covered over with a sheet. "Don't be embarrassed. What I'm going to tell you to do, you don't need to look at anything."

So, we had to bring her over to the side of the bed, like this, put her buttocks there, and all we wanted was for him to hold her, see. And I was to give her the chloroform. I said, "You straddle her, and I'll give her the chloroform, and Dr. MacMillan will go to work down here." And he said, "Give her plenty of chloroform, Janie." So I did. I got her pretty well asleep. And the fellow, he had ahold of her in the bed. And the doctor started. He got the instruments, and he had to pull, pull, pull, pull. And when he did get the baby, he went backwards, baby and all. So, we didn't think the baby would live—it was all big bumps all over its head—just the size of an egg, here and there and everywhere. And oh, its neck was stretched. He said, "It may live. Take it and do what you can with it, will you?" Then I said to the fellow, "You can go." He never saw anything, didn't know yet what happened.

So, we got her back in the bed, and of course, we had to wait till she came out of the chloroform. I went out to the kitchen, and the women were after coming back. Thank the Lord they were, because I'd have to give the baby to somebody. And I took the baby out to the kitchen and I got some warm oil, and put the warm oil all over it, and I wrapped it all up in flannel. The oil would sort of soften its little skin, you know. I wiped its eyes and face and mouth and everything, with my solution I had. I gave the baby to one of the sisters. She was very good. And I told her to keep it nice and warm, and to keep—probably little sponges, you know—wiping its mouth, clean its throat out.

So I went back and I got the poor mother, to give her a bath, got her fixed up. But oh boy, that was hard. Poor Dr. MacMillan, he was all in, when he got that baby. Oh, I think of some of those women. I think what happened to her—her pains came, and her baby didn't come with them, and then they died out. That's what happened. She didn't have any pains much, any good, after that. See, nature kind of stopped.

(*Did you lose many babies at all?*) Lose? No, I never lost—there was one baby we got, was dead, born dead. So we took it into a back room

56

where nobody would know it. And he opened it, and the liver—he weighed the liver—and it weighed as much as a lamb's liver. And it wasn't in the right place. He said, "It's a good thing this baby died," he said. "There'd be something wrong with him if he did live." Lovely big boy.

And then, we had another baby. Oh, we had an awful hard time with that baby, getting that baby. We had to get a couple of doctors in. The first doctor came, he got played out, he couldn't do any more work, and he left. Then we got another doctor that was here visiting from the States. Oh, we had an awful time. That woman—we had to do the same with her. And that baby's head was pulled terrible. Beautiful child. And it never urinated, or its bowels never moved. A child, after it's born, the bowels are supposed to move. And urinate, shortly after its birth. And it never did. I watched that baby—I did everything to try and get it to urinate. No sir, it never urinated. And a tiny little bit, the bowels moved—not much. And it wouldn't drink very much. So I said to myself, I wonder will this child live.

Then this big August gale came that night, that awful, awful gale. And the house, on the shore—it blew in the window, the kitchen window came in, smashed. And I stayed upstairs with the baby, and I was nursing the baby. I had it in my lap there, trying to do everything for it, putting warm things on its stomach. Everything. And the father came in and he said, "Well, I'm going out to get the doctor to come down." "Well," I said, "it's not fit for the doctor to come down tonight." "Well," he said, "I'm going to get him." And it was Dr. Gillis, a nice little doctor. He was a Catholic doctor. So he came in. I don't know how in the world they ever got there, the storm was that bad. It was wicked. All the boats that were out on the water were in on the shore in the morning. So he came down, he looked at the baby, and he says, "Oh, I don't know." And he got down on his knees, and he prayed. He got up, and he said, "That's all I can do."

So shortly after he went, the baby died. And look, there was about a bucket of water came from that child after it died. Wasn't that funny? Wasn't that strange? We could never figure that out, why that happened.

A little boy. She had three girls after that. But it was too bad she lost the little boy, yes.

(*When you were working, did you consider yourself a nurse or a midwife?*) Well, I don't know—a practical nurse, a practical nurse. Well, I got a lot of books, and I studied them, when I didn't get a chance to go in the hospital and train, see. I just kept up with the work.

(*Did the women ever come to you, if they didn't want any more children? Did they come to you for contraceptive advice?*) Well, I'd do what I could for them. But at that time, they did very little work at anything like that. The only advice I could give them was to use a douche, with a poison pill in it. It was a little blue pill, they could put it in the water, you know, use the douche after their connection. That was the only way they did in those days, that the women saved from not having their baby.

It's the funniest thing—the little, little, small women, I found them having babies much easier than the big, tall, stout women. That's right. I've been with little women, and they were laughing when their baby was coming. I said, "My gosh, you don't know about having babies," I said. "For land's sake, make some noise, let them know that you've got some pain!"

(*How many children did you have?*) Seven. I only have one living. I had three miscarriages, one was full nine months. I pretty near died with that one. Then I had a baby lived three months. Then I had three sons after that. They all lived. I lost one in the Second War, the air force, Ralph. And my other boy, when he was in his young twenties, he took meningitis, and he died. I have one boy living now, he's living down here on the main street. So that's all I got out of my seven children.

But at the last of it, though—well, I stopped going out. My boys, they took over the old farm, see. My mother died and they took over the old farm, and they had sawmills. Well, I had to look after them out on the farm, and I had to look after my home here in Baddeck. So, the boys were making hay this day, and the doctor came out after me at dinnertime. He said, "Come on, Janie, I've got a case. You've got to come with me." I said, "Doctor, I'm afraid I can't go today." "Well," he said, "who am I going to get?" "Well," I said, "you go and get that R.N. in Baddeck, she'll go with you." And I was glad I didn't go that time, because that baby died when it was born. I said, "Thank God I wasn't there."

Edited from a conversation with Kathy Moggridge Kuusisto.

Bill Fraser, Superintendent R.C.M.P., Rtd.

The twenty-seventh of April, 1935, I was sent to Ingonish. This was a whole new world, and I can remember the date. The time in Inverness was really all too short. When the spring came and the roads opened up, and the other fellow came back from the hospital in Halifax, they began to get ideas of moving me again. And I really didn't want to go—I liked Inverness, and I liked the people, in particular. There were all kinds. We had a lot of fun, though. It was good work. And then finally I got word, the latter part of April, that I was going to go to Ingonish. That there was some trouble in North Ingonish, and they were going to send me there. So I got word to pack up my bags and come to Sydney.

They'd found out that they really did have trouble in Ingonish. The constable in charge there, at the detachment, hadn't been heard from by way of correspondence since Christmas. Of course, they couldn't hear from him by phone because there were no phones at that time. Now here it was, almost the first of May. They didn't go down through the winter because it was almost impossible to get there, unless you wanted to walk on showshoes. So they let things ride. And I went into Sydney. They said, "We don't know what that man has done all winter. And now you're to go down there on the *Aspy* from North Sydney the first day she sails. And go to the detachment, and tell the man he's fired." I looked at him and I said, "You're asking another constable to do this?"

That's fine. I went to North Sydney and I got on the *Aspy*. The *Aspy* went down the next day and got stuck in the ice and came back. Three days we tried that. Finally, on the first day of May, we got down there and landed up at Ingonish. Not at North Ingonish because there was still ice; we landed at South Ingonish, at Dunphy's wharf. I got to the detachment and I found a man and his wife and seven children. I talked to him, and I found out right off the bat that things were really bad. He had been drinking all winter, and he just didn't do any work. I fired him, and ordered him out of the house. It was a very sad thing to see because they had no money, nowhere to go. Their home was originally in Halifax, so they went to Halifax.

But there was so much to see and do and hear. I went there as a very young man, telling another older man he was fired and has no job, and— "Here's your paycheque, and get out of here." Then I commenced to find out what really did happen was that he was drunk all winter. And he was supplied liquor by the rumrunner there. And sometime later, as I got acquainted and we started searching and finding these places, I went to this rumrunner's home. And in his bedroom, under a picture of the Sacred Heart, on the wallpaper, was a list of the rum that he had given to the policeman and another official during the winter.

I spent a lot of time that first year just trying to reorganize the whole set-up. My predecessor there had been caught in a snowstorm the fall before on Smokey. He walked out of the car and left it there. It was still there in the snow when I got down there on the first of May. The first thing I had to do was get up Smokey and get somebody from the North Shore to come down, haul this thing back up out of the ditch, and get it down to the bottom of Smokey and try and get the engine going. But there wasn't too much wrong with it—we got it going. And then the work started right away. Mostly rum, as I say.

I was only in Ingonish a short while, a very few days, really. I just got the car operating. It was about the middle of the month when I got the first urgent call by telegram, Morse code—there was a telegraph line up and down the shore there—to go north. A very serious problem. I drove all the way, thinking all the way down—I'd heard of this fellow before, and I knew what he did to our former member there. I went down, and I went to this house, and he was standing in the doorway. He had a bottle of rum in his hip pocket—a bottle of rum or moonshine or something. And I talked to him—he wasn't going to let me in, and it was none of my business, and get off his property—and so on. So I knew I had to do something. This was my first confrontation down there, really. Finally, I watched my chance, and I grabbed the bottle out of his hip pocket, and he started to chase me. I jumped over the fence. And he came at me wild, frantic. He got over the fence in about two leaps, but he didn't hit the ground on my side of the fence until I had him down on the ground, and handcuffs on him behind his back. And I dragged him like that down through the yard, out to the road to the car, threw him in the back seat, end over end, jumped in the car and started for Ingonish. The roads were crooked, and you can imagine—now he was down on the floor in the back seat—the bruises that were on him by the time I got to Ingonish, because I didn't have any mercy for him whatsoever. It was a crooked road, it was an old Ford. And of course, I had him up in court. And I never had any more trouble in that place. That kind of ended that.

The following summer there was a big dance at the Cape North crossroads one night, and there was considerable trouble there. I went down. I stopped at the crossroads, and I was searching cars for liquor. And one car came along, and out of it jumped a great big man who lived in Inverness County. I saw him one morning at three o'clock—he had broken into a building and somebody had surrounded the place. And I went out from Inverness, and he was there with a weapon in his hand. He had a pair of shorts on, and no shirt, top part of his body, and of course he was going to kill everybody who came near him with the weapon. Well, anyway, we disarmed him and took him back to Inverness. Now, here I come and I search this car in Cape North. There was a dance on, it was at the hall there. And I opened the door on the driver's side and I said, "Everybody get out on this side." And the man sitting alongside the driver got out and walked around to the back of the car. And as he got out of the car, I realized it was this same fellow. And as he went around to the back of the car, I went around to the back of the car on my side, and I didn't give him a chance to open his mouth. There was a wee short bit of a ditch there, and as he was coming up—there were lots of lights on, other cars were parked there at the crossroads—I let him have it, everything I could put into a punch. And it knocked him out so cold, he rolled down into the ditch. That was the end of it. After that, nobody bothered me any more.

This may sound fantastic to you, but it's absolutely just as God's truth as I'm standing here. Just the one crack, and I happened to get him in a good place. And I got out of that scrape down there without too much trouble.

There was a lot of trouble before I went there, and before my predecessor went there. The policeman who was there was a Nova Scotia policeman. And local boys took the car away from him, pushed it over the bank into the ocean, and then beat him up. For which they were eventually caught, went to jail. And it was following that that they had sent my predecessor there, because he was supposed to be a bit of a boxer and could look after himself. But he got down there, and the first call that he had was to go to a dance in Cape North where there was hell popping. And he went down there, and when he was there, they cut the four tires off his car. So I guess he got the tires fixed and got back to his detachment the next day and decided that discretion was the better part of valour, and that he couldn't beat them, he'd join them. So he stayed drunk all winter until I got there.

Word was always getting out that moonshine was being manufactured in Meat Cove. I got a call from Bay St. Lawrence, from Fr. Paul MacNeil, the parish priest. He would send me a message in Latin, and I'd be able to decipher it. That's the only way we could do it, because everybody could read Morse code up and down the Shore, and if he didn't send it in Latin, they would have known what we were doing. I remember the old telegraph operator in North Ingonish; he used to get cross when you'd get a message in Latin.

I was there a couple of years when this happened. So I decided, well, something's got to be done about this, and the only time you can do anything about it, really, is to go in the wintertime. In the summertime nobody would give you information. So, now listen to this: I decided this winter that I would go to Meat Cove and try to catch this man with moonshine, and get his still, if I could. And I went on my skis from Ingonish, down through Neil's Harbour, stopped at New Haven, just past Neil's Harbour, and had a bit of a lunch at Mrs. Budge's place. She saw me going past, came to the door and called me in. And I can still remember, because she did something I never saw done before—she was frying me an egg on the stove, and she put a saucer—just a plain saucer from under a cup—on the stove, and a little butter in it, and put the egg on it, and that's how she fried the egg. I never saw that done before. But I had lunch there, and went over where the White Point road is now, walked over there on skis. Crossed that long beach into Dingwall, went to the hotel and had supper there that evening, and it was the usual—you always had corned beef hash at the hotel, particularly in the wintertime. There was no fresh meat around. And I had supper there at five o'clock, and then I got on my skis and went another twelve miles across the beach and into Bay St. Lawrence, or St. Margaret's, to the parish house, the glebe house, Fr. Paul.

Had a cup of tea with Fr. Paul and talked with him until eleven o'clock. He went to bed, and I got on my skis again, and I went from there to Meat Cove in the middle of the night on skis. Packed the skis up after I got down into Meat Cove—the first hill—and then started hunting for tracks into the woods. And lucky enough, I found a track into the woods and I followed it. And I was back quite a distance back of Meat Cove, and I came upon a little camp. There were four dogs tied there. There were barrels of mash sunk in the snow, in the ground, and the fireplace was set up, and the still was set up there. So I tasted the mash—I'd learned to do it in Inverness County—and realized that pretty soon they were going to have to run this off. So I picked myself out a nice tree to lean against, across a little brook.

I was only there about an hour when I heard somebody coming—it was a man coming. He fed the dogs, and then got the fire going, and started to run the moonshine. When he got a little bit run off, he took a sip of it and kind of smacked his lips. I waited till he got a little bit more in the can, and then I jumped him. Saved the moonshine and smashed up the still, put the fire out, broke the barrels, cut the dogs loose, and said, "Well, I'll be back and get you. I've got to send this away for analysis." Got on my skis again and went back to Ingonish.

Sent the stuff out in the mail. Eventually it came back, after a month or so, and I went back up to Meat Cove. I went to Cape North on snowshoes. And I hired a horse in Cape North to take me to Meat Cove to bring this prisoner out. We arrested the guy. It was in Inverness County rather than Victoria. I put him in the sled, and stopped at MacGregor's at the foot of Cape North Mountain for the night. I had an extra pair of snowshoes for him. Got him up early in the morning, and we had breakfast, and we started out to snowshoe to Pleasant Bay and Cheticamp.

At Pleasant Bay we had to stop and have the trial before the magistrate there. He was convicted, of course, and sentenced to the county jail at Port Hood. We went on, climbed up MacKenzie Mountain, got across the top. Then my prisoner played out on me—he couldn't go any further. Nothing I could do. I knew he couldn't run away on me. I said, "Well, you come as slowly as you can, or sit down and rest here, and I'll go on down ahead into Cap Rouge. I'll get someone to come with a handsled and get you." Which I did. Christopher Aucoin and some man came up—I don't know who it was. But it was Christopher Aucoin was the first house in Cap Rouge. And he went back up the French Mountain and picked up this prisoner and brought him down. Then I took him to Cheticamp and put him in jail for the night at the cell of the detachment. Went to the hotel.

The next morning he was so hard used up that he could hardly walk. So I had to hire a man with a horse and sleigh, and start for Inverness. I put him in the seat with the driver, and I jumped on the back of the sleigh, and I ran and jumped off and ran again, and we made Inverness that night. That's another forty-seven miles from Cheticamp. I put him in jail overnight, and then got up early in the morning and took him on the passenger train to Port Hood, put him in jail and gave him warmth, and that was fine. Came back to the station and caught the freight train at eleven o'clock. It got to Point Tupper, and then I caught the evening train into Sydney. I went into Sydney and stayed there the next day, all day the next day.

And then the following morning, two of the fellows drove me out to Big Bras d'Or—it was frozen—the ferry wasn't running. I had my pack on my back and two pair of snowshoes. And I got a long pole, and I started walking across Big Bras d'Or to the ferry at New Campbellton. And the ice broke under me, and I went in and got wet. But I had my pole, and I got out. They were watching me from the shore. I got out and I walked to shore. When I got ashore, I put on my snowshoes, and I snowshoed fifty-four miles to Ingonish that day, getting home at about 10:30 at night. A woman at the foot of Smokey, on the North Shore side of Smokey, coaxed me to stay there in the evening. I stopped in there and had a bite to eat, and waited till about eight o'clock and had a bit of a rest. And then got on my snowshoes and went up Smokey. Actually, literally, and I can remember—it was a lovely winter's night—I actually jogged down on snowshoes, going down the other side of Smokey. Crossed over the Ingonish Ferry along the shore, and got home in North Ingonish at 10:30. Snowshoeing fifty-four miles that day. It didn't bother me one single bit. I got up the next morning at eight o'clock, down in the office making out reports.

That's just one incident there. I had another incident going the other way. A couple of years later, or a year and a half later—I had four prisoners in the jail. And it came that I couldn't keep them any longer, and to try to get to Baddeck with them. So, I had them all lined up, and I went and I hired three teams of horses. And I put two prisoners in the first horse and team, and one in the next horse and team, and another team behind with myself and a prisoner. So the middle team had one prisoner, but they'd change back and forth so they'd ease off on those two horses. And we

64

started from Ingonish early in the morning—it was way long before seven we got out of there. And that's a long drive to Baddeck.

Came down over Smokey, up the North Shore, stopped at D. B. MacLeod's and had lunch, fed the horses, and then came on from there, crossed the ferry, and came up to Rocky Side. Came to St. Ann's, and stopped at MacLeods' at St. Ann's, put the horses in the barn—I can remember it so well. I wired ahead that I'd be there, and asked them to have lunch for these prisoners. Put the horses in the barn, rubbed them down, took the harness off, put the blankets on them, and I gave each horse a pail of lukewarm water, sprinkled with a good share of oatmeal in it, and then a feed of hay, and a little bit of oats after that. Stayed there till about half past eight. Let the horses have a rest particularly, not so much us. Hitched them up again and came to Baddeck and put the prisoners in jail. I don't know of any other time, really, you could take horses sixty miles and come over Smokey, a hill like Smokey. But it was necessity, and the horses had a good rest at noon, and they had a good rest in the evening. And they were none the worse for it. I let them stay in the barn for two days while I stayed in Baddeck, till they rested up, and then I went back home with the three teams. That was just two expeditions out of Ingonish.

You know, in those times, the only enjoyment or sociability I had was going over to Fr. Day's, or seeing the schoolteachers. I was very close to Fr. Day. To me, he was a great man. He was a great man, a great human being, he was a great priest—no question about it. And his sermons were marvellous. I had an unusual experience with him, and he laughed about this years later. I was sitting at the hotel in North Ingonish where I stayed, at The Spruces, and there was a bunch of fellows came in this evening. They had dinner. I was there in civilian clothing, and they were talking. One fellow hauled out a bottle of rum, and they had a drink at the table there. I couldn't do very much about it then. I thought, "Well, I'll fix you fellows later." So they were going to go back to get some more. So I finished my dinner, and I went out and got in the car. And I said, "I'm going to catch that fellow tonight. This is the end of it." So I drove past the church. I was pretty religious then, I suppose maybe I am yet; and I had great faith, and I still have. But when I was driving past the church, I stopped—this is true—I stopped and made the sign of the cross, and I said a little prayer that I'd get some help in catching this rumrunner, because he'd been in existence so long.

But anyway, I caught the rumrunner. And the first person I saw the next day was Fr. Day. He was over in North Ingonish, and he called me up. He said, "They tell me you caught some fellow. How'd you do that?" I said, "Now, I'm glad you asked me, Father. I'll tell you." I said, "I was so annoyed about these men, bragging about getting that liquor from that man, that I said to myself, 'Well, I'm going to catch them tonight.'" And I said, "I started over there, and I stopped in front of your church. I stopped and said a prayer or two, and then I drove on." And Fr. Day, he said, "Bill, you shouldn't be praying for things like that!"

Fr. Day, he was a great big man; he weighed over 300 pounds. And there's a great story about him. He came to Ingonish shortly before I did. And like I did, he came down on the boat and landed at Dunphy's wharf at South Ingonish. It was in the spring, and people were there with their sleds. Some people had horses, and some people had oxen. But as Fr. Day was getting off the boat, he picked up his suitcase and started to walk—there were no taxis then—started to walk to find the glebe house. He was going past this row of horses and oxen that were parked there. And as he passed this ox, the ox let a grunt out of him, kind of put his head down. Fr. Day dropped his suitcase and went over and took the ox by the two horns,

lifted the front end of the oxen and pushed him back on his rear haunches, and said, "There." Everybody around there, their eyes just bugged out, and they talked about that for about a year. But nobody ever bothered Fr. Day, physically, after that, I'll tell you.

I asked Fr. Day about that when I heard the story, and he laughed about it, and he said yes, he just did it at that time to sort of impress them. Because, you know, Ingonish had a bad name, really. But between Fr. Day and myself, I think we kind of straightened that out a little and dispelled some of those stories, no question about it. When we left there, it wasn't so bad.

Edited from R. A. MacLean's taped conversations with Bill Fraser, made in preparation for MacLean's book, *Bill Fraser: Mountie*.

Johnny Allan MacDonald of Enon

(*Tell me your name, and where you were born, and when you were born.*)
Right here. John A. MacDonald. 1890. (*You were born—"right here" is where?*) I believe it would be in the other end of the house! Loch Lomond, they called it. But really, Loch Lomond is in Richmond County. But this is in the neighbourhood of Loch Lomond. Pretty much the same people anyway, down in Loch Lomond and here, Enon.

(*Where does the name Enon come from?*) It came from the Bible. And Salem Road was over across the lake—Salem—"and many waters there." It states in the Bible somewheres. I wouldn't be able to turn it up for you, but it's there, anyway. "Enon near Salem." That's how the Salem Road Post Office was called. It was my father that named it. And then he got a post office right here, in this house. (*And did he put the name on this place as well?*) Yes. Enon.

(*Who was the first of your people to come to this place?*) My grandfather, he was the first. John. (*Did he have a longer name in Gaelic?*) Oh, yes. Iain Mac Ghilleasbuig. His father would be Archie—Gilleasbuig. So I'm more fluent in the Gaelic than I am in the English. Though I never went to school very much. (*Where did you learn your Gaelic?*) With my grandmother here, when all the rest would be out. My grandmother, she didn't have any English. And I'd be left in with my grandmother, see, and the rest would be scattered all over the place doing something.

I used to get her mad sometimes, too. But she was very good, she was kind. Yes, I'd get picking at her. One time we were alone—oh, the rest, they went away somewheres. And after awhile, "Well," she says, "I guess it would be all right for us to have a cup of tea." And I went—and I used to make the tea anyway, you know. This time I thought I'd put a lot of tea in the teapot. And I put, I suppose, a half a pound in it. Well, I don't know whether she noticed anything or not. But she said, "That's the best cup of tea I had since I left the Old Country!" Oh, it was awful strong—must have been!...

(*Did she sing songs or tell stories to you in Gaelic?*) Ach, yes, stories, yes, always told stories about Scotland. Mostly about the peat. [And] what they call the "Big Carpenter." And his two brothers—there were two brothers left over in the Old Country—one of them was learning to be a wheelwright, and another one by the name Peter, he stayed with him. And they came over in 1829, those two. The first settlers came in '28.

He was a MacDonald, the Big Carpenter. And my grandmother would be one of his daughters.

Of course, it was log houses they had at first. And when they started to build frame houses, my grandmother had a conch, and she'd blow that conch—they could hear that conch for miles around. And they'd come— you know, there'd be a frolic, putting up the house or barn or whatever it would be. So many blows on that conch. They'd hear it all over the whole country.

(*What else do we know about the Big Carpenter?*) Oh, that was all I ever heard, that he was a carpenter and he was the builder. He had a son [Donald]—he was eighteen when they left Scotland. My grandmother was sixteen. And Donald, he was the bloodletter, you know. And when there was a doctor called [for], to let some blood, they'd send for Donald Mac-Donald. They called him a doctor, he was so quick with the lance. I believe that was the only cure he had. He was a farmer.

Angus was the Big Carpenter. My grandmother would be his daughter. And Donald would be his son.

(*Did your grandmother tell you anything about how her family happened to come to Cape Breton?*) Well, yes. Yes. This Big Carpenter—he called a meeting—you know, during the Clearance—he called a meeting of his relatives and friends. That he wanted to have a meeting with all of them. And he suggested that they all sell whatever they could get along without—whatever little they'd get for it, to sell it. And anything they kept for a year, to be sure what they'd do with it when the time would come for them to leave. That it was just as well for them to prepare to leave, rather than to be driven away. So, that's what they all did. They did away with whatever they could get along without. And they kept some little things, you know.

And when the time came, and he had the ship named the *Commerce*. And when the *Commerce* came the following year, they were right ready. There was so much space, you know, for each one. So the boat was loaded with the people. But when they came to Sydney,

Johnny Allan, holding his mother's work: an example of traditional overshot weaving

some of them went down south. You know Big Donnie MacLeod, the Member. His people came on the *Commerce*, too, and many more, that went down south [in Cape Breton]. But the most of them came up to Big Pond, to Irish Cove. And they divided there. Half of them went to West Bay, for to cruise the area over there. And the other half was—well, the mountain, between here and Irish Cove and Big Pond.

So, the people that went to West Bay, they were to meet again at Irish Cove on a certain day. So they did. And who happened to be there at the time but Dougald Buchanan MacNab, a land surveyor. He had been through all this country, you know. He followed all the brooks, streams, for mill-sites. See, a falls. And he told them he could guide them out, if they cared to come—that there was a chain of freshwater lakes littered with trout. Made no difference where you'd look, you could see lots of trout.

And he was telling the truth. I remember that myself. And it's a good many years since they came over in 1828. And all I had to do—my mother would say, "Well, it would be nice to have trout for breakfast, John." I'd take the hook and throw it out, the lake here, down below the lower field there. Throw it out, and come back in a little while. I never took more than two or three, you know. I didn't believe in trying to see how many you'd take. I always took two or three, according to the size. But they were all big trout. All big trout.

So they settled—all the ways—Munros, Salem Road; McCuishes. But

69

the lower end—Lower End Loch Lomond—it was the Chisholms and Bethunes. They were the first to come there, about the same time. But they came on another route, you know, through L'Ardoise and Grand River, and so on like that.

(*Now was there any mention at all of what the conditions were like on the* Commerce *when they came over?*) Well, he saw that there'd be lots of water put in clean barrels. You know, a lot of the ships that came over, it would be greasy barrels. And the people would die on the way; a lot of them would die after arriving. The bad water. Six weeks and six days— that's the time the *Commerce* took, coming over—six weeks and six days.

A lot of pork and oatmeal—that's what they had for food. They might have had some other little things while it would last, but it was the pork and oatmeal, that's what they depended on.

(*Did your grandmother ever say anything about what life was like?*) *Did everybody have their own room on the vessel?*) Well, there was a space—I think it was three [feet] by six [feet]—that was the space that was figured for every one. But very likely they would be together, you know. But according to this, it was three by six, that was the space. That would be figured on the boat, you know, the number of people that would come. I don't think it was cut up in rooms, I don't think.

(*So when your grandfather came to this farm, what was here?*) Nothing but forest. Nothing but forest. My grandfather first started in Lingan—very near Waterford, anyway. And he didn't like it. He didn't like it at all. And he came up this way. And here is where he started. There was nothing—no clearance or a thing. They had to chop trees and burn them and build a log cabin for themselves. Plant potatoes around the stumps. I often wondered how did they get the potatoes. (*Oh—the seed.*) Yes. They couldn't have got an awful lot. But ah, they must have been awful strong people, that would stand an awful lot. Couldn't have had many varieties, for to eat.

(*Did your grandmother remember when all this was forest?*) Oh yes. She was sixteen. A person sixteen remembers quite a lot. But, well, coming to this country, you know, leaving their old home in Scotland— whatever kind of a home it was—kind of hard to understand. (*Was she bitter about having left Scotland? Did she wish she were back there?*) No, she never wished to be back. Never did. And I never heard of any of them wishing to be back.

(*Did you ever see the first cabin, the first log house?*) Oh, I saw some of them, I saw some of them. I didn't see the ones that were here, but I saw others. (*How big would you say they were?*) Oh, about twelve by twenty, or something like that. (*Did they use the logs round?*) Round, yes. (*They didn't square them?*) No, no. They didn't square them at all. (*Not even top and bottom?*) Well, they'd have stone in the bottom, for the be-

70

ginning, you know, of the first log. (*Stone all the way along, or just at the corners?*) Oh yes, all right along the wall. Yes. And they'd have a little cellar in, too. And wherever needed, they had a ditch, to carry any moisture, water, carry it away. (*This ditch—was it in the cellar, or was it around the building?*) Well, the cellar would be dug in the ground anyway, you know. Well, the ditch would be from the cellar. To keep everything dry. They could put potatoes in the cellar, put anything in. Of course they'd have pickets in the bottom, to keep potatoes from the soil. (*What are pickets?*) Well, poles. Pole floor.

(*So they'd dig themselves something of a cellar. Was it squared right up?*) Squared right up. (*Were the walls of the cellar just the dirt?*) Oh, some of them. Some of them, wood. But they'd be preparing for to build a better house. But the one that was here, there was stone wall from the cellar up. (*And then the first log would be right on that stone.*) Yes.

(*The corners of the logs—can you remember how they put the corners together?*) Oh, yes. They slapped them together, you know, they'd notch them down with an axe. Indeed, they didn't know very much about an axe, either, because they had no wood over there for to use an axe. Of course, I don't know where they got the axes—they got them somewheres. And they used to level them off and then plant the end of the logs, you know, together. There'd be a little sticking out on both sides. But they'd take moss and—I think they called it "chinking"—chinking between the logs, to keep the wind out, the storm.

(*As you'd look at the front of one of these log houses—looking right at the face of the house—how many windows and doors would you see?*) There wouldn't be many windows, anyway, because glass wasn't very plentiful in the early days. But a door—they used to have boards. They had what they call a whipsaw. You know, they'd build this stand, oh, so high—so you could stand under it. And they'd put the log up on that stand. And they had a whipsaw. There'd be two men down below, and one above taking the saw up, and the others ripping it down, you know. (*Two would pull it down and one would take it up.*) Yeah. Of course, the teeth weren't for cutting, pulling it up. But down, you know. So, that's the way they made boards. (*And that's how the door was made.*) Yes, out of boards.

(*Were boards used anywhere else in those log houses?*) Oh, they might have been, in the floor. And soap wasn't very plentiful either, in those days. They used white sand for scrubbing the floor. (*Some floors would be this cut board. What were some other floors made of?*) Floors. Oh, made out of stone, slabs of stone. And I saw over in Scotland a house we were to, and it was all slab stone, the first floor. (*If they had a cellar, what would hold the slabs of stone up?*) Well, they'd have sticks—trimmers they called them—running across, you know. (*And slabs of stone on top of*

71

that.) Yes. (*Did you actually see that here in Cape Breton?*) No, I didn't see it here, but I know it was used.

(*Would these log houses have a second floor on them?*) No, they didn't. But they'd have, you know, with the pitch of the roof, they'd have a place to shove different things in, above. There was one down in Ben Eoin, and I think there were a couple of the children sleeping up in that hole. (*But most of the family lived just in the first floor*.) Oh yes, oh yes.

(*And there was a log house like that on this property?*) Oh yes, on every property. On every property around. (*And your grandmother actually lived in one*.) Oh yes. (*What did they do for a stove?*) An open fireplace. They didn't have a stove until they built this house here. And this house was built in 1873. And they were ready to move into it—they didn't have very much anyway, at that time—they moved some of the stuff they had. But in the morning there was no house. That was the time of what they call the August Gale—they have another name for it. We call it the August Gale, anyway. And most of the house was down at the lake. So—of course, there was a bunch of boys, and they started gathering up again, to start building.

(*You mean the house came apart?*) Ach, yes, went to pieces. Went to pieces. And they had to cut most of the frame short. That's this house here. (*Why did they cut most of the frame short?*) Because the end of the framing was—you know, it would be homemade spikes, and mortice and tenons. And that would be broke. They'd have to cut it off, you know. (*So the house was just that much smaller*.) Oh, yes. On account of the August Gale.

(*All around Cape Breton, I guess, things happened because of the gale*.) Yes. My grandmother's brother—his wife was killed. They had a new house. No, they had their old house, and a new barn. So, the gale was so savage that they thought it would be better for them to go to the barn because it was new. The barn came down in pieces, and it was across her breast here, the crowning, the beam—that's the main beam in the barn, see. It was right across her breast. She was killed. And she had a child in her arms. And the child was living. And it's only a number of years since—I suppose around twenty years—since Angus [the child] died.

(*So a house was destroyed, and a person was killed. Is that all that the August Gale did here?*) Ach, no. There wasn't a tree standing. All over the whole country. But it's a tree country, anyway. Trees grow very fast here. (*I guess ships were driven ashore all over, around Cape Breton*.) Oh, yes. I often heard them talking about Port Morien. There was a big ship anchored out in the harbour, and it was up on dry land. But I don't think it was broken up, though.

(*What were you interested in, when you were a young man?*) Well, the only thing I was interested in was carpenter work. That's the only thing I was interested in. (*And where did you learn that?*) I didn't learn it. We had a lounge here [a day bed in the kitchen]—oh, it wouldn't last long. You know, there were so many of us anyway—ten in the family. Of course, the oldest was gone away. But a lounge wouldn't last very long, between I and my brother. He was older than I, and he was awful big too. Well, I started making a lounge, anyway. And my father asked me, "What are you doing?" "I'm going to make a lounge." "Hmph. Another one for to smash up." "Yes. When I'll be through with it, I'll leave it with you to smash, if you can." [Johnny Allan points across the kitchen.] Right there, still. (*That's the lounge.*) That's the one. (*It lasted a few years.*) [Johnny Allan laughs.] I have everything, even the corners, dovetailed in hardwood, and hardwood sides.

(*But how did you learn to do that, and where did you get the proper tools?*) Oh, there were tools. Well, you know, what I had for chisels was spikes. I'd beat them out, you know, and then sharpen them on one side. That's the only thing I had for chisels. And when I needed a bigger chisel I'd batter it more. [Laughs.] Hard times!

"In Memory of Catherine, wife of John McDonald, who fell asleep in Jesus Aug 24, 1873, Aged 45 years. Came to her untimely death/ By the falling of a barn into/ Which she had taken shelter/ During the great gale of the/ Above date. Say ye to the righteous that it/ Shall be well with him."

(*And starting from that lounge, is that how you made your living, as far as cash is concerned?*) Well, as far as cash—cash came in different ways, you know. I never had much cash. But I was very lucky. Now, when I was in the lumber woods in British Columbia, I had a lot of money, made a lot of money there.... And then another time, I went to the States.

(*First, how did you get to British Columbia?*) I went on The Harvest first. And after The Harvest I went out in the woods. I wanted to see what the woods were like. I could see the picture in papers, and so on like that. But to see the real stuff. The pictures have nothing to do with the real standing of lumber.

(*When you went to The Harvest, would they expect you to be a good farmer for them?*) No, they didn't. A good many that goes out there, they're from the city, and they don't know a damn thing about farming.

73

They know nothing, only to see a horse trotting on the street—that's all they'd know at that time. And I was classed to be one of them. I wasn't long showing them that I knew pretty near as much as they knew themselves. Of course, six horses for plowing. (*Now, you wouldn't see that here.*) No. But I wouldn't tell them that I didn't see it!

So, I got along good. Got along good. And the farmer—well, there was a singletree broke, anyway. And I drove the horses over to the stable, and I tied them outside, to the fence. And the man, he came around, he saw the horses coming in—he was somewhere in one of the fields. He asked what was wrong. "Well," I said, "one of the singletrees broke." "Oh well, I'll have to go to town" —fifteen miles—"to get that fixed." "Oh, God," I said, "I'll fix that myself." "Can you fix that?" "Yes, and you showed me your tools, and I saw what you have for lumber. You have a lot of hardwood there. And you've got something that I don't need to chip very much. I'll have it in about an hour's time—I'll have a singletree on the plow."

So, one day he was talking, "Well, I wish I had a granary. I am short a granary." "And how big do you want the granary?" "Oh, I want it about twenty feet long, anyway, and about fifteen feet wide. I want a big one." "How would you get the lumber?" "In town." "Well, if you really want it, I'll build it for you. I'll build it for you." "Will you really?" "Yes," I said, "nothing to that." "I want concrete under the sills." "Okay. That'll be the boards, first, to make the forms." "Well, if you can make the forms, I can get lots of help to mix the concrete." "Okay."

So, two teams went into town for the boarding, about daybreak, ready for to go. I was working on that. You know, I wasn't losing any time. When the sun was shining, I'd be stooking [gathering up the sheaves of grain for drying in the fields]. But I'd get up, at the granary—I had the granary ready before they were ready for threshing. Had all the stooking done.... He told me when I was leaving, "I want you to come back here." But I never did. I should have, but, you know—I went to the woods, see, from there.

And then in the spring I hired on with a carpenter in a place called Milburn. In Alberta. But the first job I had in British Columbia in the woods, the man, he told me, "I want you to build a barn." And my buddy. "I want you to build the cookhouse and sleeper and so on like that." And he told me, "The lengths on the sticks, that's the lengths that I want in the barn." That would be about 150 feet long. Okay. They'd haul the stuff in, you know, with a team of horses. It was all cedar that was going in the barn. Nice wood, too. And the other fellow, it was props, you know, up and down, you know—that's the way the cookhouse was built, and the sleeping house. Got along good. Got along okay.

(*Where did you go from there?*) Came home. (*Cape Breton.*) I had a let-

74

ter from my mother to come home. And, I came. I had [an offer for] a better job than that in the States, and they wanted me to come home. (*What did they want you to come home for?*) Oh, just to fix things up, and pay a lot of bills too. Fix things up. So I'm still here. (*Once you came home, you stayed.*) Yes. Somebody had to look after the old folks.

(*Were you married yet?*) Not at that time. (*And did you go very far looking for a wife?*) No, indeed. I didn't believe in going to any distance! (*Where did you find your wife?*) Oh, about three miles from here. (*Another descendant of the Big Carpenter?*) Yes. That's right.

(*Did you have children here?*) One boy. I had one boy, and the Depression came. (*You had one boy, and what came?*) Depression! [Johnny Allan laughs.]

(*Did you have any schooling at all?*) No. Oh, I went, well, a couple of months. And then there was something to be done, and I'd have to stay home and look after stock, or water the cattle. There were so many of them—Lord, we always had between fifteen and twenty head of cows, and fifty sheep, four horses. And you know, it was quite a job for a young kid like me, you know, to clean the stables at that time. I'd only go to school when they thought that they didn't need me around. That's all. So I never got any schooling. I have made it myself.

(*Did some of your brothers and sisters go to school, though?*) Oh yes, they had a lot of schooling. (*More than you'd had.*) Ach, yes, ten times more than I had. I never had very much. (*So you were the only one of your brothers and sisters that didn't get a chance to go to school that much.*) Yes, I was. (*Were you the baby?*) Well, my youngest sister, she died when she was twelve. (*So you were the youngest son.*) Yeah. (*And it was just understood that you would stay home?*) Oh well, yes. I think they figured that I'd always die right here. And I guess I will, too!

I went to the States and I went to school. (*How old were you then?*) Oh, I was grown up. I was going to go out to British Columbia, to the woods. And I thought I'd go and visit my sister—there were four of them in the States. And one of them told me to stay—not to go to B.C. at all—stay with her. "Stay, board with me." And I went to night school. I was doing carpenter work. And only that I had to come home, you know, I would have been one of the richest guys that ever left Loch Lomond. If I had a chance—when I got word—I had a chance of working for a woman—she was a millionaire, and her husband was a millionaire.

And this man where I was working, he'd come every day, you know. I didn't know why he was coming. I was working alone on the second storey: putting down floors, and partitions, and hanging doors. You know, the contractor I worked for, he wanted to keep so many men, you know, for the spring when things would be brightening up.

75

So, there must have been three or four more working downstairs. And indeed, they weren't doing much. They were working in the hall. I couldn't see—when I'd come down, see, from up where I was working—I couldn't see anything that they did do. Only they were just hammering and making a little noise; that's about all. But this man, he'd come every day, and, "Do you smoke, John?" "No, I never smoke on the job. I never do. But I smoke when I go home. I have a smoke then. Because, we only worked eight hours. And surely to goodness, I was used to work sixteen hours, and sometimes more than that. And I don't mind working eight hours."

Well, when I was leaving, going to another job, the contractor told me, "I figured on keeping you. Keeping you to help on Dover Street, on both sides of the street. I own all the houses. And I own this building here." I didn't know he owned it. God, it was a big building. "And I own another big building over on Columbia Street. And I was going to have you to look after all those buildings for me. There's always a windowpane broke, or something wrong with a door, something wrong with the latches, hinges. And outside, too. Anything that's to be done, that you'd look after it. And you'll get the same going wages the carpenters are getting, a year." You know, the carpenters, shortly after that, the wages went—the sky's the limit. And I would have been well-to-do.

But I had word from my mother to come home, that she couldn't stand doing so much work herself. And they were alone, my father and mother. He was much older than she was. "Well," I thought, "she had trouble in bringing me into the world, and looking after me. Surely to goodness I can help her now." That's what brought me here.

And then I got married. I had my wife then to help me out. My mother was still living. But she was getting up in years, and my father was older than she was. That's what kept me here. (*Here in Enon.*) I never figured I'd be here at all.

(*So, when you got the call, you came back and you stayed with your parents.*) Oh yes, I came back. My mother would gladly go any time, to the States. Very hard for my father to leave here. He had a better chance then, staying here himself. He used to be a railroad foreman, and worked [as] a foreman on the railroad all the time. And one of the big shots of the C.N.R. took him for a train ride out west, and told him, "Now, every second section belongs to us." The head man said, "And if you pinpoint any section that belongs to us, you can have it free—640 acres—that's one section—you can have a section free." Do you think he'd accept that? No damn fear. (*Why not?*) Because he'd rather be among stumps and stones, and bogs and everything. I often told him that he was nuts that he didn't take the offer. To make his home out west.

(*And was it mostly stumps and stones that he had to farm in Cape Bre-*

Johnny Allan at home, with his son Angus and daughter-in-law Effie

ton?*) That's all that there was. And still is, a lot of stone. I spent—the Lord only knows how many great big boulders I blasted and burnt. We were cutting just as much hay with the little scythes as we were with the mowing machine, with all the big stones that were on the place. I started to bury some of them first. Digging a deep hole and turning them in.

Then, started to burn them. Do you know, I was burning them before I knew how to burn them. Have a little fire. I used to have a little fire on top of them. But a fire on top is no good if you want to break a boulder. Dig a little trench. You don't need to have it very deep. And put a lot of dry wood around, set fire to it on the side, and that'll crack right across. (*Just from the heat.*) Yes, from the heat. (*You don't have to strike them.*) No. They'll go anyway. (*You don't have to throw water on them?*) No, no.

There was one boulder between here and the road. In the middle of the road. We started to set fire on top of it. Darn thing, there was only a little went on the top. (*Little crack, you mean?*) Yeah. But, a little trench around the edge, and you don't need so very much wood, either. When it gets warmed up, it'll crack—you can hear it blasting. There were thousands of them. (*That you did.*) Yeah. (*Thousands of boulders.*) Yeah. (*Were you the first one who ever did that around here?*) I was the one to do it here. I think there were more here than anywhere else, that I knew of. (*Did other people use fire on the boulders, too?*) Oh yes, oh yes. (*That was common.*) Oh yes, that was common.

The easiest job I ever did. I got rid of all the old fencing, breaking them up and sitting around the boulders. (*Why were you cracking up the boulders? Why did you set fire to them and break the boulders up?*) So that I'd be able to turn them out, and pull them out. Some of those that were too big, you know, I'd set fire to. But other stones that weren't so heavy, I'd get a big chain around them, and the horses would pull them away.

(*You were clearing a field?*) Oh, that would be clearing the field. And there was less work to be done. Why, there's rows of big stones all over this place. Rows of them. (*And of course by the time you were doing it, the older generation—had they been moving the stones before you?*) They'd been moving little ones. But not any big ones. You know there was always a hole where a big boulder would be. And all the small stuff, I'd throw them right back into the hole. (*The small stones.*) Yeah.

(*And what would you do with the stumps?*) Ah, the stumps—set fire to them. Of course, I didn't have to do very much of that. It was boulders, the most I had to do with. (*And would you be able later to come along and use the mower, rather than the hand scythe?*) Oh yes, use the mower right through. And still, can use the mower all over the place. Clear of—there's rows of big stone. There's two rows over that way; there's another row down there, going across. (*And you built those rows?*) Well, a lot of them. (*Were you working alone?*) Oh yes, yeah. (*Heavy work.*) Ach yes, but when you have a good team of horses that you can depend on, they'll stop when you want them, and you can drop your lines and do whatever you had to do. It makes a big difference.

(*Johnny Allan, do you have any idea when horses first came here to Loch Lomond—who had the first horse?*) Well, my grandfather, he had a horse—he was a very able horse. And when he'd be plowing, he had that horse and an ox—he had that team, horse and the ox. (*Side by side.*) Side by side. And when my grandmother would blow the conch—you know what a conch is, a marine shell—for dinner, the ox would stop, but the horse would keep going. The ox was wiser—he knew that there was a feed waiting for him.

(*How did this farm fare off during the Depression?*) Okay. Better than those in the city. There was no shortage of anything. The only thing that got me going a little bit fast was tea, during the war, when tea was rationed. And tea's used a lot all over the whole country. Well, I said to Angus, my son—I didn't have the car registered at that time. You'd only get gasoline enough for so many months. I sent my son over to a McVicker fellow, so we'd go and get tea somewheres. I had a lot of hay ready to put in, but I said to myself, the heck with the hay—we've always got lots of hay, anyway.

He didn't come. But he came in the evening. I said, "What the hell was keeping you, anyway?" "What did you want me for?" "You know tea was rationed last night. And unless we get to going, and try and get some early today, we'll never get it." "Where will we go?" "We'll go to the stores around, little stores." "What about going to Sydney and going to McCoubrey, where we buy everything else?" "All right. But we'll have to tell some lies. And buy something, besides tea."

Well, I asked for a bag of flour. And the other fellow, he wanted a bag of flour too. "Oh yes," I said, "tea." "Tea? Oh, tea is rationed," McCoubrey said, "tea is rationed." "What do you mean—you haven't got it?" "Oh yes, I have lots of tea." "Well, what do you mean by rationing? I always paid you for everything I ever got here." "I know that, too. Have you got a radio home?" "Yes, but the battery is dead. I'll have to get a new battery." "My God, it's the battery kind you've got." "That's the only kind I can afford." "You know where I used to keep the tea?" "Oh, yes." "Do you know where I keep the bags?" "Yes." "Go and help yourself, and don't come to me, because I won't take your money today." [Laughing.]

So both of us went and we got bran bags and filled them with tea. He asked us, "If you're stopped on the road and they see you with all that tea, what are you going to tell them?" The other fellow says, "I'll go to jail. And by jeez, they'll have to look after my family, and make the hay for me, too!" "I'll do the same! I'll go to jail, too! Just as well. And indeed, they'll have a hell of a lot of cows to milk!" [Laughs.] "Go ahead, boys, go on! Go home." So, we got along okay.

Bowden Murphy:
24 Years Splitting Fish

My name is Bowden Murphy. I was born in Ingonish on the 17th day of September, 1890. And even yet, although I'm in my 93rd year, I feel real good.

(*What did you do that makes you feel so good now?*) Well, I don't know. I worked hard all by life, real hard. Twenty years I spent in one of those fish traps. I was splitter. Used to run the motor in the towboat. I've seen me go, split fish till eleven o'clock at night down in the stage by lantern light. Splitting the fish—there were three besides myself. There were four splitters in the bunch. You gain some days with three boatloads of fish; you know, you make three purses a day. The first purse you get out in the morning, just before daylight. And then you go out at noontime, about eleven o'clock. And then again in the evening, about four o'clock. Three purses a day. That is, if you didn't have too many fish. But of course, if you went out and got a big catch, get all your boats loaded—well, you'd only make about two purses a day.

Poor old fellow, his name was Sid Burke, he was a merchant—he owned the trap. Used to get most of his crowd over in Newfoundland. They always used to come over, a bunch of them, every summer, just during the fishing seasons. (*Were there not enough people in Ingonish to do the job?*) Oh, there were enough, but everybody was on their own, like. Everyone here was fishing for themselves. And you see, you'd make more than you'd make if you were hauling the fish traps.

(*Then, why did you work in his fish traps?*) Well, my poor old father,

80

he wasn't very well at the time. And I was only young, I didn't know very much about fishing. And this old fellow that had the trap, he had a lobster factory, too. I worked before I was only a teen in the lobster factory, picking this fine meat out of the lobster, out of the arm part. I worked for him, oh, for years, I always thought him a very nice old fellow. It made no difference when he'd meet me or what I was doing, he always called me "brother." He said, "Brother," he said, "I want you to come in the trap with me." And he said, "I want an extra splitter. You're going to learn to split." Well, I had split a few fish before that, just of my own. But after I went with him, then I split for twenty years.

And there used to be a man come down—oh, he was an expert on fish—and he'd visit you once during the summertime to see that your fish were split right. You see, when you cut down by the backbone, there's a little white stripe. Well, if you cut that stripe out, you know, you've gone too deep. But if you leave that white thread along the backbone, and don't cut it or break it, your fish won't break by handlers, when they dry it. (*So there was an interest in quality fish.*) Oh yes, oh yes. In those days, the big American vessels used to come down. You had to dry everything. There was no such a thing as freezing fish or getting clear of them fresh at that time. You had to salt them all and dry them. And then the American vessels would come down and load up and take them to the States.

I was in the boat. I used to go out and help purse the trap. And when we'd come in, then my job was splitting. Go out just as soon as it was light enough to work, you know, the pursing. Go out there lots of times, and we'd fill all the boats that we had, of our own; and probably some small boats used to go out, and we'd give them halves. See, we'd give them a boatload. When they split half of them, they got half a boatload for themselves. (*Would your own boats be really that full with fish?*) Yes, you'd fill them. Sometimes you'd take too much, you know. If you happened to strike out a heavy breeze of wind, when you were bringing it in—you'd have to go very slow. The boat would be that low in the water. We pretty near lost a boat one time. I had charge of the motorboat. And I saw she was taking water. There were two of the fellows standing in the forward standing room. And I noticed the boat was going down. The water was in among the fish, but you couldn't tell it. So I saw this lop coming—I just swung around so we were clear of it. But if she had taken another one, she would have gone down head first. (*Did that ever happen to any of the vessels out there?*) No, never had an accident. You'd try to take all you could, you know.

You'd come to the outside wharf. You had three blocks. They used to call it a block—they built a wharf—just a block of logs, and fill it with rock, and then put stringers from one block to the other. So you get out far

81

enough in the cove to get water deep enough to float your boats when they're loaded. You'd have to fork the fish all up. You used a fork then, but you had to fork them in the head. You see, if you forked them in the body of the fish, that bloodstain would never come out of the fish. They had to fork them all in the head. Of course, there were lots that weren't forked in the head. (*And where do you do the splitting?*) You have a split-house right on the outside wharf, the outside block. You split, and then everything goes overboard, all the offal of the fish goes overboard, chuck everything. A hatch is right by your splitting table, and everything goes down in the water.

There were three at the table. One fellow'd take up the fish, and he'd cut the throat and split it down, slit it down the belly. The other fellow'd take the gut out and knock the head off, and shove it over to me, the split-ter. And I'll tell you the best knife I ever had, I made it myself, and it was from a scythe for cutting hay. After it got worn so much, I just sawed it, and I took it and curved it a little—you've got to have a little curve into it, so as to get under the bone, to take the bone out.

I split all the time when I was there. Twenty years. And then, after I left him, I went with an old fellow there from Newfoundland for four years. I split for him, too. Twenty-four years, I split. (*You must have liked it.*) Oh, yeah. And when you got used to it, there's nothing to it, you get so used to it.

It was mostly haddock at that time. You hardly ever got very many codfish, very few—all haddock. You got a lot of mackerel. But the had-dock used to come inshore, more so than the other fish. You had to be at it every day while the school was on, because it only lasted for about a couple of months. You had to get them while they were going. See, we took the fish here, and split them. Then they were all salted in bulk, until that fishing season was over. Salted in bulk, you know, in a big, long building—there'd be a bulk about three to three and a half feet high right the whole length of the building. And there'd be bulk after bulk. You had to keep watch over them, in case the flies would get in them, then there'd be maggots in them, they'd rot. And then after the school of haddock was over, you'd wash all those out, put them on the flakes to dry them. And you'd work at that fish till it was all shipped aboard of the American boats that used to come in there.

Oh, I don't know. I just kind of took a liking to that, you know. I'll tell you, there were lots of times that you wouldn't get over three hours sleep, sometimes not that much, in the nighttime. By the time that you'd get home—when the big rush of the big school of fish would be on—you'd have to split them sometimes till eleven o'clock. By the time you'd get home and get washed up, get a bite to eat—you wouldn't be in bed very long before you had to get up again. Day after day. Of course, there'd be some times that there'd be more or less than others. The more fish, the harder it was right then, the less sleep you got. I never minded, no. I really enjoyed her.

(*Would they work on Sunday, too?*) No, no. No work on Sundays. And I tell you, there's some difference in those days and today. I've seen my poor old mother get her Sunday dinner all ready. She'd have everything done on Saturday, so there wouldn't be anything to do, not even carry water on Sunday. But it's different today. (*Even if there was a good run of fish, they wouldn't go after it on Sunday?*) No. All the time, during the time that I lived in Ingonish—well, I lived there all my life—never worked on Sunday. Never fish on Sunday. They never went, what they call hand-lining, or anything like that. Never did any kind of fishing on Sunday, no.

(*Was there ever any lack of fish? Did it ever fail?*) No. Well, some years you know, they weren't so good. But in the first years, well, I never saw anything like it. I've seen me go out with him—I was only a kid—and you'd haul it up, you know, and you'd put the bait on the hook and put it over, and then pull till you come to the next hook, and took it over. And by the time that you get out to the other end, get it all baited, and go back—there'd be a fish on every hook. Hardly ever missed. And I thought to myself, when I was fishing them: sometimes the last of it—you'd get those little haddock about so long. And you see, a small size haddock like that, you can't get clear of them, because they're not worth bothering with—too small for anything. I've seen when you haul the trap up—she might be half full—you pull her up till you get them up to the head rope, and dump them over the head rope, and let them go. And as far as you could see, perhaps half a mile, you'd see those fish floating on the water. Well, it wasn't only what was floating on the water, but think of the millions and millions of spawn that was into those fish. That was making away with them. And today, you can't get a haddock. That's my idea: what you were catching and keeping, and then those smaller ones—millions and millions of them were chucked overboard and went to waste. Not a trap down there today. Not in North Bay. I don't think there's any in South Bay, as far as I know. There might be a mackerel trap there, but no fish traps any more. (*A mackerel trap is different from a fish trap.*) Yeah. I said, if this keeps up, there's not going to be a haddock. And my thoughts were right.

I most always fished with my poor old father-in-law, the last years I fished. But he'd always keep his boat out as long as he could, after the others'd be all tied up. I'd see us get caught out one day—it was nice going out, the ocean was frozen over like a pane of glass. And I said to him, going out, "We'll have a nice day for our last day, anyway"—supposing

83

our last day. "I don't know, boy," he said, "I believe there's a breeze of wind outside." And you could hear it roar, like sometimes you could hear the wind on the mountains down there, you know, roaring over the mountains. And by and by, the lop struck in, heavy lop, and then the snow struck. One of the worst days I ever was on water. He made a sign. There was a fellow in the dory with me. I was hauling the trawl in. And I had a new tub of gear, brand new tub, and I wanted to get to the end. And the fellow said to me, "The skipper made a sign to put the tag on and leave it here." Getting so bad, you know. You had to take it over on the stern of the dory, and keep her bowed to the breakers coming and breaking. And when the snow struck, you could hardly see anything.

Well, we were that long out—everybody thought that there was something had happened to us. And when we came in to the wharf, to the breakwater, the sea was going right across over the breakwater. And we had to take a tackle that we used to have for hauling the boats up. We had to take it and put it into the wharf and fasten it to the boat, and pull her in to the wharf—there was that much of a suction. I'll never forget it. Just when I got to my new tub of gear, he made the sign to put the keg on. I put the keg on and we left it.

And the next day, it was out from the nor'west, blowing a gale of wind, and it wasn't fit to go out. So the second day, we went out. And when we got out to where we left the gear, there was no sign of it. But everything was frozen over, it was freezing, freezing hard. He was up forward, my father-in-law, and he was looking like this, you know, with his hands up over his eyes. He said, "I see something," he said, "outside there. I believe it's our keg." And we went out. There were two tubs of gear, and the two buoys, the two anchors, everything, were all afloat. And there was a shark on; he was as long as a horse. I'll never forget it. I looked it over, and I said, "I don't know what's on the gear, but there's something awful heavy." Well, I looked over, and I saw this great big white thing coming up. This was all that gear, three tubs of gear—you have six lines in your tub, fifty-fathom lines—all that, and the fish onto it—this was what we were pulling up. Everything else was lost. And a shark onto it long as a dory! (*And that was the end of the season for you.*) I was glad it was. (*But a storm like that—wouldn't it change your feelings about being out there?*) Not a bit, not a bit. No, you'd forget all about it after awhile. And once you did it—I don't know—everybody, I think it's the same, that likes the water. It doesn't make any difference what kind of a time you get into like that, you just forget about it. It never bothered you. It never bothered me. I just like it, just the same.

Hattie Carmichael
of the Meadow Road

I was born on the Meadow, 1888 [Meadow Road, North River, Victoria County]. I was at the Meadow until I was married, when I was twenty-three years old. And then we lived at North Sydney for a number of years. Then my husband was lost at sea. He was lost at sea down north of Cape North. His name was Daniel Carmichael. They were seagoing people, you know; most all of those Carmichaels were to sea. He was a sea captain.

He had been away, and he came home. And Captain Dunphy—you've heard of Captain Dunphy, down north—he wanted him to go to the Madeleines [Magdalen Islands] for a load of fish. And he went in the morning, on Monday morning, and at four o'clock he was gone. His body was never found. (*Was he alone?*) Oh no, he wasn't alone. The second oldest boy was with him—he was fourteen—and there was more crew on the boat, you know. They were having supper, and one of the lifeboat davits opened, and he went up to fix it. So, he didn't come back right away, and Gussie—that was his son—went up and checked. But he was gone overboard. He sank to the bottom. And they threw him a rope, and he didn't seem to care to catch it. He might have taken a turn of some kind, who knows? It wasn't a

storm and it wasn't anything. Just accidentally slipped overboard, and was lost. My son came back home after awhile. He was home some time coming on morning.

So, it was kind of rough. I had six children. And the youngest was not five years old. I was living at North Sydney at that time.

People were better to help each other. In my younger days, everybody was farming. No wonder if I feel old sometimes. Everybody was farming, out the Meadow and in here and everywhere you'd go around here, they were farming. I remember, my mother had twelve children, and my father died when I was a baby. I was the youngest of the family. And there was nobody resting—harvest time, planting time, or any time there was that kind of work going on. There was nobody resting or staying in the house. Everybody was helping each other. You'll have to go here today, and you'll have to go there tomorrow—while there was anything going on of that kind. That's the way we lived. And it was wonderful. We thought it was. We had no other activities—when we were out of school, we were working. Do most anything.

Oh, land's sake, listen. If you'd see the gardens and the planting potatoes. The women were always helping the men. And the children were just as good as their mothers. You know, there was no such thing as running around doing nothing for children when they grew to be twelve and thirteen and on, then. No, no. They played for a little while, but if there was any work to be done, they weren't playing. I don't know whether it was better or worse, but I know that they were much happier than they are today. And more content.

The parents would be in charge of the garden, you know. It would be plowed, but you had to do the rest. You'd have to take your hoe and fix the drills, put the fertilizer on what you were planting, plant the seed, and look after it after it started growing. Keep the weeds out of it. Then hoe it, and—oh dear, dear, dear—people talk about working today. (*Who picked the rocks?*) I did my good share of them. And that was one thing that we didn't like to do. Pick the rocks. When it came to that, well, I guess we were pretty sticky about doing it. Oh, we did it—there were no back answers. We did what we were told in those days.

(*What about the rest of the planting of the fields?*) Oh well, the men did

86

that, mostly. They plowed the fields, and they harrowed it. And then they sowed the seed. So that was all there was to it. It would grow. God gave it water, and it would grow. But when it came time to mowing it, then the harvest time—the men would cut it with a

Working at the potatoes

scythe. They were cutting along, you know, and the women were coming behind, making the sheaves. And by the time they'd be through with the space they were cutting, you know, they were all ready to go back to where they started again. No, there were no moments lost. (*How many men would cut at one time?*) The one man and the one woman, that's all I ever saw cutting. Of course, there'd be somebody to make the bands; you know, the things we twisted to hold the sheaves together. A younger person, or someone that didn't know their business as well. Many's the time, many's the minutes I spent at it. My mother ahead of me, making the sheaves. And as soon as the sheaf was put on it, I was twisting it and tying it up and putting it one side. Great. It was a special way of twisting it together that it would hold. It wasn't a special knot, I would say, but you just twisted it around, just turned it in a way that the end would be in when you put the sheaf on it. Therefore it would hold together.

(*What was a sheaf?*) Just bundles. And you made a strap of so many stalks of the grain. You twisted it that it would stay together. And you put that around the bundle, the sheaf. Until you'd have, oh, I'd say twelve or fourteen sheaves. Made so many and stacked it up for the grain to dry. You know, sticking the lower part, what was cut, down, kind of in the ground, and the tops would come like this together. (*The sheaves leaning against each other?*) Yes, that's right. And they'd stand up very well. Even with high wind, they'd stand after that, and dry as dry as anything. It would be oats or barley or wheat or whatever they had planted.

And then, that would be put in the barn. It would be put away over the crown beam in the barn, the whole thing, and it would be there until winter, you know. It would be in the winter they would be thrashing it. It would be kind of sticky, I figure, if you took it in from the field and tried to thrash it, the seed wouldn't break off it. It wouldn't be dry enough, you know. So it was put up in the barn, and in the fall, and coming on winter, it would be thrashed, you know, with a thrasher. You don't know what that is. Well now, this is funny. It was made at home, two sticks, possibly this long. I would say a yard, or maybe a little better than a yard, or whatever. Two sticks, and they weren't big sticks—they'd be about this much around. (*An inch and half.*) Yes. And they would be both tied together by a kind of a longer string or rope, I suppose, or maybe a wire, the two sticks. And they were thrashing: just swing it over your shoulder and hit the grain on the barn floor, and knock the oats or the barley or whatever it was, off it. (*Oh, it was like a whip, but a hard whip.*) Yes, that's right. You'd just break the grain off the straw.

(*Would it be a special day for this?*) Dear me, it would be days and days, but there was no special day. They'd do it any day that there was nothing else going on particular. (*And would the children have a role in this?*) No, not much. (*And would the women have a role?*) No. That was men's work. As far as I remember, I never saw a woman thrashing. There could be a man here and there, you know, at both ends. But most always it would be one person. (*And they'd strike the sheaf.*) They sure did. (*Was there a special place you would want to strike it?*) Oh yes, you would like to hit it near where the grain was on it.

(*So the seed would be knocked off. Now, what did they do with the straw?*) Feed it to the animals, if they would eat it, and if not, give it for bedding. Some animals used to love to eat it. But there was not much foodstuff in the straw. (*Would they use straw for bedding for people?*) No, I don't think they used straw much for that. But I'll tell you what they used to get a lot for bedding was the leaves in the woods. Many's the time we'd pick leaves. Bags and bags and bags of them, after they had fallen from the trees. A lot of people used to make mattresses of them. I remember of them being noisy. Maybe there was another mattress on top of it. You know, we used to have so many poultry and geese and ducks, and there was so much feathers. And that's what I remember mostly, the kind of mattresses we used to sleep on, was feathers. I remember very well, picking the leaves and taking them in, but I think most of the time, we had feather mattresses on top. Just a bolster—like we said, bolster.

Now, I'm going to tell you something else. We used to have geese. And do you know what they did with them? They used to pluck their feathers alive. Did you ever hear tell of that? Many's the one I plucked. To get their feathers. Because they were going to lose their feathers anyway. They lost their feathers in the run of a year, like the hens and any fowl. Those feathers had to be saved for use. They were just as good as hens' feathers. They were in mattresses and in pillows, lots of them. But I thought that was kind of cruel. I didn't like that job at all. I hated it. You'd get a barrel, and you'd throw the goose—I don't know whether they were tied or not—and you'd pluck all these feathers down in this barrel. And

Seated, right to left: Hattie's mother Euphemia MacIvor Matheson, sister Belle MacLeod, Belle's children John, Hector, Archie, dog Gibbons. Back, right to left: George MacIvor, Bessie Matheson, Hattie (Hectorina) Matheson Carmichael, her sister and brother-in-law.

the goose alive! But you know, when it came time to change their feathers, they weren't so hard to pluck them, they come out very easily. (*Would you take all the feathers?*) Every bit of them, even the feathers in the wings. They weren't saving the feathers out of the wings and out of the tail—that wasn't put in the barrel—but the soft feathers, yeah. They'd walk around naked, and pretty soon they'd be all covered with feathers all over again.

It was the women did that. Poor women, many's the thing they did that they shouldn't have done. And that was one of them, I think, plucking the geese.

You know, when the family grew up, they were all going away, because there was no father to provide. And as soon as ever they grew old enough, they were away to work. And my mother—I don't remember that she was much to talk about things that happened, and about her family. We used to often think, when the family would be away, "Isn't it strange we never hear Mother talking about John or George or this or that—what they are doing or where they are or what's going on?" We never heard Mother say that. But I must think that she worried just the same. But her worry was

89

staying by herself. She was a wonderful woman. Not that she was my mother, but.... (*She was left alone with how many children?*) Twelve. Out the Meadow. The farm was full of everything when Father died. The barn was full of animals, and there was a large farm to look after. How did she do it? How would a woman do it today? How did she do it then? That's what I tell you, people were so much better to help each other in those days than they are today.

And I remember when I came from North Sydney, a widow with five children, I still remember the difference between people then, and the difference today. When I came here, everybody was good to me. Thank God. But I was always working. And my children, all the time they were out of school, they were working with somebody. And nothing for it—nobody thinking of that. They'd give you something that they had and something that you'd need—food or clothing or whatever it would be. There was nobody looking for money.

I never worked very much away from home. Only a few months that I would work here or there. Housework. I never went far away. (*What could you get for housework?*) For goodness' sake, don't ask me. Who in the name of time saw a lot of money in those days? Will you believe this? The first time I ever went out of home to work, where I looked after a young child, I was getting a dollar and a quarter a month. Now you talk about much money! I went to work when I was doing housework, I worked for five dollars a month. I worked hard. I worked, then, for ten dollars a month, and I was doing work that the next year again, three girls were doing it. My size wasn't much, but I could work.

And I was just thinking about it today here. You know, when you're old and you're alone, doctors tell you it's not good for you to be looking in the past. Look ahead. That's the way. But if old people don't think about the past, what are they going to think about? (*And if they don't share the past....*) That's right. (*I think what the doctor means is if you dwell on the past....*) Maybe so. (*But if you share the past, doesn't the past become something useful today?*) Yes, but how can you share the past with people that don't know anything about it?

(*Would a woman have anything to do with haymaking?*) Yes. Well, goodness, couldn't she go out raking it and stacking it? They stacked the hay, you know, built stacks with a pitchfork, to be ready if it would rain through the night. And then they'd scrape it down on the sides, so if it would rain, that the rain would run down better, that the hay wouldn't get wet. Oh, they were up to their work. The women could do that, yes, they often did. And then in the morning, you'd go out and shake it out, shake it out with a pitchfork. Take those stacks, take them apart and open them out

Following the man with the scythe—raking and making sheaves.

so it would dry. If it was very wet, you know, they'd shake it out more, further on the ground. It would have to be perfectly dry going in the barn.

(*Would she load the hay wagon?*) Oh, not very much. Might throw a pitchfork full. But I never saw a woman making a load, of hay or grain or anything. A woman could go and tramp the load. Yes, many's the time I was tired of it. You were tramping all the time. (*But it would be a man that would throw the hay up.*) Oh yes, that was rather heavy work for a woman, wouldn't it? (*Didn't women do rather heavy work?*) A lot of them can do heavy work. My mother-in-law, at the house where they lived, there were three steps to the back door, before you got to the pantry. And she had a house full of boys, and her husband. And in those years you wouldn't buy a little bag of flour; you'd buy a big barrel. You know, in the fall of the year, we used to get four and five barrels. What would be the weight of it? Ninety pounds, I think, is half a barrel. A barrel is heavy, and it's big. She never would bother with a man taking a barrel in those steps. She took it in off the cart, up those steps, and into the pantry herself. Nobody ever touched it. Oh, my goodness, what a strong woman she was. (*But she still would not be asked to make a load of hay.*) No, no, she never made a load of hay.

(*So there were certain things that a woman did.*) Sure, there were certain things that a woman did, and then she wouldn't be bothered with a man. (*And certain things that a man did.*) Yes, certain things that the men did that they wouldn't have the women around. Just work of their own.

(*Would men bake?*) No. I never heard of a man baking, when I was

91

young, I never heard tell of it. And I don't think that I would care to eat what he baked. I know there's some of them that can bake today just as good as the women. (*But in those days....*) No, they never thought of it. (*What about cooking?*) If they were starving, I suppose perhaps they'd try and make a bite some way, but that was all. I'm telling you, they didn't like to bake. Or cook. In those years.

(*Whose job was it to take care of the animals?*) As far as I know, that was everybody's job. You know, my brothers, the men always fed the animals, I think, as far as that goes. Gave them the hay. The men always did that. I don't remember women going, unless there was an urgency, there was no man around. But the women used to go out and clean the stables and clean the bedding if there was any bedding, and let out the animals, and put them in. (*Would they carry water?*) Carry water? Goodness, dear, didn't we carry water all of our lives, carried the water in in buckets, out of the well. That's what we always did. There was no such a thing as running water into your house. (*Whose job was it to carry the water?*) Heavens, anybody could carry a pail of water. It wasn't left to anybody. If you found a pail empty, go and get some water.

(*Would the men help with the washing?*) No. Are men that helpful? (*Some are today.*) Some men are awful good to work, help with anything. In those days, they weren't. Monday used to be always wash days, since I remember. If it wasn't fine weather, they'd be doing washing with a tub, with a washtub and the washboard. Fine weather, they would take the washing to the brook—a big brook that was right near where we lived. And many's the beautiful washing we did there. Make a fire—there used to be a big boiler down there. And we'd fill it up and set fire under it, and it would be hot in no time, and we'd do a wash down there. And rinse the clothes in the brook, and put it to dry. On the grass. There was no such a thing as a clothesline. We always spread it on the grass. And may leave it there for a couple of nights. The longer you'd leave it there, the whiter it would get. Perhaps the dew would come on it, and then the sun in the morning would bleach it. (*Would you turn it over?*) Yes, we did at times. It was lovely.

(*What would they do for soap?*) Make it. (*Who made that?*) The women. I made both soft soap and hard soap. The hard soap is made with Gillis lye. And the soft soap is made with ashes from the fire, from the stove.

(*How do you make soft soap?*) Oh well, heavens, it's easy. You put a tub down to start with. And you put two sticks across it—I remember that so well—and set a barrel on those two sticks. And you made a hole in the bottom of the barrel. And you were putting a long stick down from the top, where the top of the ashes were going to be, out in this hole, the other end. Then you filled the barrel with the ashes from the stove, that you'd be saving for months, I suppose, and you poured water on it until the barrel was full. Cold water. It was never hot. Just let it sit. You didn't touch it, do anything with it. (*You don't pull the stick out?*) No, no.

If you pulled the stick up, the ashes would run down in the lye, through the hole, so you don't touch the stick. And after awhile it would stop dripping, you know, dripping, down in the tub that was underneath. It's just the lye goes down in that tub, it's just clean as anything. You let it sit there until you have enough lye to start boiling it. (*The water is taking the lye from the ashes?*) That's right. (*How much would be enough?*) Oh heavens, there'd be gallons. Clear as anything, and clean, because there were no ashes going out through this hole with the stick in it. It was just as good as any strainer.

And then you had a big boiler. And you made a fire outside, wherever you had your boiler lying. Put this big pot on it, and you put the lye in that. And boil it, and boil it. Perhaps you'd boil it for a day, perhaps less. And the women were used to it, you know, they used to know just how long to let it boil. (*Would you see anything that would give you a sign?*) No. I'll tell you, the only sign they'd have, was to have a dish and a spoon, and they took so much out of the pot, and put a little bit of water with it, and mixed it. And they could tell whether it was time to put the grease in it, or time to take it off, or time to put it away. It thickens, you know, thickens a little bit, but it doesn't get hard.

And then you'd put fat in it. You had to add grease of some kind. (*Where would you get the grease?*) Well, that would be saved from butchering in the fall. I don't think it mattered much whether it was fresh or not. I never remember of that. But I know sometimes it wouldn't be fresh, it wouldn't smell too good. But when once it went in the lye and boiled, that was all right, there was no bad smell of it. So it was good. Animal fat. Any animal at all. Pork or beef or sheep or lamb or anything. And it would dissolve—it didn't matter what it was like—it would dissolve. The heat and the lye. You wouldn't have to stir it. The boiling would keep it stirred enough. (*Did it take a lot of fat?*) Quite a bit, quite a bit, but I wouldn't have any idea just how much.

You had to watch it. When it would boil, it would be apt to boil over. I remember my mother sitting there. And she always had a little dipper of cold water, and she'd put a drop of that in it if she saw that it was coming over the top. To make it stop boiling, you know. Oh well, heavens, how they knew their work. And she'd be there with her knitting, and watching the pot of soap. Boy, they weren't spending many minutes idle. That wasn't a heavy job, either. Quite an easy job. But you couldn't leave it one minute. You couldn't turn your back to it. Because just as sure as you would, it would be boiled over. You had to watch it.

(*How long would she be boiling it?*) Well, I would say a whole day. And then when it was all through boiling, they were putting it in another big barrel or cask. They were pouring it in that, and putting so much water in it. And then stirring it and stirring it and stirring it, until was all stirred. And then you had your soft soap, to do for a whole year. (*Was the soft soap used for your face?*) Oh, no. Nor the Gillis lye soap, either; nobody ever used that for their face. It would be as hard and white as anything. But always for scrubbing and washing and cleaning. (*What was the soft soap used for?*) For a washing, whenever you washed at a brook. That's when it was good. We always used it in the washtub. (*This Gillis lye soap, was that made differently?*) Yes, altogether. You bought a can of Gillis lye. And it used to tell on the can how much fat to put in it.

And you melted the fat, just to warm—you wouldn't have to let it get hot—just to melt it. You would put it in so much water. And mixed it until it was all melted. Simple as anything. You poured it into a mold, a wooden box. And whenever it was cold, you'd cut it in blocks. And it was just lovely. Nobody makes it any more, and it's too bad. (*What would you wash your face with, then?*) Oh, you bought some soap. A big bar like you'd get today—Sunlight soap, you know, in two cakes—you'd get one of those for five cents apiece. I suppose that's what we used on our face, mostly.

(*And would a man do that work?*) I don't know as if they'd try, but too many other things to do. (*But it would be expected that a woman would do it, I suppose.*) Oh, sure. The man was fixing the barrel, and putting the hole in it and the stick in it, that was all.

94

Women did all the baking. All the cooking. And some with very poor stoves. If they had to bake today on the stoves that they used to bake with! Mercy on me, they were no good. Something like the Waterloo. Terrible, just terrible. But you didn't have any better, and there was no better to be gotten. Whatever the weather, you'd have to put on the fire to bake. Now, wasn't it something, the heat that stove would make? There was no such a thing as a hot plate or an electric stove. They could bake any day, whenever the food ran out, I guess. I don't think they had any particular day, any certain day that they had for baking. No, I don't think so. But Saturday they used to bake. Saturday there was a big baking day, to go over Sunday. Couldn't bake on Sunday.

(*Were you allowed to do any work on Sunday?*) No. You could go and feed the animals and clean out and milk them and all this, but you weren't allowed to do anything else. They would say, that's the work of necessity, you had to do that. But on Saturday—goodness, when we were young, we never, never passed a Saturday but we prepared all the vegetables, all the meat, what was to be cooked on Sunday—every blessed thing. We were all ready there to put it in the pots and on the stove. And then at supper-time, we had supper, all right, but we were not allowed to wash the dishes. You wouldn't bake anything, but you had to cook your meat and potatoes, whatever you were going to have. But it was all ready to put in the pot. Washed and cleaned and pared. The water was put on the stove; you could do that. But don't do anything else. Supper dishes were never washed until Monday morning.

I wonder was that good. I would say that it was religion in some shape or form, but I always think it went too far. We weren't supposed to pick an apple. If you were starving for an apple, you weren't supposed to take an apple off a tree. And you'd believe that. We thought about it every minute. I remember my sister and I going out one evening on a Sunday to take the cattle home in the pasture. And it was strawberry time. And oh, well, I saw a few strawberries, and they were so big and so tempting. I stooped down and I picked a couple of the strawberries and I ate them. And after we came home, she spilt the beans—she told Mother that I had picked strawberries and ate them. Well, she gave me such a going over. She wasn't mean, as punishing us, but oh well, the talking she'd give us. And she gave me such a talking, that I really and truly believed that I had a terrible pain in my stomach. I was just dying with that pain in my stomach, and I knew it was from the berries. But I know very well now that it wasn't, I didn't have it at all. I didn't have the pain. I just made myself believe that I did. So that's the way it was.

And isn't it funny? I think this is badness and evil, how we drifted away from these ideas. We all drifted away from the way we were brought

Women shearing sheep. Next page: (top) a spinner and a person with a niddy-noddy (a hand reel for making skeins from the spun yarn); (below) carrying bags of unspun wool.

up, I think. I know we did. (*Would you pick an apple on Sunday?*) Today? Yes, and eat it. And I don't think that's going to keep me out of heaven, if I do good things in other ways.

The weaving was all done in the wintertime. Think of all the work the women were doing. They had so many sheep—they always kept so many sheep—for wool. And from the time the lambs were born, they looked after the lambs, fed them when their mothers weren't able to do all that, looked after them.

They sheared the sheep. Maybe the men used to help with that, for to get them tied up, that they could shear them. It was the women that did the shearing. They'd wash the wool, picked it, carded it, spun it, and wove it into blankets. Of course, if they wanted dyed wool, they were dying it. They did all that.

Well, all the work that was around wool, and all they did with it, and all the blankets made in the loom. Dear, dear, dear. People don't realize what women did at one time. And they think they're working hard today. And they have everything at their fingers, press a button. I often saw Mother with three or four women coming with the spinning wheel on their shoulders, to spin with Mother. Oh boy, what a day! The wool was Mother's, and they were doing it for Mother. Because she always had so much wool, and so much to do. They always helped each other, my dear, when I think of it. (*I suppose there wasn't much pay for that.*) No thought about it, no. When they had wool to do, Mother would help, if she was not too busy. But my mother was a mother that was always busy, and that large family, and had so much to do. But she'd go and help anybody. (*Take her spinning wheel with her?*) Yes, that's right.

They used to make drugget, we used to call it. That was for dresses. That was fine stuff, you know, and it would be different to blankets. That, they didn't mill. But if it was for any special use, for fine dresses, and for Sunday dresses, they would send it away where they used to get it dressed. And would it ever be nice material. I remember one of my sisters. Mother had made for her a piece of cloth that she took with her when she went to Boston. And a dress-maker made the dress for her. And where she was working, whenever they had a special occasion, like a big supper or anything, that was the dress she had to wear, a homespun dress that she took from home. It was beautiful.

(*Did women ever go around the butchering?*) Oh heavens, no. Unless a woman would go with a basin or container of some kind, to get blood or to get whatever went in pudding. They made black pudding, blood pudding, and a white pudding, scads of it. A woman didn't have very much to do with the butchering, on- ly that she cleaned the coats for the puddings—the intestines. The women used to wash the intestines in a brook, if there was any brook to be got. If not, there was lots of water in the well. They'd clean them inside out.

Make the pudding. You'd get the suet from the inside of the animal and the suet on the kidneys. It didn't matter—one was as good as the other. Cut it up. And you put cornmeal, flour, rolled oats if you wanted, pepper and salt, lots of onions, that's all. Cut it all up, mix it, and put it inside the intestines, and tie both ends and put them in a pot and cook them. And were they ever good! I don't think there was ever a recipe for them. Mother would put so much of this in and so much of the other.

(*There'd be black ones and white ones—what would be the difference?*) Oh, a vast difference. The white ones, you just had the suet, and the cornmeal and the flour and the whatever. But in the black ones, you have that darn blood that comes from the animal. And it was soft. You'd have to put it in the coats with a spoon or something. Fill them the same way and tie them up and put them in a pot and boil them. (*How long did you boil them?*) Oh well, no recipe. You would just try the coats, you know, with a sharp fork or a darning needle, and you could tell on the feeling of the coats, whether they were ready to take off or not. If they're not done, they're still tough. But if they're all ready to take off, they're quite tender. Pierce them a little bit. You can't pierce them too much because if you do, you're skunking yourself.

I wish we had a scad of them right now. But that was one thing I always disliked, to help Mother with the black pudding. I didn't mind the other. I could make white pudding all day. But I would eat them—they were awful good. I'll tell you what Mother used to do. Oh, my goodness, there used to be so much butchering and so much pudding. She used to dry them. Put them on a string on the kitchen loft—you know, it was always warm on the kitchen loft, from the stove. And they'd dry just as dry as anything. Then, when you were going to use them, you'd parboil them for a little while in water, and then fry them—and they were just as good as the day they were made. It keeps them—there was no refrigerator. That was the only way you could keep them. But everybody didn't do that—a lot of people don't care for that.

In latter years I can't work, because I'm too old and I get too tired, and I can't think of doing things that I did years ago. But I think I lived a pretty busy life. If I wasn't working for myself, I was working for somebody else, helping. Maybe I was more like my mother. Of course, poor Father left us before we knew very much about him. I lost my husband when I was forty-three. (*And no insurance, I suppose.*) Not a cent. Look, my dear. The day my husband's clothes came home from the boat, from down north, I just had one ten-cent piece. No insurance, children small, no income, nothing—only myself and the children. We were buying a home, and I had to let that go, because I couldn't pay for it. And we got along

98

some way or other. I don't think there was any of them hungry at any time. People were good to us. I don't think I was idle many minutes that I could do something for somebody else, or myself. I sewed for them. I—oh, what do I be talking like this for? I bought sugar bags, I bought flour bags, I washed them, and got the letters off them, and dyed them. I made shirts for the boys and clothes for the girls. I made their overalls, knit them mitts and socks, and did everything for them. And thank goodness that I was able to

do it. If I didn't, I don't know what would have happened..

I know every woman wouldn't do it. I know that. Because I know of some young women that don't know how to sew a button on their children's clothes. Darn them.

I remember a young woman that was here the other day, and she was talking about how busy she was and all the things she had to do, and she was talking about something about the men's work. Now, she said, "The men—they don't know what it's all about." I don't like that kind of talk. I think the men do their share. And I think they are very good to do it, some of them. But I know that they don't take a woman's place. I know that they don't take a woman's place as far as thinking of doing a thing, and doing it, too. (*That's right, the thinking of it is very important. I think a man gets reminded by the season.*) Yes. That's right. (*But a woman has to be alert in a different way.*) I know she has. Yeah. And some women are different, too. Some women are shocking as far as I'm concerned, shocking to think about, how little they know how to do anything. And I don't know why they are like that. But they are, some of them. And I guess we can't help them.

99

Bill Forbrigger
and Coastal Schooners

(*There must have been a lot of boats here in the Strait of Canso at one time.*) Oh my dear, I guess there were. In those days, nothing but boats—all kinds of them. There were seven of them in that little place. Port Malcolm had seven schooners alone at that time, and that was only a small village. Everyone here had schooners those days. (*And a lot of traffic?*) Yes. In 1916 the ice was in here the 24th of May, the place was blocked with ice. There came a gale of wind that night from the southwest. And we all went out next morning, and we never saw a cake. There were 107 sail of vessels left Port Malcolm and Hawkesbury when the ice went out—107. An awful late spring.

Some from the States, from Lunenburg, and some from Barbados. They were waiting for the ice to go through, to go north, on to Prince Edward Island and Madeleine [Magdalen] Islands and New Brunswick. An awful pile. Seven three-masters. A couple coming from New York with hard coal for Charlottetown. And others were coming from Barbados with molasses.

I was born in Port Malcolm, down seven miles from Point Tupper.

Vessels in the Strait of Canso near Port Hawkesbury and Port Malcolm, circa 1900

1900. My father sailed on big ships for about twenty-two years. Square-rigged ships, going around all over the world. Then he fished out of Gloucester [Massachusetts] for twenty-five years. First one, he went from Buctouche [New Brunswick] with a load of oats for China. That was his first trip—a cabin boy. (*How old was he?*) Nine. And his mother didn't see him for about twelve years after that.

He wanted to go to sea. My grandmother left here when he was a baby and went to Souris, Prince Edward Island. Her husband had died. He grew up till he was nine years old. He went out with a fellow fishing in a boat, and he jumped on a Madeleine [Island] vessel going to Buctouche, and he shipped on a big ship going to China with a load of oats.

He stayed on those big ships. I don't know where he went from there. He'd wait on the tables—a big crew of them was out there. Making the beds and waiting on the tables and running the little errands. Till he got big enough. I don't know how old he was when he went before the mast. Able seaman.

He left that and he came to Gloucester, fished out of Gloucester. They fished all year round. Fished winter and summer on the Grand Banks. When he came from Gloucester, he got sailing on schooners here [Port Malcolm, Cape Breton]. My grandfather—my mother's father—had two schooners; he sailed on one of them for awhile. My grandfather had a big business in Port Malcolm. He had a big grocery store. He supplied the American fishermen and the Dutch fishermen with bait and salt and ice. He used to cut his own ice out here. And kept oilclothes, and kept oars and dories and molasses—he kept everything. He had his own wharf. He had two schooners bringing his supplies from Halifax. My father sailed one of them at that time. Bringing bait from the Madeleine Islands.

(*Where did you grow up?*) Port Malcolm. I left home when I was fourteen. Went to schooners with my father. Started in Campbellton, New Brunswick, in 1914, the year the war broke out. We sailed on a smack for a packing company, lobster smack. Well, they canned lobsters in the lobster season. When the lobster season was over, they canned everything—blueberries and plums and apples. We sailed a schooner from about the first of April till November—all in the Baie Chaleur. There were no wharves those days. We used to lay to an anchor, and they'd boat the stuff off. Everything in cans. Nothing back. Came back light.

And lots of storms. We had one the first year I was in Baie Chaleur. There was an awful lot of people lost—fishermen. A gale of wind from northeast, snowstorm. We were loading lobsters. We hove an anchor short. She had a wooden windlass spit. And she made a dive, and she took the windlass out. So we had to slip our chains, and we went around to Miscou Harbour. And that night it came a gale from the northeast. At the

8th day of June, it snowed one foot, one foot of snow. There must have been about twenty lives lost—small boats, six in a boat. There were three brand new ones they just built that winter; they were all lost. An awful gale of wind.

I was in school till I was about nineteen years old, going in the winter. Go away in the summer, and go to school in the winter. I was only getting a few months. (*When you were nineteen....*) I just stopped. (*You were only getting half a year.*) Just about, yeah. (*Did you know then what you would like to do with your life?*) Yes, schooners, go to sea, yeah. (*"Schooners," "go to sea"—you like the words, don't you?*) Yeah. I loved schooners. I did that till '29. I had two schooners of my own.

(*Did you stay with your father?*) No, I worked with my older brother after that. He had schooners, too. He owned them and sailed them. The same as I did—coal and lumber and potatoes and salt and brick—everything you could get. (*Where would you get the coal?*) Sydney, Pictou, Little Bras d'Or, Kelly's Cove. Carried railroad coal from New Campbellton to P.E.I. Only place you shoveled was when you took a load to the Madeleine Islands. There was no one to shovel it over there. Fishermen wouldn't shovel it. They'd give us a horse to hoist. We'd shovel it ourselves. In Charlottetown and all those places, they always had free discharge. Had a horse to hoist, and three big tubs, and three men in the hold, shoveling. And all we did was tend the guys, one on the gaff and one on the tub. Two-hundred-fifty-pound tubs. They'd fill them and hoist them up

In the Madeleine Islands, one trip I was there, they were hauling with their cows. Milk them in the morning, and then put a half ton of coal in them and haul it up. We'd take coal all over Prince Edward Island—Souris, Georgetown, Summerside, Charlottetown, Grapaud, the north side, Malpeque—that's where I used to go. We took potatoes back. Not always. We came back light most of the time. Spring and the fall, we'd take potatoes. (*Did you go to the farms?*) No, no—merchant. The merchant would get them from the farmers and we'd buy them from him. All loose. In later years they were bagged in ninety-pound bags.

(*So you'd fill your hold with potatoes.*) Right. Wash her out [after the coal]—water and buckets—sweep her out, and then wash her down with water and a broom, and then slack lime all over to dry her up. It wouldn't take long. Splashing a bucket of water, and then a fellow with a broom, eh? Then you pump it out, pump the dirt out. Slack lime. (*Powdered.*) Yeah. Just throw it around. That'll dry it right up.

Sometimes we had the potatoes on freight, chartered, and sometimes we owned them. We'd go where we could sell them—Canso, Mulgrave, Hawkesbury. We had to go to Sydney, or all the way down through the lake, Baddeck, right through to Louisdale. Just go in, and go to shore and

Bill Forbrigger's father Frank; Bill's mother Ellen Malcolm Forbrigger;
and his grandfather William Malcolm

see if they wanted them. Wherever we went, we always sold some.

(*Where did you pick up the lumber?*) Oh, Buctouche, for the Island, and
we went in the Lake for Sydney, North Sydney, New Waterford. All up
above Whycocomagh, up to St. Patrick's Channel. I loaded a lot in Nyanza. I loaded a lot in Little Narrows. Bucklaw. Carried railroad ties from
there, too, to Sydney. St. Patrick's Channel and Nyanza and Baddeck and
Big Harbour—I carried lumber from all those places. Kempt Head.

(*Was it difficult to get a load?*) No, no, no—it was all right. I never had
any trouble. (*So while the season was on, you were on the go.*) All the
time. The last year I carried coal steady from Pictou to Canso. Slack coal
over to the fish plant, Maritime Fish Plant.

(*Where did you get the money to buy your own schooner?*) Oh, saving
it up. The schooners didn't run the year round, you know. We just ran till,
oh, sometimes till New Year's. Old Christmas. We used to tie up then at
Lower River Inhabitants. Freeze in for the winter. Then after that, I'd go
to work in the fish plant in Hawkesbury. I liked work. I did mostly anything. I worked in the shed—loading fish, unloading sawdust, working a
lot of overtime, too. I got all the overtime I could get. Ten hours a day for
$1.25 a day. I liked to work—days weren't long enough. They're still not
long enough.

It was hard work. When you're young you don't mind working, anyway. It was cold. I wasn't putting any hands in fish; that wasn't my work
at all. We did mostly loading in cars. And we cut ice for the same plant in
the winter, too, in the harbour there—a big pond there—it's all filled in
now. But that was the hard work, loading big bobsleighs. Two men with
ice hooks, loading them on these high sleighs—boy, your old arms were
tired in the night.

And we were shacking. There was a bunch of men in an old place you

103

could see through the roof, hard old place. Yet there were bunks there, and you cooked your own meals. Took the fish from the fish plant and cooked them yourself. We took bread from home. And meat and stuff, we got that at the stores right close. Just what they call bunks, made out of boards. (*Mattress?*) A kind of a bag full of hay, I'd call it. Oh, you were warm enough, when you covered up.

(*So you would do that for the winter.*) Not all winter, but part. Then we had wood to cut in the woods for the winter, my father and I. Go in the woods for a couple of weeks, cut forty loads of wood, and haul it out. Big "two-top-master" to haul it out—an ox! We'd cut about forty loads. Some for that winter and some for next, too. Hardwood. We'd burn both, green and dry pulp.

(*Did you do any work on the schooner through the winter?*) No, not till the spring. About the last of March, middle of March, somewhere around there. Start painting them up, and caulking them on the water line. Put all this stuff—booms and gaffs and chains—on one side, and list out. (*You'd put them to one side of the vessel, and she'd list.*) Her main boom with the sails on it, and her fore boom—she had quite a list. Then turn to the other side and do the same. Always paint them all over in the spring. That's all we'd do while she was listed, the copper paint. Then the topside is out of water. We used to—if it was blowing—we'd take the rope aft, tie it to the bit, and then pay our chain, and she'd turn side to the wind. Then we worked to leeward—no wind at all, calm. (*Would your father work with you?*) Well, I worked with him. When I was with my brother, I worked with my brother. Mostly just the two of us, till we got ready to go. We'd always get another man after that. (*What would you do for a crew?*) Oh, just go around—as a rule, you got it right in the place where you lived, in Port Malcolm. They were mostly all sailors there. (*So there'd be just the three of you aboard?*) Just three. One was the captain, one was the cook, and the other fellow's the deckhand. (*But when it came to work, everybody had to work.*) Right. Hoist sails and hoist anchors and steer.

(*After awhile you had your own schooner,* Speed.) I forget what I paid for it. (*It was a schooner?*) Oh yeah. Well used. Built in Newfoundland, she was a good schooner. She wasn't that big—56 registered tons. Carried about 120 ton of coal. Good in wind. Good off of the wind, too.

My brother lost it at Burchell's Mines in Little Bras d'Or, with a load of coal. You get your tide there, where you've got to go through the bridge, to come up the Lakes. You had to tow through when you loaded. Such a tide, eh? You couldn't sail through. You get a slack tide and they'd tow you out. The towboat towing him through—and they hit the Little Bras d'Or bridge. Got up in Burchell's Cove, and it must have knocked a plank off, for she sunk there. Saved the sails. Where they put her, the water wasn't that deep. But it cost too much money to take the coal out of her. So we got another one after that.

The *Stella* I got in Arichat, West Arichat. I think it was $1200. And I sold it for $1400. I didn't have her too long, about four years, I guess. (*With your own schooners, were you ever caught in any rough storms?*) No, no. Not once. I had great luck with schooners.

(***Family:** Bill, was it you or your brother who took the schooner in to Sydney that time there was some kind of a strike on, and they couldn't get the schooner unloaded?*) My brother Raymond. It was the steel plant was on strike. The mines—the whole thing. He was seven weeks there with a load of pit timber, trying to get unloaded. He was in at the Pier and then they chased him out of there, and went up to an anchor in Sydney, till the strike was over. (*Couldn't he have gone somewhere else?*) No, no, the pit timber belonged to the mines. He had to stay; he had to wait. But I was going all the time—I didn't get caught in that. I was carrying potatoes and coal. Wasn't caught in that at all.

He [finally] got unloaded, he took the vessel around to North Sydney. To load coal. And come the August Gale, and he lost her there in North Sydney. They had a French consul there—he started to build a wharf. And he built a pier way out in the harbour—and he never finished it. And my brother drug into that old pier and knocked the stern right off the vessel. So he lost her there, and he lost the other one in Little Bras d'Or. He had hard luck. I was awful lucky with schooners—never had any trouble at all.

My father, he was out in the August Gale, the big August Gale, in a small schooner. He came from the Madeleine Islands. He was down in Pleasant Bay when the wind struck, and he laid to, what they call laying to—the foresail, the middle sail, and then you put the wheel hard down, and they go ahead a little, and they drift—and that breaks the sea. But when the foresail blew off her, ran her bare-poled before the wind. Then when it jumped nor'west, he was up off St. Paul's, and he ran her bare-poled the other way. So he was down off of Port-aux-Basques, New-foundland, when it died out. He rode it out. There were an awful lot of vessels lost—Lunenburgers, and American fishermen. Oh, an awful pile lost, an awful pile of schooners.

(*Where were you during the August Gale that sank your brother's schooner?*) On the beach, up in the Lakes. Drug ashore. Widow's Light. That's just below St. Peter's. Next to Cape George. We anchored pretty close that evening. We had the little anchor out. We gave her all the chain on the little one. We had just given her the big anchor. We were about fif-teen fathom out. That's all we could give her. We were getting too close to the shore. So we were just going to put a tackle from the horse pipe back to the bit—that'd ease her, the way she was jumping. She was driving about, oh, just picking the water up in chunks. When she parted the big chain and turned to the wind for the beach. It was beached away up, oh, sea was hitting her. Her rudder irons were out of water. She was out of water about five feet, I guess. And the tide was terrible low. If it had been as high when we went on as when we came off, we'd have gone in the pond, and we'd have had to dredge the pond, to get her out. But it was right down low. We just stayed there [on the beach] till the gale was over, southeast.

In the morning we only had one anchor. We thought we had no anchors by the way she went for the beach. So we had a big six-inch cable aboard. Brand new. We put that ashore to a big pine tree. The wind jumped down nor'west. No wind where we were. All trees. But we put the jibs on her and the foresail, and slewed her bow some. But she wouldn't come off. And the tide had raised away up—about three or four feet, I guess. Wind driving out into the nor'west. We got her off with the sails and the wind. Hoisted the jibs and the foresail and then threw her down on her side. That bow slewed around, and her stern still on. But then we put a piece of mainsail on her. Then she went afloat and hung by the big pine, big cable on it. So we just ran from one to the other and let the sails go right on deck, and she swung to the pine tree and we laid there all day. Till it died out that evening. (*No damage, really.*) Oh no, no, never hurt it. All sand.

When the wind died out, we took two boats and we swept, and we hooked the fluke of our anchor. One boat [went] around the other, then we hoisted our anchor, put a chain shackle in it, and we were all set.

Lots of times you'd get a calm. You just stayed there, you never moved, till the wind struck again. It didn't happen too much around here. There was always a little breeze of wind closer to any of the shores. So just lay there. Lay down and read a storybook. Nothing to do. Sometimes a couple hours; sometimes all day. No wind at all. (*Was it a holiday or was it work?*) [Mr. Forbrigger chuckles.] No holidays on them. We had lots of rest, of course. Sometimes we'd be in here in the Strait, going north. There'd be a nor'wester, we couldn't get out, we'd have nothing to do for a couple of days. No work at all when you were sailing. All you had to do was steer it. Cook a bite to eat. The work was when you got in and unloading lumber, or unloaded brick or potatoes, or anything of your cargo—that was the work. We didn't shovel any coal—only in the Madeleine Islands.

We raced lots of times to get to dock in Charlottetown first. There'd be a bunch, probably twenty vessels making for Charlottetown. Well, some of the fellows would anchor on the flats. I was one of the fellows that'd go right in the docks and stick her in the mud—to get ahead, unloaded first. Get in there the middle of the night, dark as the devil, and tide there. I used to do a lot of that—sneak into the wharf. Sometimes stick her in the mud way up, low tide; high tide, she'd flood. To get ahead, eh? I'd be foxy.

(*Family: Dad, what about when your brother had the toothache?*) Oh, no. They'll all laugh at me, why should I tell that? (*Which brother?*) Raymond. Oh, I hate to tell that. It's the truth, but none of them will believe it. Well, I suppose I'll have to tell you.

My father and I, and my brother, the oldest fellow, were beating up the Lake, down by where the new bridge is there now, Seal Island. Well, above that—Man-o'-war Point—between that and Big Harbour.... See, she's laughing at me already. So he took the toothache. Oh good God, he was going right crazy with the toothache—ready to jump overboard. So my father took a nail and he pointed it, and told him to pick his gums with it till it bled. And go ashore and drive it in a tree that he thought would never be cut down. So I rowed him ashore—he was screaming. And he drove it in a tree. And on the way back, he was laughing. Toothache left him just like that. And the tooth all went to pieces and fell out. They won't believe that.

My father also gave him a little prayer to say—but I never heard what the prayer was. I didn't hear. I tried the same thing at Point Tupper, with a nail and a great big old tree we had there—I knew it would never be cut down. At that time, anyway. So I picked my tooth, and picked it, got it full of blood, and I drove it in the tree. But I think I made it worse! (*You didn't know the prayer.*) Didn't know the prayer, no.

TB was bad those days. TB and whooping cough. I had three brothers died with TB. They didn't have the smallpox in Port Malcolm, but there was an Island schooner here loaded with potatoes, bound for Halifax. And they took the smallpox aboard of her. There was an old doctor here, old Dr. MacDonald—Dr. Pat, they called him. They took those fellows, six of them, to a small cabin out the old Sydney Road, and my father went out there and looked after them. One died—but he saved the other five. I remember when he came home, before he came in the house, he walked right in the basement from outside, the back of the house. He went in there and he took all his clothes off and took them out in the field and he burned them. There were no bathtubs in those days. He got a great big tub of water and he washed himself with something before he ever came in the house. He had the smallpox, fishing out on the Grand Banks. So he was all right. He saved the five of them, and one fellow died.

Oh God, the flu in 1917 was Canada-wide. Terrible. Oh, it was bad at home. There was nobody but my youngest sister, Gladys—everybody was knocked out. One couldn't get off of it to help the other—all in bed. She was the only one. She trained for a nurse in Sydney, after. She was only a young girl then, fifteen. She looked after the works. Cooked, and cut the wood out of the woodpile. We had no wood. We had all kinds of wood in

107

the woods when we got sick. But none at the door. We had a great big ox. Snow, God, the snow must have been three feet. Talk about snow. So she hitched up the big ox and went ahead of him out to the wood, and got a load of hardwood and brought it home and sawed it up at the woodpile, and brought it in to keep us from freezing. Only for that, I don't know what we'd have done. Nobody could move. We all got flu—father and mother, all hands. Terrible. It was that way—everybody was the same, all over the place. Everybody had it, everybody, everybody.

I never was so sick in my life. Couldn't eat, couldn't sleep, you couldn't sit up, you couldn't do anything. Just lay there. It must have been some fellows come from overseas, I guess. That's what they say, where it all came from, from the German gas. They were dying like sheep out in the trenches of Europe. (*How long were you down?*) I must have been out about ten days altogether. And then you could just about walk when you did get around. I was weak for so long—oh, it was terrible.

(*And your sister...?*) She never got it. She did everything. We'd have all died in a pile if it hadn't been for her.

(*Family: Why did you have cats on board the vessel?*) I never had a cat on them. (*Didn't you sail on one once that you had a problem with a cat?*) Oh, that was an old fellow I went to the Island with for a trip. We had a cat in the fo'c'sle, and a dog in the cabin. (*You were working with him?*) Yeah, I was that fall.

We had sold one of our vessels, and we only had one. He couldn't get anyone to go with him, terrible hard to get—the war was on, First War. He laid on Port Malcolm I don't know how long. (*And the boat in such bad shape.*) Oh, she was that way when he bought her. She was never any good. (*It wasn't that he didn't take care of her.*) Oh well, that's part of it, too, yeah. Because he was a poor sailor. Like the bridges and stuff—he always hit them when he was going through them. He was an awful poor sailor. (*Why did you go with him?*) I went to get the stuff for the winter, from the Island. For my family. Potatoes and turnips and a pig, and that stuff. Our own vessel wasn't going to the Island: we were carrying lumber out of the Lake, my father and my oldest brother.

So we laid in here two weeks. Down nor'west, blowing a gale every day. And we were squidding—we got lots of squid. Drew a dollar a bucket. We were selling them for bait to the fish plant.

So we finally got going. And the old vessel he had, she was all rotten. She was all falling to pieces. So we got out halfway between Cape George and the Strait here. It started to blow. He still had the staysail on her. The staysail was a sail that went from the end of the topmast down to the foremast. The light sail. We had the four lowers on, and that upper sail. And

108

he had hit the Grand Narrows bridge—I wasn't with him then; I just joined him in Port Malcolm—and he had broken some of the rigging. So I went to try the rigging, see if it had much strain on it. I looked aloft, and the old masthead was all bent. I hollered and told him, "Your masthead!" "Oh by Jove, Billy, no," he said, "that's a new masthead." "Well," I said, "it's gone." So we hauled down the jib. I tied that up. We took in the mainsail. We didn't get it tied up. The boom fell on the davit plank. And down came the old masthead, topmast and all. So then we had to get the mainsail tied up, got the foresail down.

He was steering, the old fellow. He was going to make a beeline right to Souris from the Strait, but I told him, "The wind might haul down to the westward—you'd better keep up for the cape." So we did. Anyway, we got that piece of foresail on her, and I hauled the jumbo down. She took one roll, and the big topmast went right out of the cap, went about twenty feet away from it. So we just had the masthead then, hanging to the springstay. He wanted me to go aloft and uncheck it. I said, "No sir, I'm not going up aloft with that swinging there."

Anyway, I took the wheel and steered, and he—the fellow we had with us [the cook] was seasick—he was only a young fellow. The old fellow took the pump—and he pumped and he pumped and he pumped and he pumped. Damn near sunk.

That was about at four o'clock in the evening. We had nothing to eat, had no dinner. About two o'clock in the morning we got off of the breakwater in Souris, and the wind jumped down nor'west. We clubbed her there. Two anchors. We let the two anchors go, and we hung on there till next morning we got into the wharf.

When we got in to an anchor, that was two o'clock in the morning. We had nothing to eat since we had our breakfast. So the young fellow went down and made a fire on in the fo'c'sle. And we went down to eat. And we heard the cat howling and howling and howling. We looked in the flour barrel and we looked [in the oven]—about the only place that was dry. The deck was leaking; she was leaking everywhere. The cat got in there— it was dry in the oven. And the young fellow shut the door and made a fire on. Thought of the oven, and opened it, and the poor old cat fell out on the floor—pretty near cooked. He got feeding the cat milk with a spoon, but it only lived about an hour, I guess, and she fell over on her side, dead.

(*You sold your second schooner, the* Stella.) In 1930. (*Why?*) Because coasting got so bad, with the car ferry to Prince Edward Island. Well, that wasn't it altogether. But things were going bad, and I got a good price for the boat, so I gave it up. Trucks took over. (*Was there still some work, if you'd wanted it?*) Oh yes, I could have still, there could still be some work.

(*You got married in 1929.*) That was most of it, giving up going to sea, I'd be away all the time, mostly. It was my own decision. Oh, the schooners were going down, too, along with it.

(*Did other people keep on with schooners?*) Oh, most of them. Then when the war started, they boomed then. There was all kinds of work for schooners then. It was in '39 that times got good again for schooners.

1930 I sold the *Stella*. Times got bad, and I got a job on the railroad. Painting. Painter. Painting on the bridges and buildings. Stations and bridges. I was pretty good to paint, so it suited me pretty well. I had hard luck on the railroad. Although I liked it, too. Come pension time at sixty-four, I'd like to have stayed for another ten years.

(*What all did you break when you were on the railroad?*) Broke two shoulders. Hip. Smashed my hip all up. Pretty near broke my neck, too. Time I got hurt in the motorcar. I went in the hospital. My hair was as black as hers there. In two weeks it turned grey. That's how I suffered.

(*How often did you hurt yourself on the schooners?*) Never. Oh, I fell overboard a couple of times.

(*Did you mind being ashore?*) I guess I did. I wasn't built for railroading, I was built for sailing. I think I could have done all right on the schooners. If I'd have known another war was coming, I'd have been all right, I'd have put her up in the harbour. Then I'd have made all kinds of money. Carrying coal to Newfoundland, and Madeleine Islands. Coasting got right good. Newfoundlanders all started smoking cigars! All the captains I talked to—"Lots of money now, boy." The war—everything went right up.

Working on the Grand Narrows bridge [painting], and I saw this schooner

coming way down by Kempt Head with a main topsail up, all her sails up. I said, "That's the *Stella* coming, all right." So I got in a little hole, and I stayed there till she was away out in the Lake. The fellow bought her was carrying salmon from Newfoundland to Halifax. I stayed there till she went almost out of sight. Didn't want to see her going through at all.

Mary Ryan:
A Woman's Account

I was born in Canso, Nova Scotia—Guysborough County—in 1895.

I went to school in Canso until—I was only fifteen when I had to leave school, and help my parents. Then I went to work—just housework—for a few months. I tried to go back to school, but it was impossible. At that time there was no compulsion.

So I kept house then for a lady who was sick all the time, for three years, in a village called Hazel Hill—just three and a half miles from home.

Then I decided I wanted a change. So I went to Antigonish. Got in with the Sisters from Notre Dame. Then I asked questions about entering a convent. And they sent me to Sisters of St. Martha.

So in October of that year, I got ready to enter. Sister sent me home for more preparation. And on December 8th I entered the convent. I received the holy habit. And I hadn't been sick a day until eight days after I received the holy habit. I broke down with some kind of rheumatism. And I was crippled in bed for two months, and for nine months I couldn't walk very well.

So then I got sort of discouraged with myself, and I asked to leave. I went home with my parents, and then, looked for a job.

So, there was a widower, whose wife had died two years before that. The children were alone. So I went up to see what help I could be to him. I stayed around with them and worked with them: looked after them, cleaned them up.

And after awhile, things got happening. And the priest asked me if I would stay home instead of going back to the convent. I had permission to go back to the convent again, if my health got better. But then I told Fr. Michael McCormack that I would stay and look after the children.

So after awhile, the Love Bug came along. So I married the widow[er] with five children. One year afterwards, I had a child of my own. Then we fostered a couple or three.

So, the Depression was coming on, and we decided to move to Cape Breton. So we moved to Cape Breton—a place called Plaster Mines, just outside of Baddeck. We bought a farm, and we started farming. And my husband started a little fishing—lobster fishing.

So we got along very well, until our house burned in 1938. And at that time we were in quarantine with scarlet fever, and we couldn't go anywhere to live with other people.

So a lady from Sydney Mines—they got in contact with this lady. And she told us to go live in her summer house, and use anything that was there. So we spent the night in that house that had been vacant for three years. We didn't have any beds—only just the beds that had been, and they're all damp and soiled. So, a man came along—we did find a place for the children to lie down. But a man came along at dark with a mattress on his back. We threw it on the floor and we spent the night there—my husband and I.

But my husband had to go away to earn a living.

Well, time went on, the children were sick. One of the girls almost died. And I had the five children with me then. Two had already left home. And, one of the girls got awfully sick, and I had to send for the priest. Fr. Rankin had 52 miles to drive over a dirt road. At last, he came.

Well, things went all right—my daughter got better. Then when the fumigating time came and we had to leave the house—I started to fumigate. We thought we could live in one part of the house while they fumigated the other. But the doors didn't fit well, and the fumes began to come through where we were living.

So I had to take the children to the beach—about a quarter of a mile away from the house—in a fishing shack that my husband used for his fishing tackle. Well, of course there was no room for beds there. The children laid on the floor, on blankets. And I sat with my five-month-old baby on my knee, in a basket—while I held the door up that didn't have any hinges—till daylight. And I heard—all I could hear was the splashing of the waves, the quacking of the ducks, and a crane yelled all night.

When daylight came, I sent my daughter up to the house to open the windows and let the air in. And in the meantime, we had taken our breakfast with us. But we couldn't get a fire—the stove smoked—wasn't well secured. And we couldn't have the breakfast. So we rallied up the hill after daylight—went back to the house—and we had our breakfast.

And we stayed there until December, till the cold weather drove us out of that—because the place was not in any condition to live in in the winter. So we moved to another farmhouse farther down. We stayed there for three years. And after three years, we moved to a village called Havre Boucher, so the children could get to school.

I'm ahead of my story. And while we were living in this old farmhouse, I had to teach the children myself, from Primary up to Grade 8, with the help of correspondence course.

Well when we moved to Havre Boucher, the children went to convent school there, with the Sisters of Charity. And one of the girls entered the convent—St. Martha—and the other entered the Sisters of Charity.

So, one of my little sons—twelve years old—from the effects of the scarlet fever—died.

Well, in 1944, we moved over to Canso, and occupied our old home. We lived there ten years. And when the ten years was up, we were burnt out again. Now where were we going to live?

So we had another little shack at the shore where my husband used to keep the fishing tackle and other things that he used around the boat. Cleaned that out, and we lived there for a year.

When the winter came—the priest was coming to the house to give communion to my husband that was a semi-invalid. And while he was hearing my husband's confession, I had to go out-of-doors, in February, and wait there while—till confession was over. And when I went in the house after the priest gave the communion, he said, "This is the first time I ever came to a place where I had to drive the old woman out-of-doors while I heard the old man's confession!"

Well, of course he made a joke of that. But it was no joke. Because it was very, very cold.

113

But, we got along all right. We built the house. My husband built the house in-between times. We moved in the house on the 16th of December, 1949.

Well, we didn't have it finished, when my husband died six years later.

Then, a new life started for me. I came to Sydney, and lived with my sister, until it was time for me to retire—to the MacGillivray Guest House, where I am today. And so happy to be here, with the affiliations. And all I do is thank God that everything happened so wonderfully for me and my family.

God bless you all, and goodbye.

Sr. Helene Comeau interviewed Mary Ryan. Mrs. Ryan raised eighteen children. Her husband brought five to the marriage. Then her sister died leaving six children, of whom she raised two. Her husband's sister died and left two more. Another sister died, and she took one boy. And she bore eight children of her own.

Frank Murphy:
The Steel Plant Was Family

This visit is taken from a conversation at Frank's during the last days of the Blast Furnace and the Open Hearth—the last days of the old method of making steel at the Sydney Steel Plant. The last heat in the Open Hearth Furnace was on June 17, and the last cast from the Blast Furnace was July 2, 1989.

Frank Murphy begins, reading from his notebook:

"The first heat tapped on the Sydney Steel Plant on December the 31st, 1901. And the first heat on that electric furnace tapped on November the 18th, 1937. And the first million tons was tapped on December the 28th, 1969, at 2:25 Sunday morning."

And the first time we ever made seventeen heats [in twenty-four hours]—that was on March the 31st, 1969. (*Seventeen heats....*) In twenty-four hours. On the big furnaces. And that was an all-time record. (*And a heat is what?*) Is 200 tons of steel—200, 250 tons. And [so] it was 3578 tons in one day.

That's why it kills me to see this place go down the drain. And I think today, what they should do is put a crepe on Number 1 Gate and call her dead. That's my feelings of Sydney Steel. It's the end of a complete era of—our island is gone. We'll never get over this. To me, now, this is like, cut the head off a turkey and, it's over. Because—as much as I hate to say it—I have no faith in [that new] electric furnace. BOFs [basic oxygen furnace]. Maybe so. Who knows? I hope I'm wrong.

(*But you worked with electric furnace before.*) I worked twenty-five years on one. They built it in 1937. And I worked right on that from 1937 up to 1953. And then I went back on it again, you know, on different times. In fact, I worked about 1960 on it.

(*And can you remember your reaction to the company bringing in an electric furnace in 1937?*) Oh, we thought it was fantastic. You know? Because [then] it was only a ten-ton furnace—it was a specialty furnace, for making gun barrels and gun breeches, gun blocks, propeller shafts for the Navy. See, we'd pour a shaft, and in one ingot it would be taken to Trenton and machined down—be forged and machined—be probably 100-150 feet long. Just one piece of steel.

That electric furnace—that's where your specialty steel was made: chrome, nickel, titanium—all those. It was a special furnace for alloys.

We were refining right down to the finest thing. We were making all the special axles for the C.P.R. and C.N.R. And we were making wire rope used for the pits, for the cables. As I said, we made gun barrels, gun blocks. We even made steel at one time for bobby pins. And steel wool. Now, you imagine going into a store and picking up a little package of steel wool—we used to make that in 200-ton lots. Coordinate the steel for it, and we'd send the steel away. We didn't make it—we made the steel to make the steel wool.

That was our [trouble]—we were shipping our raw materials out. Instead of having our factories here [in Cape Breton], we were shipping our raw material away for somebody else to finish it. (*Was that good or bad?*) Oh, that was bad, because we lost all the industry. We were just making the rough material. We'd make it and ship it away.

At one time, we made about 200 different grades of steel here. We made rails for the North Shore, Quebec, to stand the frost, and we made them for India to stand the heat. We made rails for Poland, Malaysia, South Africa, New York Central, British Columbia. We made rails—Sydney Steel spanned the world.

(*These different places would each require a little different kind of steel.*) Every one of them. Had to make them to their specifications, whatever they wanted. And we made them all here just as—like a woman making a pot of soup. Make your additions and everything else.

And we were using, like, we were using tungsten, which only melts at 3200 degrees. So, you can imagine the heat we'd have in a furnace to melt at 3200. We had to be using nickel and copper, chrome. We made steel here for the bottom of warships—the lowest carbon you could possibly make. It was just like sponge—it would stop a torpedo. It wouldn't ex-

A view of the Open Hearth at Sydney Steel in 1958. Frank Murphy, coming home off the back shift—the first shift he worked—May 9, 1934. Photo taken by his mother.

plode. Like, if it was 35- or 40-carbon, you hit it, it would shatter. What we made was like a piece of dough—it would go in, and just leave a bulge in it.

All this stuff was made here. The sad part of this: our story never got out to the world, what we did here. You know? And now—we were owned by an English firm, let's face it. And if they didn't show a profit of 18 to 20 cents on the dollar, 50 years ago, they weren't staying. I always say, we were like Cuba—pardon the expression. We had outside owner-ship, see. The Americans owned Cuba. They ran it, they put whoever they wanted there. Until Castro overthrew them, and then they got clear of this American ownership. And we had British Empire Steel, which was ours. Then we went to—we were owned practically by—all the board of direc-tors never sit here, they always sit in Montreal, and told us what we're go-ing to do down here. This is what killed us.

And then we got into the government, and that was worse again. Be-cause all the political hacks got jobs. We had fellows out there who didn't know their...I'm sure—they were just out there—they were friends of a party, and they got a job. The board of directors, now, for Sydney Steel—there's not one steelworker on it. And when the Liberals were there, the Liberals gave their friends the jobs.

(*And you don't think that's any way to run a steel plant.*) You can't—how can you run a steel plant when you haven't got steel men? You have

117

to have men that know steel to be able to run a steel plant. [There was a fellow there,] he was an engineer of some kind, but he never ran an open hearth furnace. I don't believe he was ever in the Open Hearth. He was never in the Blast Furnace. How the hell could you run a job when you don't know what's going on?

It's great to read a book. Technology is wonderful. I've got a stack of steel books out there. One of them: *Steelmaking for the World Over*. I read it cover to cover, but it didn't tell me how to run an open hearth furnace that was in trouble and it wasn't getting its gas or its oil or the steam, and I'd have to get out and find out what am I going to adjust to bring this heat into control. This [book] didn't tell me anything about that. It told me how to make it.

(*And this book here,* The Making, Shaping, and Treating of Steel. *It's put out by the United States Steel Corporation.*) U.S. Steel, yeah. Everything is in that book, from the blast furnace to the finished product. (*And U.S. Steel is no longer there.*) No. U.S. Steel is finished. (*It was the biggest in the world, wasn't it?*) The biggest in the world. Bethlehem Steel, Lackawanna, Buffalo; Pittsburgh, Pennsylvania; Virginia—every one of them. Not one open hearth—fifty open hearths. Fifty! Going full blast.

So the war comes. The Japanese are defeated. The Germans are defeated. And what do they do? Germany built up—Germany is stronger than ever they were. They built up Japan—that's cutting their throat today. With steelmaking. Shipping it in there—they're paying five, six, seven dollars an hour. And what's happening? The Americans are buying it.

Now, R.B. Cameron, when he came here, he was here a year or two. (*This is after Hawker-Siddeley pulled out and the government took over.*) We made a million tons of steel [in one year]. We burned the steel plant down doing it. Took it to the core. And what did R.B. do? He takes our Nail Mill to Dartmouth. [So] he's got a Nail Mill up there, he bought it from the government. And he's buying his steel from Germany—offshore steel, to make his nails up there in Dartmouth. He didn't buy it from Sydney Steel. He gets it cheaper from Germany.

So where do you stand? And the union can complain all its life. We've complained—I was in union here. In fact, I was one of the organizers—I helped organize this union in 1936. But what happens: they don't listen to people that work. Governments don't listen to the working men. Never did. The only way the working man can do is revolt. As one fellow said here—I just forget what his name—he put a paper out here. He says, "We have nothing to lose but our chains." That's all we have to lose, if we revolt.

And I hate to talk revolution. But I'm sure, today, if we loaded buses with about 5000 people from the city of Sydney and landed in Halifax in front of that Provincial Building in Halifax, we'd get any damn thing we wanted. If we showed enough force. But the sad part of the Sydney steelworker—Fr. Tom Boyle told me this a long time ago. He sat on one of our first conciliation boards. He was a terrific labour man. And he told me, he said, "Frank, we're too complacent." He said, "When our stomachs are full, our brains are dead. And when our stomach gets empty, our brain goes to work. Too late. We should be thinking of our future on a full stomach, not on an empty one." And it was the greatest piece of philosophy that I ever—this man, he was so right. When your stomach is full, go after it. When things are blooming, not when they're going down. It's too late to fight when they're shutting it down.

You know there's been over a billion and a half dollars spent here in twenty years? A billion and a half! Everybody in our island could be on a pension about—yes, $15,000 a year. With the billion and a half dollars, you could pension off all Cape Breton! With the money that we wasted down there. See, this is where we stand.

It's a sad picture.

(*It is a sad picture. Tell me, where does it begin for your family?*) Well, my father was the first. My father went there probably in 1913 or '14, before World War One. John Murphy. Originally they came from Ireland, but they came from Newfoundland. Came to Sydney. And he worked on the steel plant up until—I just forget the year he retired—1952, probably—'51 or '52. He worked in the Open Hearth....

(*Did your father want you to go on the steel plant?*) Oh, yeah. Well, he got me a job in the Open Hearth. See, that's where he was. My brother Pat went first—Pat went down—he was the oldest. He went to the Open Hearth. He worked at the stripper, where they take those ingots that you saw poured yesterday, and take that casing off of them. He worked up there. And my brother Tom worked up there. And my brother Sam worked up there. Three of them.

But I went on the furnaces. I liked the furnace. So I went on the furnaces in 1953. I was twenty—just turned twenty.

(*When you say you went on the furnaces—surely they don't just give you control over a furnace.*) Oh no, no, no. You go on as a third helper. Then you work your way up, from third helping to second helping to first help. Then you learn to run the furnace. On your way up, you learn the operation.

(*As a third helper, what did you do?*) Well, you had to carry all the stock for the furnace. Make your tapping bars to punch the hole out. There was no such thing as oxygen then to burn out a tap hole, or bombs—you had to punch them out with a big steel bar. You'd have two big billets bolted together, with a clamp. And there's a big pit, and you stood on the

119

edge of it. Sometimes fellows fell in the pit. You know, they'd slip on the edge of the bank and fall in. We'd probably get them out before the steel came. But if they didn't, they were gone. (*Did that happen?*) Oh, yes, we had fellows killed. We had fellows killed in the Open Hearth—tap holes breaking out while they'd be working down below. The furnace would be working, the heat. The tap hole'd break out, and there'd be men burned, that they would die from the effects of it, you know....

(*Tell me, now. You were hurt on the plant.*) I lost my leg in the Number 4 furnace there. (*How did that happen?*) Well, what happened was—we brought up our manganese—it was late getting up. I guess it was around four o'clock in the morning. And we wanted to get a pan off to take to another furnace. I was first helping then, on Number 4 furnace. So when the crane operator, when he lowered down the hooks—there's holes at the end of the pan—you had to reach in to get them. So Joe Cormier, my buddy, he was on the inside by the furnace. But when I reached in to get the chain, I put my foot on the track to reach the chain to push on in to him, you see—the two of them are together. He was in the heat. And I pushed the chain in. But they were charging the next furnace, and the fellow just hit the charge, and the wheel went right over and cut my foot off.

The wheel of the car. And it was loaded with manganese—one of the heaviest materials you have. So it just cut the foot right off, right at the instep.

(*When there's an accident like that in the Open Hearth, what happens? Everything stop, or what?*) Oh, no. They just take you away, keep going. There's no stopping them. They just take you—pick you up—they put you in a stretcher and take you to the hospital. But the job keeps going. There's no such thing as stopping.

They had to get a stretcher. They had to stop charging the furnace until they took me away. But that was only, probably, ten minutes. (*Where did they take you?*) Up to the emergency hospital. That little building that you saw when we were going down—that little white building. And in those days, you couldn't have your family doctor. You had to take the company doctor. When you were injured on the steel plant, you couldn't go to St. Rita's Hospital or the City Hospital—you had to go to the steel company hospital. They had their own doctors. This was the sad part of it, too.

(*Why is that?*) Well, they weren't competent. See, under compensation, we have a meat chart. And the less that's taken off, the less compensation you'll get. You were paid for what you lost. If they had taken me off below the knee, they'd have to pay me more—I have more of a disability. I'm only listed at 40%. (*Because you only lost your foot.*) Only lost my foot. They give you 40% disability. (*And it was the doctor at the steel plant that made that decision.*) Oh, yeah, they made that decision, yeah....

And 19 months after I lost the foot, I went to Halifax and had my leg taken off below the knee, so I could walk. I couldn't walk on what I had.

I don't want to tell you horror stories of compensation, but I could write a book on compensation. It's a horror story. They did skin grafts on me that were unheard of. They did five skin grafts on my carcass, where they could have taken the leg off the night I had the accident, and then it would have been all over.

When I [finally] went to Halifax and saw Dr. Allen Currie, the first question he said to me, "Frank, what butcher operated on you?" And he took my leg off in Halifax in October 1954, and I was back on the Open Hearth furnaces in May of 1955. Seven months and twenty days after he took the leg off, I was back on my own job. And I [had] spent nineteen months going back and forth to this emergency hospital for those foolish operations. They even flew doctors in from Montreal to do the job. (*That's the steel company.*) The steel company. Just that meat chart.

So there's horror stories of compensation.

I went through two-and-a-half years off work, with a wife and five kids. I had just bought a house, just got into my home. I got in the hole about $6000. Thanks to a good grocery man that carried me. Compensation then was $37 a week. So you can figure what $37 would go. Paying a mortgage and feeding a family.

And when I went back to work, I had to go down to the credit union where I have some good friends, and I borrowed $6000 to pay off my bills. The first thing I did, paid off all my bills. Then it took me about eight years to pay off the $6000. This is all compensation. (*You mean the results of the way compensation works.*) That's the way it works. Even today, it's very unfair. The old awards, they don't give you anything. I got a raise the

121

other day in my compensation: I got $9.63 a month. And as far as I'm concerned, they could have shoved it.... What the hell is nine more dollars good to me now, at my age? (*I see. When you needed it....*) If they had given it to me when I needed it, yeah. When I had a mortgage and a family.

(*Yes, I understand. Well, I want to know....*) Let's get into the steel! (*Tell me about your work.*) I started in the Open Hearth in 1935 as a third helper on Number 3 furnace with Danny Yakimchuk. Now you may see a name in the paper now, Danny Yakimchuk, head of the pensioners' union. Well, that's that fellow's father that I worked with. Danny Yakimchuk. He was a first helper. He was a melter. They were called melters, then. They weren't called helpers. When you ran your furnace, they considered you a melter. You were in charge of your furnace. You made the heat. The foreman came down and tapped it out, and put your name on the sheet, and his name on the sheet. And the time—everything went on the sheet of paper. And those records are still there, right back to 1901. I don't know if they kept them all or not, but they had—a few years ago, they could tell you what heat you made.

Now, if we got a bad heat. And five years afterwards, something turned up, they could go back and say, "Frank Murphy made this heat on February the 5th, 1955." They could tell you right to the—and tell you what you put in it. (*In other words, if a rail failed in New York City....*) We made rails for New York Central. We made them for San Francisco Railroad, British Columbia, North Shore Quebec, C.N.R., C.P.R. And overseas, we made them for Poland, India, Pakistan. We made them for Malaysia. We made rails for everybody.

(*But I'm saying, if a rail failed in Malaysia, they could trace it back....*) Right back to the heat number. Because every rail that went out of here had the heat number on it. (*And to the person who....*) Man that made the steel that made that rail. (*That's an interesting sense of responsibility.*) Yeah, they could pinpoint you right to the minute you tapped it.

Learning on the job was something that, when the first helper—if he liked you—he would sit down and tell you the actions to watch for in a furnace. Like, a bottom boil, on the bottom of your furnace, it would be a roll. She'd roll. But if it was an ore boil, she'd be shooting up. The sparks would be coming through the steel. And if it was a stone boil, you'd see it getting thick on the top. You'd have to put fluorspar in to cut it up. The stone'd be making it thick—like putting dumplings in a stew. That's the expression I've used: like dumplings. Well, then you'd know your stone was up. And then, if you got a bottom boil, she's boiling on the bottom, she'd roll and roll. Well, the only way we could kill a bottom boil would be put manganese in to try to stop it from rolling on the bottom.

You'd watch for even the flame in the furnace—you had your blue

glasses on. You could tell [by] the flame if your furnace was hot, or cherry red, or cold, or.... (*Never cold.*) Well, what we called cold here, when she was chilling off—2500, she was chilling off. You'd want 2800 or 2900 degrees to tap out on her, rail steel.

(*So you said, sometimes, if the first helper liked you....*) He'd tell you all this. But if he didn't like you, he wouldn't tell you anything. (*So how would you learn then?*) Well, then you'd have to—well, you'd probably go to another furnace or something.

See, our big trouble in our day, the men weren't educated like today. We had men operating a furnace that couldn't sign his sheet. He could make steel with anybody. They could tell you what they were doing, but they couldn't put it in writing. They'd tell you. And this is where you gained your experience.

Now, when they broke a test—they'd break it, they'd look at it. Then they could tell you what was in it. But then they would show you the different way the grain of the steel was. Or, if it got rusty right [away]—soon as you broke out, that it got kind of dark, and kind of like a rusted form right off the bat. They knew then they had phosphorus or sulfur; the heat was dirty. By looking at that piece of steel.

You see, it was fantastic, those men, they were steelmakers....

That's why I say we had the best steelmakers in the world here. But mind you, some of those men, now, before they learned it, we had fellows up here from the United States, from Pittsburgh, when they built the steel plant. And they were the first helpers we ever had here, were Americans. They brought the knowledge with them and they passed it on to everybody else.

(*And it was a matter of passing on. In other words, am I correct that*

123

there weren't classes?) No classes. You learned it—you either learned it, or you didn't learn it. No books. No nothing. Watching it. That's the way you learned.

I was in the fortunate position of getting with a first helper that was very, very good—Sid MacGillivray. God have mercy on him—he's dead, now. And I had the job of floating with him. That would be taking a shift off of every furnace. You know, we went to the six-day week. We were working seven days a week. But then we went to the six-day week, I went with Sid MacGillivray, floating. And I worked on every furnace in the Open Hearth. And I knew every heat—he was a wonderful teacher. And he would say, "Now, Frank, this is what's happening here. And this is what...."

So, when it came my turn to take a steady furnace, they wouldn't give me a steady furnace. They wanted me to stay floating. And the reason why—I knew all the furnaces. I could go to Number 3 furnace and look at it, and turn the gas or turn the oil or whatever the hell was on it, and adjust it to suit the situation. Where if they had a new man on there, he couldn't do this.

Every furnace was different, worked differently. Every one of them. You couldn't take Number 1 furnace and adjust it, and go down to Number 6 and do the same thing at Number 6. (*Even though they were all built the same.*) Yeah, all built the same. But they all had their little kinks or queeks, whatever you want to call it—they all had their little things—what you had to learn, how to get your temperature up. It was an education in itself, steelmaking.

(*The first helpers, did they associate together, or did they consider themselves a group?*) Yeah. He was a little bit on a pedestal, the first helper. He was kingpin—Huey Long, you know. "You do what I say." See. That was some of them, not all of them. Some of them were very, very good. They would take you and explain the thing to you. But some of them would try to hide it on you. Oh, yeah, they didn't want—they always figured—you see, the days before the union, if you learned [their] job, maybe they'd say, "Well, you're after my job." Especially in the foreign element, you know. Like the fellows that came from the Ukraine and those places, they always figured, "Well, my English broke, I can't talk a good English. You get my job—I go back helping." This is the theme.... But as a rule, a lot of them were very, very good. I can say that. But there were some, a few that—"You look for my job."

(*Did the workers on the Open Hearth all get together outside of work?*) Oh, yes, we'd have our banquets and everything else. We'd have a bowling banquet. Or even the shifts would get together for a party, for a lobster party. Just the shift itself. See, we had—when I started, we had the A, B,

124

and C turns—three turns, three shifts. And each shift, like, when they got on dayshift, in the evening they'd get together and go bowling. Or they'd go for a lobster do, or a fish fry, or something like that, you see.

The men were very, very close. The men in the Open Hearth. Open Hearth men were noted for being close.

For instance, if I was in Number 1 furnace and my furnace got in trouble—she was boiling on the bottom or something, or boiling on the back wall—those men are all right down with their shovels and help you. Every one of them. But that's gone today. If I was in trouble today on Number 3, and Number 2—that fellow'd be sitting on his ass. You know? The attitude—the camaraderie—is all gone out of it today.

For instance, if one of our fellows died, everybody would go to their wake. We go in a body. If he was sick, we'd all go in a body to hospital to see him. It was a close-knit shop. Because everybody that was on it, it was someone that you knew personally. Now, when you became boss—I couldn't send you home, because you're so-and-so's son. So I'd hide you away and cover up for you. You know? I couldn't—geez—how?—Christ, I worked with [his father]—how am I going to send this boy home? So you take him and you give him a lecturing, you know. (*Even if you had a good reason to send him home.*) Even if I had a good reason to send him home. I'd hide him, probably lock him up in one of the shacks until he's sobered up or something, if he was drunk. Instead of getting him off. And then we'd do his work. We'd carry him for the shift. He'd still get his pay. This shows you, this was the camaraderie of the thing.

It was a real close shop. They were very, very close. Everybody was close.

(*It seemed to me, as I watched certain things at the plant, that there are times when you are waiting and can sit together.*) Oh, yeah. Sit together and talk. For instance, when you put your metal in a furnace—when you charge a furnace up—you put your limestone on the bottom, then you put your ore in, then you put your scrap in. Well, you've got an hour, generally, with getting your scrap soft enough, melted down enough, to put your metal in. Well, you had an hour.

Once you got your furnace cleaned up. That was the first thing, when you charge a furnace, was clean the floor. Clean the track. Then you sit down for about an hour. Well, then you talked about fishing, or going shopping, or whatever you were doing. We had a lot of fellows who were very close-knit for fishing buddies, you know.

(*In that hour....*) They'd be telling stories about the Old Country, about Newfoundland, fishing off the Grand Banks. And they'd be telling you about in the Ukraine, when they were kids in the Ukraine, they'd be telling you stories. And fellows that came from Italy, you'd hear stories from Italy. And we had all the ethnic groups that worked on the steel plant, all in this ward. The ethnics—that would be the Chinese and the Blacks and the Ukrainians and the Swedes and the Newfoundlanders. Before 1949, Newfoundland was a foreign country. Then we had a Polish Village down over Ferris Street hill, right by the steel plant. Was practically all Polanders.

(*When you were in the Open Hearth, were there many black people working in the Open Hearth?*) No, no. The Blacks were on the gas producer. That's where they made the gas for the Open Hearth furnace.

I'm going to tell you a story. The first Black that ever worked on an Open Hearth furnace, I had him—he came with me. During the war, I was short a man on the electric furnace, and I went in the shack, the labour shack. And I wanted one man. There was a black fellow sitting down there. And I said [to the foreman], "I'm short a man," I said, "on the electric furnace. And I want a man." He said, "Frank, there's no more men in the yard. General Yard," he said, "got all the men out. Can't get a man for you." I said, "What's wrong with him?" He looked at me like I had horns. I said, "Come on, boy, come on with me." And that was the first Black that ever worked on the Open Hearth furnace—Jerome Gibson. After that, we had Blacks. I said, "Boy, he got two arms and two legs and he can shovel—that's all I want. I don't care what his colour is." I never did.

(*So when we say there were all kind of ethnic groups in the....*) Yeah, but the Blacks were barred.... For some reason or other, the Blacks—I don't know how it started or where it started—but I know there were no Blacks on the Open Hearth furnace. Never saw one on it till I took that Jerome Gibson.

(*Were most of the people the same religion in the Open Hearth?*) No, no, we had every religion. But it was predominately Catholic. Although we had quite a few other fellows, the majority of them—in those days, the Open Hearth was known as "the Vatican City." Because Peter MacIsaac was superintendent. And in the Blooming Mill it was known as the "Orange Lodge" because Bob Moffatt was the—he was an Orangeman or something—he ran the Blooming Mill. And then, in the Rod and Bar Mill, MacKay ran that in my time, and that was "the Masons." The Masons worked there. It was pretty well broke down. Although there were some Catholics and Protestants in all departments, predominately your religion decided where you got your job. Yeah, that went on here. Yeah, religion played a part in it....

Now, for instance, on the backshift. Now, it'd be nothing to have a big feed of herring and potatoes. We'd bring out the potatoes and the herring, have a big bucket and.... Between the furnaces, we'd just pour the hot metal on the ground, and put the bucket on it and boil it, and have a big feed on the back—or corned beef and cabbage. And a bottle of rum'd be

800,000 TONS OF STEEL, DECEMBER 16, 1964, HEAT #4034
Left to right: Frank Murphy, Stogick, Donald MacDonald, Ned Carew, Don Hanrahan, Alvin MacDonald, John Neilie Campbell

in the cupboard, and you'd have a drink of rum or something. The oldtimers are more so for the rum, you know.

You'd take your furnace shovel and you'd just wash it off, and then you'd put the capelin on it, and put it in front of a peephole. In the furnace, where you take the test out. And you'd fry your capelin there, right on the shovel....

(Have a meal together.) Oh, yeah, they'd sit down. The furnace crew would do that. Whatever crew—like, if I was on Number 3, we'd have herring and potatoes, probably, and next night we'd have corned beef and cabbage. But you still bring your lunch out. Because we worked the long hours. We were working eleven by day and thirteen by night. We'd go to seven o'clock in the morning and come home, and then the other shift would come out at five o'clock and stay till the next morning. And on Sunday, if you were changing, going from backshift to dayshift, you went out on Sunday morning at 7, and you came home Monday morning. Twenty-four hours you never came home at all.

I was there for—I was nine days short of forty-five years.

(*When we went in the Open Hearth yesterday, there was one furnace....*) In operation. When I was there, there were twelve. (*And you could look the length of that and there'd be all these men working at the....*) At their furnace. Every one, different times, they'd be tapping out. Each fellow would be doing something different in that time. And you knew every one of them, and you knew what they were—you knew what their family—they'd come and tell you their family troubles and everything else, you know.

That was one of our big downfalls here, you know, was this being a family plant. It didn't make any difference [whether] you could do your job, if you were a son of so-and-so. (*Is that right?*) Oh, yeah, you got a job. If you didn't fit in on that job, they put you somewhere else. But if you were in Hamilton or Algoma, they'd fire you. You couldn't do it. But here, they just moved you somewhere else.

Well, you see, we were born with the steel plant in our back door. Look out in the morning and you'd see the smoke come out of the stacks. And you'd go to school—school was right up here, the convent was right up here—the steel plant. Every kid going to school knowing when the Blast Furnace was dumping or charging. Then at nighttime when they used to dump the slag in the water, the sky'd all light up, everyone would know. So everybody knew what the steel plant was.

There were twenty-seven men worked with me in the Open Hearth— we were all born in the same year. And if we had all stayed till we were sixty-five years of age, they would have lost twenty-seven men off the furnaces in one year. If we all had gone our limit. All 1914 babies....

Went to wakes and weddings and everything, together. We went in a group. We'd leave the plant at eleven o'clock in the night and go to a fellow's house. The wakes were all in the houses then, you know. If one of our men died, everybody went in and knelt down and said the rosary, no matter if he was Catholic, Protestant, or what he was. Everybody knelt down and said their prayers. That was common. Common thing. And they'd all go to the funeral. If he was on our shift, that died, we'd all change the whole shift to go to the funeral.

(*And what about paying for the funeral?*) Well, we always took a collection up. And anyone who was off sick, the men took up a collection. You could get anything from $2000 down to $50. (*Does that depend on the time, or whether the guy was liked?*) It would depend on the man himself, mostly. You know, if you were well liked.

And anyone that was joining the priesthood or becoming a minister or anything, they took up a collection for him, to send him away. Say, for instance, if I had a son who wanted to study for the ministry. Well, they'd take up a collection and give him maybe 100 or 150 dollars. The men would all chip in. (*The men on the Open Hearth.*) Yes. On the Open Hearth.

(*I bet if someone was getting married....*) They'd do the same thing.

128

Everybody got a wedding present from the shift. No matter who died, there was always a mass card if he was a Catholic, got flowers if he was a Protestant, we sent the flowers. That was organized. We had our own little mutual benefit, in our own time. We paid 25¢ a week into it. And if you were off sick, you got $10 every week for thirteen weeks, from our department. But that was our own self-organization. We did that on our own. (*It wasn't the union.*) Oh, no, no, no, just the men themselves. In fact, I was president of ours.

(*What about construction of homes?*) Well, if you worked in the Open Hearth and you were building a house—we had thirty-five or forty men up there that worked on the backshift. And there was no such thing as a cement mixer. We'd have four big boards going, and mix it all by hand, and build a foundation. Maybe it took you ten hours to build it. And then you went back to work that night. You put in the whole foundation before you left, by hand.... Come and help you build it and everything.

It was family. The steel plant was family. All family. And it didn't make a difference if you were black, white, or what it was, if you were building a house. We had an old coloured fellow down there—he was putting a foundation under it. So we'd go down there and we'd dig it out, and we'd put in his cribwork for him and all his forms—bunch of men. And our electricians went down and did the wiring—fellows that were electricians on the steel plant—they went down and did the wiring. Everybody helped everybody.

But the sad part of the whole thing was—and I hate to say this—when we became unionized, there was something about it that dropped off.

Because you were guaranteed five days or six days a week. Now, when I went in there, for instance, if the mill was going down half time, we didn't lay anybody off like they do today. We would split the shifts. A married man worked four, and a single man would take three. And nobody was laid off. We all got a share. But once the union came in and demanded you get six days a week, well, that went out the window. That was sometime in the '40s, during the war.

But in the early years of my time, from '34 to '40, we wired houses for fellows. We even took a bunch of electricians out, when they built St. Augustine's Church out there on Grand Lake Road, and wired it for the priests down there. It was all steel company.

(*And would people also make things on the plant that could be used in their homes?*)

Well, it was all coal stoves then. They'd make pokers, and they'd make grates for their stoves. The foundry had all the patterns for practically every stove. If I wanted a grate, we'd say, for an Enterprise, if I'd go up and I'd see the foreman in the foundry. And on the backshift they'd pour you—

they'd make a grate for you or they'd make a damper for you. If you'd want something done, they'd do it. And if you knew him, or if you were a good friend of him up there, he'd pour you a brass hot-water front for your stove—one that would last a lifetime. And if I ask him for five of them in five days, five weeks—I got five brass hot-water fronts.

And if you wanted a poker made, or a set of tongs to take the clinkers out of your furnace, you'd go out there. And the next thing you know, they're laying there. No one sees it, but they're laying there. You don't know who put it there, but you know where it came from. No one would come down and present it to you.

For instance, like, now, when a foundry car would be coming down, he would call me and say, "Now, look at Number 2 box there." So I'd go over to Number 2 box and scrape the sand away, and the hot-water front would be buried on the car. Well, he never gave it to me. I found it on the car. I don't know who made it. I never saw it being made. But it was there.

(*How would you get things like that out of the plant?*) Oh, it took a little bit of conniving to get it out.

If you had a friend that had a car in there. And if you were—like, the superintendent—if I went to the superintendent and said, "Look, I got an iron front made," he'd give me a pass to take it out as scrap. You'd carry it out. At that time you could go up and buy scrap. Well, say you got ten pounds—oh, 50¢, or $1.00, at the general office, and he'd give you a slip to take it out. Same way with nails. If you were building a house and you wanted nails, you'd get an order for 50 pounds of nails. So you'd go in on the plant, and you'd come out with maybe two kegs of nails. When you'd pass the fellow at the gate, he got the slip. He doesn't check—they never checked you out in those days. (*So it went out as scrap.*) You bought a piece of scrap. Actually, it was brand-new nails.

Now, you could buy scrap barbed wire. Like, for instance, when it was going through the machine, she'd have a cobble, she'd catch, and you'd only get a half a roll. Well, you could buy a half, or you'd go in and you'd buy the scrap. But in that scrap you'd throw in three or four complete rolls. And you'd pass them in the slip.

(*Well, it's ways to augment your income.*) Yeah. I remember one time one of our watchmen caught a fellow with a lunch can full of nails. He was over before the chief, and the chief gave the watchman hell for saying a word. He said, "Why don't you catch some of those fellows that are going with ten kegs of nails?" he said. "Never mind the fellow with the lunch can." Gave him hell for catching the fellow with—that's the way it was.

Everybody knew everybody. If I had a friend of mine that got into trouble, I could go up and talk to the chief. I knew him. I'd say, "Look," I said, "Chief, he's got five kids. And he's just getting along, and he's having...." "Oh, send him back to work."

I don't know what it was, but there was something that—I had a camaraderie with all of them, that I could talk to most any of them. From Clem Anson [a former general manager]—one fellow asked me, he said one time, "How can you talk to Clem Anson like that?" I said, "Clem Anson's only a man." As I said before, he's no better than I. He's got a better job, and I call him Mr. Anson. But there's no reason why I can't talk to him. He's not God. No, he was just another human being.

And that's been my philosophy all my lifetime.

(*But you do make it clear there was the sense of family, the sense of caring for one another in the Open Hearth—or in the steel plant in general perhaps.*) Generally—the whole thing. Like, the Blast Furnace had the same thing—they had their own benefit society, that they paid people $10 a week. And $10 a week then was a lot of money.

Now I can tell you this. I remember being laying in my bed home, after my leg was off. And two men came in the bedroom. And they threw a bunch of money on the bed—couple of bagfuls. There was anything from a one to a twenty, and silver. And I counted $2000, that they collected at the steel plant for me when I was off. They made it plant-wide—they got at the paymaster—made it plant-wide. I got over $2000. And they did that on two different occasions while I was off work.

So when you're dealing with those kind of people, those people are human. They're human beings. You're not just a statistic or a number with them. Those are people that—you associate your life with, and you're working with them. And if they don't feel good, now.... For instance, if a fellow came out and he said, "Geez, I've got an awful cold." "Now, you go in the shack and stay there for the night. And we'll open the hole and we'll mud the runner."

You looked after them.

(*And you're telling me the truth here? You're not trying to make the Open Hearth, or the workers, look better than they were, are you?*) Oh, no. This is the way they worked. It was one big family. (*Ah, but there must have been some rotten people like in any family.*) Oh, yes. We had a few of them, too, now. That's why I say, I don't want to name any of them. But we had fellows, too, now, were just as miserable. We had fellows who wouldn't turn their hand to help you. But mind you, they'd pay for it in the long run. Once you knew them.

I remember going to a man one time, taking up a collection. And we were only asking 50¢—that was a lot of money, then. And he said, "No, I save my money. I'm not going to give you any money." Okay. But that man got sick one time. And who did he call, looking for somebody to take a collection? He called me. And I said, "Boy, you remember when I asked you for 50¢? Now," I said, "tough.... You go and get somebody else to take up a collection for you."

And you knew everybody. You knew the fellows who were carrying stories to the bosses. You'd set traps for them, you know. I can tell you of one incident, we had one fellow, boy. We were wondering how the stories were getting out. We couldn't fathom it at all. But we had an idea. So anyway, this fellow came into the shack one day and he sat down. And I started running down one of the superintendents. He had just come on, boy, and I was calling him—he was from England. And I called him everything under the sun. And about an hour afterwards, this man walked in the shack. And he came right to me. "Oh, Frank," he said, "you think I'm quite a prick, don't you?" And I started to laugh. "Well," I said, "thanks, Jack," I said. "I didn't mean a word I said. I think you're a wonderful guy. And so do all the fellows here. But," I said, "we had a fellow carrying stories. Now I know who he is."

(*And then what do you do with a fellow like that?*) Well, then you ignore him. He has no life after that at all. You just ignore him. Walk by him like he was a stick. Natural that after maybe two or three months you'll find he either shifted to another place, on the back of the mill somewhere. But he doesn't stay on the furnace with you. You ignore him that bad— you make life so miserable for him that he doesn't stay there.

[From Frank's notebook:] "July the 24th, 1971. Number 1 furnace, first test, 11 carbon, 100 sulfur. That was 4:06. We tapped her at 7:30, on 65 sulfur and 3 carbon. We put 15 bags of coke in the ladle. Heat boiled in ladle, added 10 boxes of manganese extra, and 6 more bags of coke. Heat finished, 58 sulfur, 23 carbon, for tie plate."

But the story behind that was: when I went out there at four o'clock in the afternoon, Gonzales said, "Frank, we'll take her for scrap." Rather than make [steel]—the sulfur was 100 sulfur. I said, "No, we'll make something. We'll make tie plate." Because I knew they'd [allow] over 60 sulfur on tie plate. He said, "You've got no carbon." I said, "That's all right." So I put the oxygen right down on the bath. And I got her stinking hot. And I kept adding stone, and taking slag off.

So anyway, we threw everything in the ladle. And I got all the helpers out of the way. I said, "Okay, take her over, boy." Took her over, and the flames went right up clean to the roof of the Open Hearth. We had no carbon; we had to add coke. But the heat finished 23 carbon and 58 sulfur for tie plate. We made something [of it].... We made a product that you could sell.

I said, "Geez, we can make something out of that, we can sell," you know. So, you keep at it. Like a bulldog, you stay in there, you stay with it, until you get something.

But all this stuff, you know, is—you just keep notes as you go along. "Number 5 runner's in one hell of a mess." (*This is sort of your diary.*) Yeah. (*But your diary is comments on the condition of your work.*) You run into things on your job that are not ordinary. Like getting a hole in Number 1 door and a hole in Number 3 door, and steel in both doors. And you want to get the steel out of the furnace. So you've got to burn the bridge between 1 door and 3 door, and burn a trench down there about two feet deep. Let the steel run from Number 1 door into Number 3 door, where you can turn the furnace over. Because Number 3 door is right at the entrance of your tap hole....

We were steelmakers. The period of steelmaking has gone to computer. Everything that goes into this (new) furnace, what I gather—everything is computer. They just push the buttons and they make everything—all the additions are done.

Well, in my day, boy, you had to wrack your brain, boy, to know what was going on. When that heat went in the ladle, you were a human calculator. Everything was by the clock. I'd look—I had—my manganese is going to be in five minutes, and then it's going to start to disintegrate. I'm going to lose it. So I've got four and a half minutes to get the manganese in. I've got to get a tap hole open, and I've got to get the silicon into the ladle. And nobody talks to you—even the superintendent don't bother you then. The wheels are—everything is going full blast, knowing your calculations and what you're going to do.

And then you get a furnace that breaks out on you. And you've got 100 carbon, and she's going out in the ladle. And you want to keep the oxygen on to get her down to 75. And you know you're losing X-number of points per minute. And you're saying, "I've got 3 minute—I've got 90 carbon—I've got 80 carbon—I've got 75 carbon. Turn her over!" You know, your timing—you know, you get so many points per minute....

When you see the flame go right up through and set fire to those cranes, that you had to get up with a fire extinguisher to put the grease out. The crane'd be burning—the grease'd be burning up on the top of those girders. And they'd still be pouring the heat, and there'd be men up with fire extinguishers putting it out. Walking out on those girders over that hot ladle.

You know, sometimes, in order to catch a heat. Say a carbon is down, we'll say, to 40, and you're making 70-carbon rails. That means that you have to put 30 bags of coke in that ladle, and every one of them weigh over 60 pounds. And you had to throw it in. And you have a bunch of men lined up, and they just put their coats over their heads and they just throw

133

one at a time, and keep going around in a circle, trying to get the coke in for you before she'd foam out of the ladle, you know....

And all those little technical things that they don't print. They don't put this in books, you see.

You know, I could talk steel all day, I could talk steel for a month. That's all I do! [Frank laughs.] Ask me anything else, I wouldn't know!

Frank and Thelma Murphy, Whitney Pier

Anne Morrell, Margaree Valley: "Seasons of My Life"

(*Where were you born?*) Trenton, New Jersey. 1948. But I was raised in Pennsylvania, because Trenton was just a half a mile across the river. That's where the hospital was. (*What kind of situation were you raised in?*) Typical lower middle class. Working parents— my father worked in a bank, and my mother was a housewife who became a secretary to put us through school. Actually, she was a secretary before she was a housewife. She went to business college.

(*You didn't grow up on a farm?*) No, but my grandparents had a farm. My mother was the farm girl that married the city boy. So we spent a lot of time on the grandparents' farm. They had about a hundred head of Holstein cows. (*So this is not a big change.*) Not really. Because I used to love going out to the farm. And then when I became a teenager, I got into horses and I worked on farms. Rode, showed, fox-hunted, taught kids how to ride. I had half a horse for awhile. My parents couldn't afford the board for a horse. And my grandparents wouldn't let me keep it on their farm because of [dairy] regulations. So I split it with a friend. The two of us bought a cheap horse and trained it, and split the board. And then I worked at the stable to help earn money to pay for it.

When I first came [to Cape Breton], that's what I did. I bought a couple of horses locally—young racehorses—and retrained them for rid-

135

ing horses and jumpers. Showed them in Sydney, in the Exhibition. And then I bred quarter horses for awhile, showed them in Sydney and Antigonish; took one down to Truro once. And I taught all the kids around here how to ride, had a 4-H club. But they all grew up and went away to school and got married, and that was the end of it!

(*You and Garry, when did you meet each other?*) High school. We went to high school together. We were always friends, because my brother and Garry were close friends. They had the same interests: motorcycles, old cars, stuff like that. We came up here to visit my brother, and really liked it.

I wanted to have my own farm. I was working for a guy in the States, and it was a great job, I got a regular salary, but I wasn't getting anywhere. I just felt like, if I had my own place and I was doing it, then at least I'd have something in the end. [Garry] had just finished graduate school, just gotten a Master's degree in Fine Arts. And he wanted to get away from the craziness of the States and just have a place to be able to do what he wanted. Which was playing with machines, and doing a little bit of art, and farming. It was the "self-sufficient homestead" days.

The first day we came, I came with Garry and his sister. We drove up in a VW bus. And I had a photograph of the house where [my brother] lived. So we come to this stretch of road; it says "Northeast Margaree." "It's got to be around here somewhere." We're driving around in circles, through the loop around the river. Finally, this guy comes down the road riding a little kid's bicycle. And he comes up to us, and he says, "Oh, I saw the Pennsylvania license plates. You must be Allan's sister. Well, he lives right here, and his truck broke down in Inverness, so he'll be awhile. But go in and make yourself at home." And of course that just blew me away. I said, "How's this guy know all this stuff?" Of course, that's how it's been in Margaree ever since.

The first trip down was just to visit. It was lucky that I could take about seven weeks off from work. We visited my brother, and went to Newfoundland, drove around there for a few weeks. Put a garden in here and started looking for land. Then we came back in the winter, on Boxing Day, and spent another three weeks. Kind of did the same thing, got the feel of the place, and kept an eye out for some land. And my brother found a piece for us, which the three of us bought together. And we immigrated that following summer, as soon as Garry got out of graduate school.

When we came up here, we had about $1200 and a truckload of stuff, that's all we had. It was kind of a way of starting over. You finish school and you're ready to start something new. Garry didn't want to get into the 9-to-5 rut in the States. He used to say he'd sit and watch his father pay bills every night, and he didn't want to have to do that. Of course, you have

Garry and Anne Morrell

to do it anyway. (*But not 9-to-5.*) Not 9-to-5, no. The thing is, you had a variety of work. Fixed up the old houses and got the property back in shape, repaired the barn and fenced. Then we started getting stock, and farming it.

(*Is your background Quaker, or is it just a philosophy you're interested in?*) Well, both. I guess you're born Quaker when both your parents belong to the Quaker Meeting. It's called being a birthright Quaker. My parents still keep up my membership for me in the Meeting I was raised in. Really, it's become more of a philosophy of life. You know, the basic principle of non-violence, and equality, and living simply.

(*Had Garry ever had a job?*) Well, he was assistant professor in graduate school: he taught art. Oh, he worked at the steel plant, too, in Pennsylvania—summer job. But he was a jack-of-all-trades, he could do anything. So he had no problem earning a living here.

I've never officially worked, where I've been on anybody's payroll. I've always just created my own employment, either through the horses or the cattle, or the quilt business now. But Garry never had any problem working, because he was a good mechanic, he was a good carpenter, and he moved houses. He could do whatever he wanted, really. All he had to do was tell somebody he needed a job and they'd hire him. So he would work during the season when we needed money, and then he would either run this place, or set up a sawmill or do his painting, in the odd times between. It's nice to be able to have a choice on what you wanted to do.

We went back to the States and got married on my grandfather's farm. It was a little easier than having the relatives come up here. Then we came right back. I spent my honeymoon—one night in a tent, with my brother—because the three of us went down. My brother had a Morris Mini Minor car, and a two-man tent. And he said—my brother's about 6-foot-2, right? So he said, "I'm not sleeping in this little car, either." So that left Garry in the car, and my brother and I in the tent!

We went on our honeymoon on our tenth anniversary. Kind of. We went to P.E.I., but Garry was very sick at that point. And I went to give a riding clinic to the pony club over there. Kind of a working holiday with a sick husband. We stopped at the V.G. [Victoria General Hospital, Halifax] on the way for his checkup. The doctors wanted him to go in immediately. And he said, "I have to go on my honeymoon! It's been ten years— my wife will kill me! This might be my last chance!" And they said, "Well, I really don't think you should go. You might not make it back." But he went anyway. He made it back, survived another year.

(*So where does quilting come into your life?*) Quilting started just about the time I first came up here. I got interested in it kind of as a hobby. It was something to do in the long winter nights up here. And then, gradually it took over as a business. And I guess it's my creative outlet, and it's my way of earning money. The farm supports us food-wise, but there's no cash. So the quilts provide the cash.

(*Why quilts?*) I'm not sure. I think it's probably, like a lot of women say, it's just this womanly thing with fabric, that you're attracted to fabric, the feel and the texture and the colours of fabric. After you get a quilt made, it feels really nice to the touch. And it looks nice, too. And it's something you can pick up and fold up and stick it wherever you want it. I did a little painting. And I never liked oil paints because I was not patient enough to wait for them to dry. I wanted to keep working on them. And with a quilt, of course, you just keep working on it till it's done. I've since realized you can do that with oil paintings, too.

(*You look on quilting now as a full-time occupation, as a business.*) Pretty well, from fall till spring, and then the farm takes over.

(*We're going to discuss just one quilt. Go over it section by section.*) [See photo of quilt on page ii.] It's called "Seasons of My Life," because the squares around the outside are arranged seasonally. It's 102 by 112 inches. Top is summer, left side's spring, right side's fall, and the bottom's winter. And you notice the symbols quilted in the corners between the blocks? You have sun in the summer and a tulip in the spring, and a snowflake in the winter, and a maple leaf in the fall.

It's a quilt I'd wanted to do, but I knew it was going to take a lot of time. And I felt I couldn't afford the time to do it just for myself. And this show came up called "Mirrorings." And it was to be women and their roles in life and community, and the way they see themselves. It was just Maritime women artists. So I submitted a proposal for that. And I made

138

the first selection, the first twenty-five. And then those twenty-five had to start on their work, and go to Halifax with it, and show it to them. I did that, and then I made the final selection. And they took fourteen artists in the end.

(*So you may have made it eventually sometime for yourself.*) I don't know. I needed an excuse to do it. And so there was my excuse. Even though the quilt wasn't for sale—I could have sold it if I wanted; but I didn't want to; I didn't make any money off of it—it was still a good thing, because it made the show, and a lot of people saw it, and it traveled around and got great exposure, and it started me on more of a reputation as a Canadian quilter. Instead of just being back here and making them for the tourist trade.

(*It says, in sewn thread, "This is the story of my life in 1982./ These are some of the things I do." How do you follow it?*) Well, you can read across the top, which is just a few verses of coming here, like a brief history, what the quilt's about. And then under each block there's a little verse about what each block is about. And then on the bottom there are the family names and their birth dates, and where they were born. Because, when people are doing research on quilts, they always want to know about the maker and the family—anything they can about the maker and how they made the quilt. So I thought, rather than have people have to research that, I'm going to write it right on the quilt. And I needed a way to quilt those sashes between the blocks, anyway. I spent a couple of weeks, probably, thinking about how I was going to quilt it. And then just one day I said, "Oh, I'm going to quilt the history right into the quilt!" I think it's added a lot to it because people enjoy reading it.

(*It says, "From the break of day to the setting sun/ A woman's work is never done."*) Right. Because the quilt was pertaining to women and their roles. So I stuck that one in. (*"This is the valley of Margaree,/ Tucked in the mountains not far from the sea." And then: "Cape Breton had become my home./ No more did I feel the need to roam." And: "Keep love and truth in sight./ Mind the Light."*) That's the Quaker influence, there. Anybody could see where I came from. The Light is that of God in every person. That was kind of one of the sayings of Quakers, and it was also the motto of where I went to school. The school seal, symbol, whatever, was a little oil lamp, and it said, "Mind the Light." It's really like, follow your inner feelings, follow your conscience.

(*And the last across the top says, "Just because I know you'll ask/ It took 316 hours to do this task."*) That's because that's the first thing everybody asks me when they see it, and I just point to that corner.

[The quilt] covers a lot of time, really. But I made it in 1982, and most of those things I was doing in '82. Some of them I had done previously,

and hadn't repeated. (*"Planting transplants, planting seeds,/ Growing enough to meet our needs."*) I grow all our own vegetables, almost all our own dairy products. I always kept two cows milking; this is the first year I've just had one. But I really still haven't bought milk, other than powdered milk, and eggnog at Christmas. And we have our own beef and our own chicken. And we had our own turkeys, and we have our own lamb. And we've had pork in the past; no more, because it's too expensive now. To buy feed for it. So the only things we really buy at the store are paper products, flour, some spices—I grow my own herbs—and sugar. That kind of stuff.

(*In the quilt, you're alone in the garden.*) Yeah, the garden was always my project. Garry would help get it plowed and harrowed, and then I was on my own. But then I got a rototiller so I could do it all myself, I didn't have to depend on him.

We had a division of expenses. I took care of the food, and all the kids' other needs. And [financially] did major house repair. And Garry took care of the vehicles, the machinery, and major land things, like reseeding and liming, fertilizing a new field, that kind of stuff. Garry cut the wood [for the house]. But after I built my studio, I would have to buy my own wood for the studio.

(*You were able to keep those things separate?*) Pretty well. It's just that if I wanted something special in the food line, I had to buy it. And if I wanted to do something in the house, well, it was up to me to pay for it. So it just kind of naturally became a division that way. (*You kept two accounts: your earnings and his earnings?*) Yes. And I had my own savings. So if there was something really special I wanted to do, like the one year I had to buy a new cow—if I didn't have any money in my savings account, we wouldn't have had a cow.

(*Most marriages just dump everything together.*) Well, see, we each had our own priorities, and so it was up to ourselves to look after them.

140

Like, I would never spend any money on a vehicle, a car or a tractor. That was his interest. Or if he saw an old motor he wanted to buy—it was his money, fine. And if I decided I wanted new kitchen cabinets, it was my money, fine.

(*Interesting. Something like that has broken up many marriages. Or maybe you see it as saving yours.*) Well, we never had any problems in our marriage. Maybe that's part of the reason why. I would have liked—I mean, I thought it would have been wonderful if some guy would take care of me and I didn't have to worry about money. But he wasn't like that. So, I always had to worry about getting money to do what I wanted to do. (*So it wasn't you were deeply, deeply liberated—it was, that was the fellow you loved.*) I guess, some of each. He had no guilt feelings about [not] being the breadwinner. It was just, do your share and that's it. It's up to the little woman to do the rest!

(*"Spreading manure, renewing the ground,/ Using farming practices that are sound."*) That was a statement on our kind of organic philosophy of farming—that we try to do things naturally, the way they were always done, rather than try to use chemicals. There were some old hayfields that Garry insisted we put chemical fertilizer on. Which I wasn't too keen on. But at that point, that was his project. But it wasn't land that we were growing anything other than hay. And we just did it one year to get it started.

(*It's you on the tractor.*) Yeah. (*You with the manure spreader.*) Yeah. We used to take turns at that job. Actually, in the beginning, he looked after the cows and I looked after the horses and the sheep and the chickens. So, I had to spread the horse manure and the sheep manure, and he spread the cow manure. And we had to shovel it all on by hand, at that point, too. And then we started doing it together, because the spreader got kind of finicky, and one guy had to be on the spreader and the other guy on the tractor. Actually, I lost the job after awhile, too, because the spreader got so finicky that I was accused of not operating it correctly. Now I'm back on the spreader. But now I have a friend that comes up with a front-end loader and puts it in for me. Can do it all in a day, instead of three weeks of shoveling.

I'd go out and do maybe four or five loads in a day. And that was it. My back couldn't take it after that. Shovel it onto the spreader. (*And take it out with the tractor and spread it.*) Come back and fill it up again. I didn't enjoy doing it. But some jobs had to be done, so you did them. And I always say, you can see [that] reflected in the quilt. The jobs I didn't like doing, the squares are simpler than the ones I enjoyed—there's more detail on them.

(*"Tilling the garden at least twice/ Makes the seed bed soft and nice."* And, *"Sawing logs at the mill,/ Some for the walls, some for the sill."*) Down at our sawmill. Garry bought that, together with a guy who used to

live down the road, because he was building a house. And at that point, we had lots of building projects. And of course, Garry loved machinery. And the guy sawed up wood for his house, and then sold his share back to Garry. Garry just sawed up wood for our own uses, and the neighbours that wanted stuff sawn. We sawed all the wood for my studio together. I was the guy that threw the slabs into the truck and piled the lumber, and sent stuff back up to him. He was the sawyer. And if I couldn't help him at the mill, the kids would go down and help him. It was kind of a rainy-fall-day job, usually. Did most of it in the fall or the spring.

(*"Burning brush is not much fun,/ But it's work that must be done."*) All this land was grown up in pasture spruce, when we came. So we had to clear all the fields. Which meant ripping out the trees with a tractor. And then piling the brush and burning it. Every year there was a burning project somewhere. I never really liked doing that job.

(*"Lambs and calves are coming now./ What would we do without Elsie the cow?"*) After the first couple of years, I took it all over. Garry finally said, "Look, I really don't like milking the cows and looking after the animals, and you do. So why don't I get the kids off to school, and make their lunches, and put them to bed at night, and you do the chores." I said, "Fine with me." So for the last five or six years, that's the way we did it. You know, he'd help if I needed him. But otherwise, I was on my own.

I delivered maybe three or four [calves]. Most of the time they were okay on their own. That kind of stuff doesn't bother me. I always felt I had a better sense of what the animals were going through. Like, when we went out at night—say we were someplace and we were having a good time—I'd say, "We have to go home and milk." I knew how the cow felt, full of milk, having nursed children. You know, I just felt I had a better sense for the animals in that way, and what they were going through.

(*I think a lot of people went to the country for freedom and things like*

142

that—but you pile enough animals on yourself, you never see your own gate.) Yeah. We started getting more animals when the kids were little. We said, "Look, we're stuck here with kids, anyway. We might as well have the animals." And there's a few times that it's been a drag. Like, going away together. I think we only went away together as a family once. And we were just fortunate that we had a friend who had no children, and was raised on a farm, and knew how to look after things, who was willing to come up and spend two weeks. But other than that, it's just—you can never get away together. And I miss that. But it's one of the things you have to sacrifice, I guess. There's times now I think I should get rid of them, and then I'd have freedom to travel and do stuff. But I still have a house. You've got to keep everything from freezing. What are you going to do with the dog, the cats? It's all or nothing.

(*"The sugar maple, it's time to tap./ Fill the pails with sweet sap."*) That would be early spring. That was from the days when we used to make our own syrup. When we first came we put a steel roof on the barn. So we tore off all the old shingles, and we had this huge pile of dry shingles. So it was great for boiling down sap. And then when we re-did the house, we had another pile. So whenever we had a good supply of scrap wood, or a lot of slabs from the mill that were dry, we made syrup. The last time we made it, actually, was when I was pregnant with Ezra. He was born in April, just at the end of the syrup season. So that last week, I just sat by the fire and threw shingles in it, and boiled down sap, and read books. I gathered the last sap on the day he was born. It never got boiled down.

(*"Christmas dinner with our friends./ And so another year ends."*) We really miss it. We were talking to friends the other day. She was complaining: in Nantucket she feels like she'd like to invite somebody that doesn't have family or would really appreciate a nice meal, but she doesn't know anybody there like that. She remembers the days that us hippie immigrants that had no family here

would get together and have a nice Christmas dinner and good time. (*And eat organically.*) Right.

(*"Cleaning out the barn is a chore,/ Compared to housework it's not a bore."*) I don't like housework at all. But when you're dealing with live animals, it's a whole different thing. There is always something different and something new. You get a response. From a house, you get nothing—but dirt the next day.

(*"Cook the meals, bake the bread./ Sit down when the children are in bed."*) That's the way it used to be. Work all day. I always had to do all that, all the cooking and baking, and then help Garry on outside projects, and do my own work. At the end of the day, it was just like, GROAN. Get the kids to bed, and you'd say, "Oh, wow, alone at last. SNORE."

(*"Canning fruits, jams and pickles galore./ There's not much need to go to the store."* And, *"Taking Chester for a ride/ With Pepper running along beside."*

(*"Picking apples under the tree./ Which tastes best? Ezra will see."*) Every year we go apple-ing, and we get enough to make about—oh, we used to make about 20 or 30 gallons of cider. And maybe between 40 and

100 quarts of apple sauce. When the kids were little—Amish, at that age, was very helpful, and he'd fill buckets and bags of apples. And Ezra would just sit under the tree and eat 'em!

(*"Butchering time is good and bad./ It's best to think food and not be sad."*) You know, when I first came [to Cape Breton] I was a vegetarian. The first sheep we had, somebody gave us a pet lamb. We raised him on a bottle. He was like a dog. He followed us everywhere, he went swimming with us. Every morning when I'd cross the river to get the horses—they were on an island—he'd swim across with me. A couple of times we almost lost him—he got in heavy, fast water, and then we'd go rescue him. But he started getting us pretty mad at the end. First of all, he used to go across the road and eat her rosebushes and her tulips. She wasn't too pleased about that. And then he learned how to open the house door. And if we went away, we'd come back, and he'd be in the house, asleep on the couch. And there'd be a string of lamb turds all the way across the room. He learned how to knock down my jars of whole wheat berries and soybeans and stuff. You'd go in and you'd find broken jars, and this little fat lamb with a smile on his face.

When we killed him, I was pregnant with Amish. And Garry was sitting there eating this lamb chop, saying, "Oh, you won't believe how good this is. You've never had anything like this. It just melts in your mouth." I said, "Okay, give me a bite." And I've been eating lamb and beef ever since. And we only missed Frank the lamb a teeny bit. (*Frank?*) He had eyes like a friend of mine named Frank.

(*"It warms you once, it warms you twice./ Burning wood is awfully nice."*)

(*"Every morning and every night,/ In the barn you'll see this sight."*)

(*"Keeping the potatoes weed free/ Takes the pony, Garry and me."*)

(*"Stooking bales in the sun/ Haying time has begun."*) See the black flies around my head? Haying has mixed reviews. It's

nice when you have help and there's this community feel to it. But when you don't have any help, it's awful. And there were lots of days where Garry was baling and I was the only one putting it in. He would try to be at the bottom of the conveyor and the top at the same time. There were times during hay season that if somebody shot me, I would have been grateful.

(*"Tourists come and tourists go./ Some buy, those that know."*) Smug, huh? (*So you used to sell right here from the house?*) Yeah, I still do. Actually, now, it's more taking orders for custom work. But I've always been in the *Buyers' Guide to Arts and Crafts*. And you don't get too many people up. But usually if somebody comes up, they're pretty serious about buying something.

(*"Judging horse shows during the season,/ For all my decisions there is a reason."*) I usually do about one horse show a year, now, still. It's a way to kind of keep in touch with the horse world. And I enjoy doing it. I still enjoy a good horse and a good rider. But I do less and less just because I've kind of dropped out of that whole circuit. Right now I just can't leave the farm for that length of time.

(*And then the whole centre of the quilt is your farm and family.*) Yeah. And the house, before it was re-shingled. (*You have a dress on!*) Yeah. I did that from a photograph. We were going to an antique car show. So I had made a dress that had an old feel to it, and Garry had on kind of old-time clothes. See, the whole feeling of the quilt is—I wanted to portray, like the verse I put in there—the feeling of using the best of today with the best of traditional. So the blocks have a feeling to them that, even though they're done [with] a modern method—they're done with machine appliqué—it still has an old folky feeling to it, to the whole quilt. And it kind of echoes the lifestyle, in that we take advantage of technology that doesn't really harm the environment, it makes life easier. But at the same time we still value the traditional things like organic farming and that.

(*I like the boldness of it, in the sense that it isn't the family's quilt. It*

146

Garry and Anne Morrell's sons, Ezra and Amish

really is your own. It would have been quite a different quilt if it was the life of Garry Morrell.) Yeah. Actually, I thought, I really should do one about him at the same time. But you know, it was just a matter of, I didn't have an excuse to do it. And I almost did one after he died, so I'd have one for the kids with the same feeling to it. But then I thought, Well, how am I going to decide which one I give to which kid? Who gets the father and who gets the mother?

For Ezra, I talked to him before about doing one with the house, and the changes through the years. I mean, that would have a whole story for him, too, because he'd see himself growing up, and then he'd see, there'd be Garry absent. And after that, who knows what's going to turn up on it. So, it'd be kind of fun. It would bring back a lot of memories for him. "Remember when we put the greenhouse on." "Remember when we put the root garden out front." "Remember when we tore this down." I'd just have to gather up the old pictures of the house.

I can still see the house as we first saw it when we drove up here, with thistles all growing up around it, and the shed falling off the back, and all this stuff thrown around inside. So that would be the starting point. And the first couple squares, Ezra wouldn't be there.

That's the plan, whether or not I ever get around to it.

The quilting photos shown here are from twenty-three squares that border a huge central quilted portrait of the Morrell family home in Margaree Valley in 1982. The entire quilt in full colour can be seen on the back cover of Issue 45 of *Cape Breton's Magazine*. A black-and-white photo of the quilt appears on page ii of this book.

147

Yvon LeBlanc, Architect: Building Fortress Louisbourg

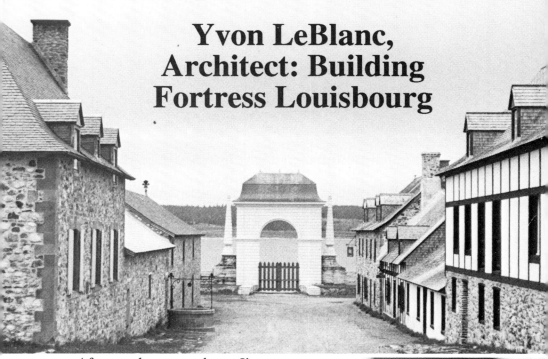

After twelve years here, I'm still enthused by the view of the thing. Every morning when I come to work, seeing it under different light, it's still quite taking. You know, when there's fog, when you just see it through—beautiful sunlight and all that—oh, it's a dilly. And I was lucky. I came here for the last part of my career. Because for other people, younger ones, coming here with a young family, needing social life and all that—oh, it's awfully hard. (*To live in Louisbourg?*) Oh, yes. It is out of the way. And especially French-speaking ones. That is why we never could get French-speaking people here, as much as we would have needed. Be-

The de la Plagne house, faced partly in wood, partly in stone

cause it is a fringe region to people from inland.

(*Would people from the eighteenth century, living here, have felt as cut off?*) Oh, they must have. The few comments we have are usually bad. They were cut off, far away. Although they had quite a lot going on here, you know—dances and gambling and dinners and things like that. Especially during carnival time, which was from the beginning of the year up to Lent. They had lots of dances and balls and dinners and meetings—especially in the second occupation [1749-1758]. In the first one [1713-1745] we don't have as much information on those activities. We wish we had more—letters, more personal things.

We know that they had certain celebrations. The Feast of St. Louis, for instance, 25th of August. In the first period there's a description of a celebration they had on the occasion when the king, who had been sick, got well. And there was some celebration at the birth of the dauphin, the king's first son. Because King Louis got several girls all in a row. Then finally, he got a son in 1729, and that was the future king. So they had some celebrations. (*And your studies for the architecture of Louisbourg, they include even this?*) It's the people. That's the part which was interesting to me here: working for people, trying to imagine people who have been dead for 250 years. In other words, building for clients who have long been dead. In order to try to make up my mind about how their house was.

This was one of our latest buildings [photo above]. It's called the de la Plagne house. He was the nephew of one of the officers here, de Penses, who owned this land. And maybe it was his uncle who built it, we're not sure. We found the foundations. Very soon after it was built, there was a lawsuit. A soldier came and stole something from it, and he went in front of the court. It's a very sad kind of story. Most of our stories are rather sad. This one was a young soldier who was on guard one night, not long after the house had been built. And he came out for—as he calls it—his necessities. And he was right at the corner of that fence we see here today.

There was a latrine there, we think; we're not absolutely sure it was still there at that time. Anyway, he was there, doing his thing, and he saw this house; and he remembered that he had worked here earlier as a servant, and he knew they were fairly rich. This all comes out at the interrogation.

He climbs over the gate on the other side, comes inside, lifts one of the window panes, puts his hand inside, unhooks and goes in. And he steals some money and a pair of white gloves. The next morning, the Negro slave, the servant in this house, came down and saw the pane hanging out. That's how the theft was found out. And he was reported and he was caught. He was in a tavern. He wasn't a very bright fellow. I think he was a very young man, an orphan, about twenty years old.

Then, of course, the outcome of the story is very sad. There's a first account. And then there was another account of it, which says this: that after he went through the first trial, he was sentenced, and some people thought the sentence was not hard enough—so the whole thing started again. All through the whole interrogation and everything. And in the course of one of the interrogations, a very touching scene happened. The judge was making a review of the information, of the testimonies, and he interrogated Mrs. de la Plagne. And he asked her if she had anything to add to her testimony of before. She said something like, "Yes. On a certain date, I was in front of my house, and a young soldier went by with guards. He broke away. He came and threw himself on his knees in front of me, and said he would never do it again—asking me to pardon him." And then, that second time, he was hanged. So, we have the whole series of questions and answers. We could put that on the stage as it is and make a beautiful play out of it. A touching story.

As far as the building itself [the de la Plagne house], we had, when it was sold, mention of this: it was boarded inside and out. It was a wood frame building, garnished, as they call it, with stone and brick. In other words, stone and brick between the frame, inside the wall. We presume it's that. That's all we can do. Then boarded inside and out. That is why, on the inside, where we see one of the walls, we filled the bottom part with stone and the upper part with brick—presuming when they said with stone and brick, maybe they went one floor stone and the other floor brick. And then we sort of deduced things from that, assuming that that was it. For instance, in the archeological work, we had found in the foundation some traces of the wood plate on top of the foundation—not very very strong, but some trace. It seemed to be about twelve inches thick, twelve pouces—which was the old French—a pouce is about one-sixteenth more than our inch. So from that, we deduced that probably the ground floor framework of the wall was twelve pouces by twelve pouces, as we knew some others were, by documentation. And at the upper part—

it often happened that the upper floors of buildings were thinner, making that, say, eight inches or so—and so we filled that with brick. So it's a lot of detective work, really.

We also know that the glass of the window panes was held in with points, and then on the outside there were strips of blue paper. In the 1720's, there's an account in France, saying there's this new thing, this putty, that you put on the outside of the window—it stops the drafts from coming in. But they say that now, since that hardens very soon, you can't take the panes off to clean them. In other words, when they had paper around them, they took each pane out to clean them. Now we know that here at Louisbourg they had strips of paper also. Because this fellow, when he went into the house, he lifted one of the panes, he put his arm in. And the next morning, the slave saw the pane hanging out. Therefore, this house, built in about 1740, had the paper holding the glass in. But we put putty today, because we have to. We haven't found a proper paper and glue which would answer to some extent our present need for maintenance. So for the moment—and since we do know that they were starting to use putty here occasionally—we've taken the liberty for the moment to use some putty. Though some fine day, you may find little strips of glued paper.

(*But you really want to be that precise?*) Oh, we're trying to be as precise as we can. We have to do things for modern needs, but we go out of our way to do it as close as possible as it was. Now, quite often we're not absolutely sure. As close as possible as we have reason to think it was. If we have to do something else, for some reason, we like to have it written down that we did it, but knowingly. Sometimes we have to guess. And that is why, when I first came here, my whole point was to try to sort of imbibe myself of everything I could find out about building anything of that time, so that when the time for guessing comes, well, I guess with that influencing my guess. That's the best we can do.

The boarding of the de la Plagne house—that's purely invention, but justified by this: the gate down at the bottom of the street, the Frédéric Gate, is built in wood—we have a drawing of it. And it shows strips of wood like that, with the deep joint. These both were built about the same time. We know this house was planked, or boarded. And since we knew that they were fairly well-to-do, we figured that, well, this house could very well have been boarded like the Frédéric Gate. But we have no real firsthand reason to think that.

Now, we're still mystified about what we're going to do with the stone part of the de la Plagne house. Because the foundations that were found are very, very clear, that this part was obviously an addition. We had to presume that it was there in 1745; we're not absolutely sure. We have a drawing—a general view of the town, seen from outside—where we see

151

this building, what we think is this building. And this end here, the extended part of the building, is not very clear. So, we hemmed and hawed a long time before building that part. There's a later drawing, 1758. It's a strangely interesting drawing; it's a sort of a bird's-eye view of the town, based on imagination, largely. And it's all sort of distorted. But it's amazing how you can recognize some of the buildings. And this building, we see it. We see the number of windows. But we don't see any difference in the wall surface. It was very, very small scale, you know, and it's a thing which the artist might not have noticed. But on the other hand, it could have meant that either the planking continued over the stone extension, or that the same paint would have been applied on the stone surface. The stones could have been given a coat of mortar, and then the whole thing painted the same colour as the boards. And that's what we may do, eventually. We don't know yet. For the moment, it's raw stone, and we're still deliberating. Oh, there's lots of little decisions to take yet.

That is why now, since I'm leaving this summer, I'm preparing a summary of all the buildings. I have to include a comment on each building, saying the things that now, by hindsight, we could have done differently.

We worked in a team, a design team. There's a historian, an archeologist, a draftsman, and the architect, who's chairman of the team. And we gather all the information from those different aspects. And then we put all that together, see what we can deduce. And then I fill the holes by going into architectural background, how people lived at that time, secondary historical documents, archeology—what different pieces might mean. It's a question of putting things together. And then, from what we know of the individuals themselves. Now me, as an architect, I've always been people-oriented in architecture. So, I went as far as I could to get as much as I could about feeling about the people themselves.

The de Gannes house was one of the earlier buildings I worked on. And I don't think I worked in enough of that. I had not imbibed enough of the people at that very early stage. That is why, now, I'm going to recommend that we change the interior batten doors, to put doors which have a bit better finish. In a house like this, the doors probably were what we call the emboiture doors, that is, the doors which are flush. All sorts of little things haven't been solved yet. Or things that I'm getting solved now, after years. It takes a long time. As a matter of fact, it was only after about four years here, that I began to feel a little bit comfortable about guessing, that I could trust my imagination, that it would be sufficiently coloured by all that I had imbibed.

De Gannes was a captain of one of the companies here. He was born at Port Royal in Acadia, to a military family. But he's not an Acadian, as such. He was born there—but to us Acadians, there's a difference. He was

152

born there; his father was in the military there; but he was not a settler, he was not an Acadian, not as the people who had settled down there. If you lived in England, even if you were born there, it makes you an English citizen as such—

The de Gannes house

but it doesn't make you an Englishman. (*I had heard that de Gannes was wealthy enough to build a house like de la Plagne. But because he was from Acadia, not France, and had experienced Maritime winters, he chose a smaller, more humble house—but one easier to heat.*) That's interesting. That comes from me. Because, as an Acadian, I'm trying like mad to find out what the Acadian houses were like. We have extremely little on Acadian houses. Now there is this: he was born in Acadia, but we don't know too much about his youth, whether he actually lived there. Because, at that late period—this house was built in the 1740's—he built with piquet. The piquet type building—that is, with the vertical logs in the ground—was a type of building which was built at the very first in Louisbourg, as a very quick way of building, a nearly temporary way of building. That's my opinion. Because, it's a very inefficient way of building, logs in the ground. Although we are amazed how some of them lasted; one built in 1713 was still there in 1745. Still, it's quite astonishing that he, an officer, thirty years after the start, still built in that technique.

And we found the foundation, and we found the traces of the piquets in the ground. It's on account of his building here that way, that we wonder whether the Acadians did not build like that in Port Royal as well. We don't know how they built in Port Royal. In some of our other buildings, you'll see the piquet technique exposed. Here, during the archeological excavation, we found little bits of plaster in the foundation, so we presume that the interior was plastered, or partly. We don't really know. We tried both. We covered some with boards, and some with the plaster. And you'll notice we arranged the plaster to show slightly the form of the piquet underneath. But by far, the interiors seemed much, much more often boarded than plastered inside.

Building this modest little house in 1742, de Gannes must have gone through a very low time, a difficult time business-wise. Because he had owned three lots in town, on which one had a house from quite early, where he must have lived. He died in '52. And we know that in the early

'40s, when he sold his lots, he was living on another of his lots. So therefore he had two houses. We know he sold those three lots in a fairly short period of time. We know he'd sold all his lots, so it's by that that we presume that he was living here. This house shows on the first English plan in 1745. So it's by all that surmising that we figure he was here. What we really only know is that he died here. Because, when he died, it's definitely this house, by the inventory.

But why would he build such a house? His wife was from an engineer's family, de Catalogne. She died in 1750. Around that time, his daughter got married. She got a dowry of over 10,000 livres, of which he had paid 8,000 at his death. Therefore, he must have been quite well off. Oh yes, and when the family came back after the first siege, three of his daughters came back with him. They had interesting names. Whereas, usually you're Mary or Anne or something like that, they were Mademoiselle de la—Something or Other—Mademoiselle de So-and-So. That seems to mean that they had become attached to some property in France. They came with four servants. And they presumably settled down in this house. Three girls and a son, the father and mother, four servants who might have been living there. So therefore, they must have been fairly well off. But it's not a house which seems to indicate that kind of living. (*Because of the use of piquet?*) And small, and sort of temporary. The modesty of the building does not seem to add up. Whether it was a choice, or influence, or perhaps he built it when he was in low means in the '40s. We just don't know. When he died, he had lots of stuff, but there were lots of old things. And it appeared that his family was not living with him— there was no evidence of the family in his inventory. Although often they didn't inventory the things considered belonging to the children or others. So that is why it makes it difficult for us at times.

But to come back to the house. The Acadian thing—that is partly me trying to explain why he did that. And maybe this is some little indication of how some houses at Port Royal might have been. It's very thin, our thing. And I'd like to find out. Now, when the archeological sources tell us, "a fireplace, centrally located in the house"—that can really be two fireplaces. It is a normal thing to do in a small house, because you can heat two rooms with one mass. Now, I've heard it said how the engineer was stupid building his great big house, whereas this guy, de Gannes, up the hill there, he was much brighter—he built a small house around a fireplace. That is the kind of myth we have to debunk, because we just don't know. It goes without saying that a house like this was more comfortable. Is that why de Gannes built it? Intentionally and all that? That's another story.

Now look at the roof—this was re-roofed recently. That's one of our maintenance problems: things that don't last very long here. This had to be re-roofed after only six or seven years. That's a problem with the climate. I would like to paint some of the roofs. (*Does anything stop you?*) Oh yes, yes, yes. See, we always hold our heads, and everything has to be thought out and justified with great care.

The Duhaget house, seen from the back

And I would like to paint some of them because there is some mention of paint in our papers. None connected with roofs, except there have been pieces of shingles found with traces of colour on them. But any mention of paint is just as often to complain that there was not enough of it. There were some paint shipments arriving, there's some yellow ochre and quite a lot of red ochre. But we know there was a lack of paint. So we are still hemming and hawing and discussing all that, because we have to reflect. We want to be very serious.

For the Duhaget house, we have no inventory, no nothing on that. We think there was some paint on it; there might have been some paint applied. That is, in one of the rental agreements, there is some hint—but we're not sure, we're not sure. And we'd like to paint it, because our houses are deteriorating with the weather and all that—the exposed wood. Oh, it's a big worry we have. And we'd like to paint them all. If we could get evidence. Although we have no definite evidence one way or the other, there are certainly indications that a lot were not painted. There's no doubt about that. So that is why we're a bit leery.

(*The Duhaget is one for which you've not made decisions on the interior.*) That's right. It's a bit bigger than others. We knew it had two floors. We knew that Duhaget was captain of a company. We have reason to believe that he may have been not too badly off. We also tend to believe that he built that rather big house, planning to have a family, but he didn't have any. And then, there was a later view of it which showed it fairly high. Therefore, it was quite a substantial house. We had a terrific controversy about the roof. When I arrived, they were just starting to work on it, whether it should be the gable roof or the hip roof. Some of the views were contradictory. Working by team, you see, and working by a sort of majority vote—it was not easy for an architect.

The placing of board: vertical on the upper part, horizontal on the lower part. We knew this house was framed—we found traces of the posts

155

The Lartigue house

and all that. And therefore I think we presumed it was boarded, or maybe we had some reason to believe it was boarded. Now, as it was high, and a sense of the place, that it was a fairly large house, boards all the same width could have been very dull. Since we do see buildings with a different kind of finish on the ground floor part and on the upper part—well, using wood both places, the only possible way to vary it was one horizontal and one vertical. So that's really how we came to that. It's purely to give it a bit of a shape, of a look, on account of the size. That's the only reason we did that. And it's quite plausible.

Most of the houses that I worked with, what we find—the foundation and the location of the fireplace—usually gives us a pretty good idea of how it was divided inside. But this one has me stumped. The way the fireplace is—I haven't found an interior distribution of rooms which makes any sense. So it's got me stumped. It's the only one, really.

But when there's something definite, we of course try to stick to that. For the Lartigue house, for instance, we have a document which is dated 1753—probably done after that—when Widow Lartigue was showing the state of her estate, the houses she owned, pieces of land here and there. So we followed this, but with great, great care. There are so many errors, we had to make up our mind on a lot of things. There's a note on it saying how the pieces of frame were twelve by twelve pouces pine wood, filled with rough stone between the posts—put on a foundation of stone, about one pied and a half above the street. [One pied is 1.066 feet.] So we could observe that very well.

But there are little mysteries again. Here we found the foundation. What was found did not completely reflect the drawing. For instance, there was very clear evidence of the floorboards and joists and things. But they were found below the top of the foundation wall. That would mean that you would have gone up two steps, and then gone down. That doesn't add up. We never figured that one out. Also, there was some paving in the house, at the back, some stone and brick paving at two spots, which were down at the level of the floor. We know that this building was used much later by the English as a stable or something else like that. And for the moment, we attributed those things to that second occupation, and had to leave the mystery. The mystery is still there. We're building for 1744, and all we can surmise is that the floor was at the level of the bottom of the door. That's the way we built it. But we haven't really solved the mysteries yet.

The Lartigue house is interesting, because there were quite a lot of people living in there. And at first glance, they could have been quite squeezed in. But it worked out that they could have had about eighteen people in that, without being all that overcrowded. The way it was laid out. (*Do you mean, the way you chose to lay it out?*) No, the way I found out that it probably was, by following the indications. I chose because I was being led—that there were the two fireplace bases, and all that. And also, led by a typical way that houses were at that time: houses of a certain size, where the rooms were in groups, in suites. You find that in elaborate townhouses, great big houses. Even in this rather small one, as far as townhouses go, you could have a group of three rooms on one side of the stair. And often the rooms go one into the other. We had enough room to make a hallway; and they often had that. Because the sense of privacy at that time was a bit different from ours, since beds had curtains around—a room was a room, not necessarily a bedroom. A living room could easily have a bed in it. Or a bedroom could also be for living in, on account of the curtains. So, people travelling through a room was not that unheard of. And in this house, it would reflect that quite easily. Although, we knew something about the house: we found the foundation and we had the elevation [a drawing of the face of the house]. That's all we had. And the date that he died. And the number of his family, including a daughter who had married. As part of the dowry or wedding arrangement, we knew Lartigue was going to lodge them for a period of time. And with them in there, with a couple of children—I think there were some servants—they could have fitted there quite easily, not more than two per room. Some of the rooms were smallish. And still leaving a big general area where they could have dined, where the stair came down—leaving a largish room for him to conduct his business as a judge.

(*Do you ever have these people come to you in any way?*) I dearly wish that they would! Oh, I dream of that! It's not that I dream of them as such—no, I haven't dreamt of them. But I find myself speaking in the present sometimes, of that time. People have a good laugh at me, that I speak of them as present, or speak of "us."

For instance, about the Royal Battery out there. It's a very sad story about that, how it never was used. Because at the first siege, they were in the process of doing some repairs on it, and they felt they could not defend it. It had some weaknesses; there were some hills around. But it had been made to shoot at the entrance to the harbour, to protect the harbour. So anyway, they decided to abandon it, when the English were coming. (*Because they came by land.*) Yes. That is a very sore point to me, because the engineer, Verrier [here from 1724 to 1745], he's really my predecessor here.

When they decided that they could not defend the Royal Battery, and decided to give it up, they discussed the possibility of blowing it up completely. It was Verrier, the engineer, who was instrumental in stopping that decision, making the decision that they should spike the cannon to stop them from being fired. And then withdraw all the ammunition. Now, that was decided. Some people have looked very crossly at Verrier for doing that, that he did that because he was very proud of his Royal Battery, he didn't want to see it destroyed. Well, I think that's not so at all. I think he was hoping that it could be protected, and that they could get it back after and still use it. But they got panic-stricken, and they didn't properly spike the cannon. So that a couple of days after, the English were shooting at us with our own cannon and balls. And look, I find myself saying, "They were shooting at us." Which makes people laugh.

We've all got our own people that we prefer or like, that we get more involved with. And Verrier, he was a sort of dullish kind of person. But he's accused of all sorts of things, and I feel bound to try to put things straight. They accuse him of wasting money on building the big gates, monumental gates. They say, if he had been working at his fortification rather than at that, it might have been better. But what I tried to make them realize, it ain't necessarily so. Because at that time, in the times of kings, the monumental entrances to a town were extremely important. They express the prestige of the king. And in architecture and in the mores of the time, that part was a functional thing. These gates are not embellishments. They are part and parcel of fortress building at that time. And these are rather tame compared to a whole lot of others elsewhere. Usually, they bore the name of the direction in which they were going. But not here. Why was it called the Maurepas Gate? And another, Frédéric Gate—because they're the same man. He was Frédéric de Maurepas, the Pontchartrain Comte de Maurepas. He was the Minister of the Navy—oh, he had lots of functions. He was the Grand Master of the king's household. He controlled France. And he was the one that we are in constant correspondence with here. So that would be an interesting thing to speculate on: how come he got two gates named after him? Whereas there was none after the king; there was one after his son, the Dauphin Gate. We understand how that came. The king had had several daughters, and he was hankering for a son, and finally he got one. So there was a big celebration. And they were planning the gate in that year, so it became the Porte Dauphine in his honour. There's a little wee gate called the Queen's Gate, that was on the other side. Now, why did the queen get such a small gate to her name? Poor Queen Mary, she was a shy kind of girl; all she did was make kids for the king. She took a second seat; she wasn't very outgoing. She was the daughter of the king of Poland, who was exiled in eastern France because he had lost the throne of Poland. And they needed a royal personnage to marry the king.

There are some ghost stories starting to come around here. People have been hearing things, have been seeing things, over the last several years. One day, somebody saw a person in a red costume coming, and they thought it was me. The people who saw him did not recognize his face, or see it very much. I'm not too sure. Because those stories, you know, they sort of grow. There's also somebody hearing things, steps in the house—in the Duhaget house. In the bakery, the baker one day swore he felt a presence behind him and saw something. It's all things that could be imagination, there's no doubt about that. But anyway, I hear that, and I say, Geez, wouldn't I like to see one, to talk to him, because I'd like to know this: it's either of two things. Either our work is so good that they feel at home. Or it's so bad that they're coming to haunt us. So I'd dearly like to know.

I'd like to come back in fifty or a hundred years. To see how this thing has lived. Because right now, you see, the reality of Louisbourg is this one, not that one from the past. It's this one, because it's here and it's living. With all its problems, its present-day conditions. And this is the one which is interesting to me, to see what will have happened to it, how it will have lived over the time, how it will have adapted. One thing that I can see is that in time it will become interpreted completely in English, in its English reality, which is the "now" one. Which starts with the sieges. It's just a feeling I have. Because when you come to think of it, all this heritage business—nobody has any heritage from Louisbourg, nobody at all. It's meaningless. Except to, maybe, the descendants of the New Englanders. They are the ones who have ancestors buried here, who came and suffered here, and died here. Maybe the descendants of some of the French ones, too. We Acadians, we have no real heritage here. Canada doesn't, because this is a very short interlude of French history, and is only connected with Acadia in a by-the-way sort of thing, because the Acadians were up there in Nova Scotia, and traded with Louisbourg. And only a few came to settle in Cape Breton.

The ones who have really close feelings are those Americans. So, to me, that is the reality of Louisbourg. And I would be willing to bet that in fifty or a hundred years, that will be the one which will have taken over. It has been rebuilt as much as possible as a French thing—that's fine. But with the other thing superimposing itself on it. (*In what way?*) That it becomes lived in by English-speaking people, who can handle it and tell the story. I illustrate it this way. When a study has been made of a certain subject, they're taken mostly from French text sources, and then digested, made into a report. And then when they need to be done in French, they are regurgitated in French from the English intermediate. And that shows. It shows in the form of language that comes out, as well as in the thing itself. It cannot but be so. You've heard him called Captain de Gannes here. That is a thing which is not French at all. You don't say "Captain de Gannes" in French. You say, "Monsieur de Gannes, Capitaine." So that when you hear it, it sounds English. A very subtle little thing which grates. A thing seen by English eyes being put into French by—unfortunately in Canada here, by the very nature of things—translation, reflects English. So, what comes back there, and comes out—an English-seen kind of thing, and an English-felt kind of thing. So it cannot but gradually go in time and become the richest part of the interest. It cannot be anything else.

Here is the Dugas house. He's the only Acadian, really, that settled here from Acadia. He was a carpenter. And his wife was a Richard girl. And after that she married a la Tour, Saint-Etienne de la Tour. (*Did you have a great deal to go on when you did that house?*) Oh, yes. We knew that it had been built in conjunction with a fellow by the name of Detcheverry as a double house. And Dugas, he got the right to live in it as his remuneration for building the house. And they had made a pact, the two of them—if one left, the other one would buy it all. Dugas settled down in his side. In the 1720's, he bought the whole house. And then he died in 1733, and we have an inventory of that time, on which we based our plan. And then Marguerite Richard, she married again, la Tour, so that by 1744 it was really—we used to call it the Dugas-la Tour house. And then, they would have had six unmarried girls [two daughters with Dugas, two of de la Tour, and twins of Marguerite Richard and de la Tour].

To build the house, we found the foundation, which was fairly insubstantial. We were sure it was not a stone house. Now, as far as charpente, we deduced that from the fact that there was a foundation wall. But the rest is imagination. The piquet fill, for instance, that is our own thing. We didn't know. We put some piquet fill because the foundation was sort of light. And since there was the occupied upstairs, we presumed that there

The Dugas-la Tour house

would have been a knee wall, therefore, the roof a bit higher. And since he was a carpenter, we thought we might try to give something special to his house. So we have put the piquets at an angle within the charpente framework, in the knee wall, just for a little change. Because having pieces like that in the framing members is quite common in many French frame houses. We thought, well, maybe Dugas remembered that. But we don't know at all. This is purely our own thing. It's a pity, because everybody sort of likes it. We thought we could take this little liberty as a plausible thing that might have happened. And it might have been, but I wish I knew if it was really so.

(*You're aware of an inventive art, but at the same time, you're determined to get it as right as you can.*) Well, that's the challenge, you see, that I have myself. Because, from an architecture point of view, it's not worth much, if you take architecture in its sort of superficial way—the design visual and all that sort of thing. But from a thing of reconnecting with the people of the past, with real people—the challenge I give myself is to reflect as close as possible what I can make of it, either by finding out or by re-inventing. That is why some imagination comes in. And creation, too. (*You read and then you try to apply that when you deal with these buildings.*) It's not so much that I try to apply it, but I figure that all that is there, and somehow I hope it will come through in the making of decisions and in the making of how I feel about the whole thing. I manage to get a little of that feeling through—very, very, very little, I'm afraid—but maybe more than I think.

While not being great architecture by any means, or exceptional or

161

Yvon LeBlanc, dressed as the eighteenth-century engineer Verrier

anything like that, it's extremely interesting. Because it's a good example of vernacular, quite functional. And it's amazing the number of French architects, especially the ones connected a little bit with historical architecture, are quite taken by the simple kind of functionalism and classical look about it. Because it was built-in at that time, a sense of architecture, in a sort of unconscious kind of way. Rhythm. See, they're not carefully, consciously designed. But they're made with a sense of the form, of the shape. A sense of form that was innate in people. Many, many people have a natural sense of the placing of things. That is the difference between our young civilization and a much older one. So, no, it's not great architecture by any means, but it is interesting.

Some of my architect friends in Moncton think I'm nuts, getting into this foolish thing. But I said, I've had the best of two worlds. I've had ten years private practice and I've had this. But it was easier for me, going into this, because I already had some of the other one. I didn't have to worry about what I would do in ordinary architecture afterward. I wouldn't be good for it at all, now. I'm ruined!

Annie and John Battiste:
A Mi'kmaq Family History

Annie Battiste of Chapel Island told this story in Mi'kmaq to her daughter Marie; Marie
has written, from her notes, into English. It's a Mi'kmaq interviewing a Mi'kmaq, rather
than our typical situation of one culture calling to another. This is a long, complex story
which retains the pace of family sharing.

A crystal clear memory is hard to find in many people, a tragedy of old
age or an inattentiveness to the world. But my mother Annie Battiste has
always been known for her memory of details that others, including myself, have never attended to and could not remember. I have always been
in awe of this trait and in the spring of 1992 when my mother, at the age of
eighty-one, spent some weeks with us as she often did during the years after the death of my father, she sat and told stories of people and places of
the past. Although I had heard these stories often, I marvelled at how new
and fresh and interesting they were to me. My memory being so bad, I
asked if I might use paper and pencil to take notes. Then we started at the
first memory of her life.

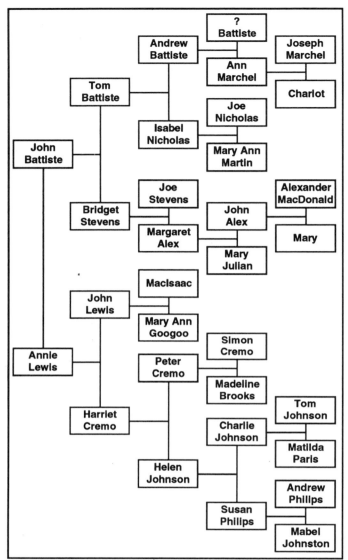

Born December 16, 1910, to Harriet Cremo Lewis and John Lewis in Barra Head, Una-ma'kik, Annie lived all of her growing up years in Potlo'tek, Barra Head, Nova Scotia, now known as Chapel Island Reserve. Barra Head was among the largest Mi'kmaq communities at that time, being the capital of the Mi'kmaq Nation where Mi'kmaqs from everywhere gathered annually each summer for their national assembly to meet, pray, socialize, and discuss political issues of the day.

At the age of five or six years old, my mother remembers her whole family had the deadly dreaded disease called smallpox. The Mi'kmaq word for this disease was lapekut. Her father John Lewis worked with cutting pulp in the woods. Since in these days there was no speedy transportation and the distance from work required him to remain away from home, my mother's mother lived with her father's family in their home.

This was the home of Peter Cremo and his second wife Mary Ann Googoo. His first wife Helen had given birth to two children—Simon and Harriet Cremo—and died in Canso where she was buried. Mary Ann worked like most Mi'kmaq women of those days. She was a basket maker within an extended Mi'kmaq family enterprise and sold the baskets, peddling them from village to village by train and by foot. At that time, the people in Barra Head usually would take a horse-and-wagon to the village

Annie's parents: John Lewis and Harriet Cremo

of St. Peters, and from there they took a train to various points. It was not unusual, however, to walk the full seven miles to St. Peters, although [in] winter they skated across the Bras d'Or Lake to the town.

On one such peddling expedition, Mary Ann came to a Scotch home where she was invited to come in. She discovered immediately that the people in the house were sick with smallpox. The trip home must have been a long one for her as she carried the news to the family. Her husband Peter was away cutting pulp, and when she got home she cried in despair that in eighteen days she knew she would get the deadly disease of smallpox. She had no one to turn to who would help her for she knew that whoever stayed with her would also get the disease. This disease that began with the prolonged fever could kill or permanently scar one for life. She knew that. It was well known that many people died from this disease. And every home where there was one who was sick with smallpox was quarantined for months and no one would come to the house. Food would be dropped off for the sick family at a distance, but no one could come near as the disease could rapidly spread.

Upon her arrival, Mary Ann cried desperately in fear and panic for what was to come, relating to her stepdaughter Harriet the fate of this deadly disease. Harriet, already a married woman, agreed to stay with her stepmother, together with her children Annie and Mattie, to help her through her sickness. Knowing they also would be ill, she agreed to help her stepmother and nurse her as long as she could. With luck perhaps they

165

would both live. When Harriet's husband John came home, he also agreed to help his family and stayed with them as well. Peter Cremo stayed away although he helped them from afar delivering food and provisions nearby where they would pick it up.

As predicted, in eighteen days Mary Ann became ill and the family was quarantined for the winter. No one could come to the house. Their smallpox sickness was as great as its reputation and many times they felt that they would not live. Harriet watched her failing mother, and later John watched his failing wife and finally resigned himself that his daughter Annie would not live through this fever. He started to think about the burial, for at that time people who had died of smallpox would have to be buried far away from other people. As John sat thinking about the sad events that were to happen and the prospect of where to bury his child, his daughter Annie awoke from the fever and asked for mashed potatoes and turnip. With great joy he fixed his daughter her healing meal. They all survived the disease that winter and in the spring, the house had to be smoked out to cleanse it from traces of the terrible disease.

As part of the family's livelihood and traditions followed by their Mi'kmaq ancestors, the family made their annual journey by boat from Chapel Island to Canso where they fished swordfish by boat and lived in a tarpaper shanty on the side of the waters of the town of Canso. Nestled in a cove warmed by the shelter of woods on one side and accessed by a water inlet in a cove, Mi'kmaq families made their homes and lived for several weeks through the summer while they fished the southern port. There were about five wigwams and camps huddled together that housed about five large families.

The fishing expedition provided the families with trade goods that many stores easily purchased. And the woods nearby furnished the makings of baskets that the women made and sold. Before July 26, they all would return to Chapel Island for the annual St. Ann Mission in their new store-bought clothes and with their provisions for the ten-day stay on Chapel Island [Miniku]. At the end of the mission they returned to their homes in Barra Head.

Sick times probably are most memorable in one's childhood, especially if one has life-threatening diseases. At the age of ten or eleven, my mother again fell ill to another deadly disease: scarlet fever. Only Annie who was about ten, and her brother who was seven, fell ill to scarlet fever. The sickness of the fever was so great that she remembers her skin peeled off. She remembers the quilts that were put around the doors and windows to prevent drafts from coming in as the shanties were only wooden frames, without insulation.

When Mi'kmaq families travelled or made camp, they always stayed

166

John Battiste's parents: Bridget Stevens with John, and Thomas Battiste

together in groups, taking their children wherever they went. The children took part in all the events and the tasks of the home, learning how to survive by their hands and talents. The families stayed among themselves, immersed in the Mi'kmaq language and culture, rituals and traditions. A few may roam about more adventuresomely among the Scottish or French people, learning their languages and listening to their stories—only to return with colourful and humorous stories for the fold.

The Mi'kmaq are a friendly people, gregarious and affable, who always can find humour and funny anecdotes in everything they do. John Lewis, Annie's father, was like that, a fellow who loved to tease and tell funny stories. His mannerisms made him a popular guy, well thought of and highly respected among the community. Like most men, he may have a drink when he went to town, given to him by his non-Indian friends, since Mi'kmaqs were not allowed to purchase any liquor, but he rarely brought it back home to drink. He was known to be a fine family man.

For two weeks one summer, my mother, her brother Mattie and her uncle Simon, her father John, and her grandfather Peter Cremo worked on making a fishing boat. Two Frenchmen from L'Ardoise helped them make the boat. In return, the family shared their food provisions and provided beds on the floor for the two men. In those two weeks that they worked on making the boat, after supper, they sat and talked and shared stories and laughter and language. My mother was just a young girl, but she still remembers the French language they taught her. She repeats with pride the

167

numbers in French: "Yon, der, trah, cat, sank, sees, set, weet, nuff, dees"—she counts out and then goes on to fifty just to show how well she got it down. Then she names the days of the week in French and the family names they taught her for mother, father, daughter, son, etc. If she had had more exposure, she laments, she would assuredly be trilingual today.

Annie did get some schooling in Barra Head as there was a school in the community run by various employees sought out by Indian agents. Annie went to school for about six years. She repeated the last grade; she reports it was very difficult. The books were very hard to read, she remembers, because she had little experience in English. Her father and mother, both literate in English and Mi'kmaq, helped her. Her father liked to read to her. Some stories were particularly memorable, like the story of Bertha, a young girl who had many problems and was very poor. Annie remembers after first hearing of Bertha, she was so sad for Bertha that she cried as her father told the story. She laughs at herself as she remembers how sorry she felt for Bertha and the story her mother related to friends of her father making her cry.

She remembers one of the teachers at the school. He had a temper which could flare up at various times. His abusive power over children was well known. Once when she asked for a pencil, he threw it at her and stabbed her hand. These were not isolated incidents and she suffered under his tutelage. Her father and mother finally insisted that she stop going to school. As long as Annie could spell "poison" and could read "danger," her father reasoned, there was no need for her to have to go to school and get abused. Thereafter, Annie stayed at home taking care of her family, helping with the household chores, learning how to make baskets to help the family economy, and led a carefree life of a young person in the Mi'kmaq family network. Her father and mother continued to teach her to read both in English and in Mi'kmaq.

Annie's mother Harriet was a warm and affectionate mother who had learned well the skills of family care from her mother. She cooked, cleaned, sewed, and made baskets for her family and for people in town where she worked as well. She was a smart woman, energetic and thorough in her work. Her beautiful care in making baskets made her peddling go easier as they were frequently purchased, but Mi'kmaq baskets as everything else, were bought for very little money. Her baskets sold for five cents to two dollars. Harriet had many responsibilities when her mother died and cared for her father Peter Cremo as well until he died.

At the age of fifteen, Annie's family moved to East River Point near Chester Basin in Lunenburg County because the lumber for making baskets was abundant there. They made baskets all summer, using the maple tree which was soft and white and made beautiful fancy baskets. After a

168

day of making baskets, they would then peddle the baskets in the town. Many times Annie and her mother would have to look for lodging for the night in the town as it would be too late or dark to go back to their camp. For those who took them in for the night, Harriet would leave a basket behind. But when her father and brother went peddling, they would have to return even in the dark to the camp to protect the women.

They camped in an all-wooded area where there were no houses. They washed their clothes in the big river where they camped and dried their clothes on bushes. They owned a big heavy iron which was heated by the fire in a cast-iron pot to iron their clothes. They always appeared clean and well-kept, a trait they took pride in. Their camp was always kept clean, tidy and inviting for guests who may come to visit. Especially important was the Sunday visiting. While going from house to house peddling, they made many friends and were invited to return to visit. They returned to homes where they had stopped along the way and shared stories and laughter.

One day Mother's family went to visit a friend, Mary Rose Johnson, in the Nova Scotia hospital. When they arrived they found that she had died the day before. They then went home for the funeral and wake. It was the tradition then, as it continues to be today, to help out the families where one had died by being with the person throughout the wake and sharing one's goods and hands with the grieving family as they care for their visitors with food and stories. The larger community shared in the grief and aided all the grieving people in their hour of need. Their prayers and their faith held them together. Rituals of prayers and songs for the dead and dying continue today, as do the wakes and charity auctions which follow the funeral. Everyone comes, bringing with them their most cherished possession which is given to the auctioneer for charity. The proceeds are then passed on to the family to cover the costs of the wake and funeral and other expenses of bringing in distant relatives.

When Mi'kmaq were on the road, peddling or making baskets, their spirituality never went without nourishment. They prayed often, always before meals, and said the rosary. They also would find a church in the town and even though it may not be a Catholic church, they still went to it to pray. One summer for five months, John and Harriet Lewis' family went to the Church of England, not the Catholic church they had been baptized into, because none was available in the town where they lived and worked. In those days, such a practice was not encouraged by the Catholic Church. So when they returned home, they immediately went to confession and confessed that they had to go to another church because a Catholic church was not handy.

John and Harriet became well-known among the folks in the small village of East River Point. John's friendly nature and Harriet's warm and

169

inviting smile were welcomed throughout the town as they made their way around with their baskets and stories. They visited people, went to church, and sold their baskets around the town. John liked music and even danced, although his wife was quite shy and did not dance. When the Lewis family got ready to leave and prepared to return to Barra Head, many people in the town asked them to drop by before they left to say goodbye. When they arrived at these homes, they were given baskets and boxes of sandwiches and cakes to take with them on their journey home.

Home for Harriet and John Lewis was a little house, a shell that was built by the money provided by the Indian agent. Most people got a shell. But from profits from their baskets, John and Harriet bought sheet rock and hired a Frenchman to finish their house. They had hardwood floors and an oilcloth flooring in the kitchen. They had two bedrooms upstairs and kitchen and living room downstairs. These houses were not big, but they often had to hold a lot of people, especially during the annual Pestie'wa'taqtimk. This was the occasion for feasting and fêting with friends and family.

Pestie'wa'taqtimk started on Noelimk or Christmas Day. The preparations for the event had gone on for a least a month or two before that. Food was gathered and stored and readied for the thirteen days of feasting and the all-night dancing at each of the little houses in the Mi'kmaq village. Each consecutive night, a different person's name was honoured. As each name was honoured the people would gather and then walk to the house singing Christmas carols or talking.

As they approached the house, a gun shot would announce their arrival. The host would open the door and invite them to enter. When they entered the house the leader of the procession gave the host a shaved wooden cross and a medal or tie or cloth wrapped around the cross. After asking the host if they might dance, they danced the traditional ko'jua dance around the stove until the house rocked to the rhythm. A loud "Ta ho!" would end the dance and they would then eat the meal prepared by the host. When they had eaten and visited with the family, they then would start out to the next house and continue throughout the night until all the names for that night had been honoured.

My mother remembers these days fondly as they were a fun time for the people. They feasted and frolicked every night for thirteen nights until the last day, January 6. This last night of Pestie'wa'taqtimk festivities commemorated the three kings' arrival at the manger bearing gifts for the Baby Jesus. On this last night there was a square dance and people would come and dance all evening. A king and queen would be selected previously to host the evening's dance, and they would come dressed in a king and queen's costume.

Fond memories of the past always give way to tragic moments as well. John Lewis died on September 15, 1933, from appendicitis, at the age of forty-three. He had gone to the doctor in St. Peters with a pain on his side. The doctor had diagnosed an abscess and sent him home with some aspirins for the fever. Several days later, John realized that there was something much greater wrong and kissed his family goodbye and he took the car ride to the St. Peters train station. He traveled in anguish by train to the hospital in Antigonish. Three nights later he died.

Mother remembers that night and the sign that came to her foretelling her father's death. She was alone at the house. Her brother Mattie was in the woods cutting pulp, living among men in camps. That night she decided to try to work on some baskets to keep herself busy. She had been most anxious about her father's sickness. As she sat at the bay window pulling together her strips of wood for her baskets, she heard a loud thud on the roof of the house, like a large stick of wood had been dropped from the sky. It rolled off the roof. She took the lamp and rushed out to find out what had fallen but found nothing to account for the noise—no sticks [that would account for] the sound. She shuddered as she realized that this was a forerunner—a sign of the impending death of her father. In Mi'kmaq these sign are known as amulsiktmat. When her Uncle Simon arrived that evening to find out if there had been any news, she decided not to tell him of the forerunner. Uncle Simon was well-known in the community; he was the [person] who went from house to house sharing the community news. He had not yet heard anything and she dared not share this fear and sign with him.

The next morning as she was cleaning the house, she saw from the window her grandfather Pie'l Sosep, and Big Mali, coming down the road. She rushed out in panic as to the news they might bring. "You are scaring me," she told them in Mi'kmaq. "What has happened?" "Nothing," they said, until they could get nearer and could help her gently take the news of her father's death. Her mother was forty-one and she was twenty-two years old. Her brother Mattie was still in the woods working and the men went out to find him to tell him about his father's death.

Not long after the death of her father, Annie's mother became ill. "Women's troubles," she put it. She had her period for seven years on a constant basis. The doctor insisted on a hysterectomy, but she had no trust in doctors since they had misdiagnosed Annie's father, and Harriet saw this as their killing her husband. She slowly withered by the loss of blood and the sickness, which today Annie diagnoses as cancer. For each day for two weeks she lay in her bed upstairs sick. Each morning Harriet called on her daughter to bring fresh water so that she could privately wash herself. Her daughter Annie obliged her. She washed herself and dressed herself

171

even to the last day. On that day she called for her water and washcloth and towel. Everyone left the room while she washed herself, and then she asked for her white nightgown. Later that same day she died.

Harriet was disillusioned with modern medicine and never sought modern medicine to help her, just Indian herbal medicine. Harriet knew she had to take care of her family as best she could. And when she died, she left Annie and Mattie to care for each other. Mattie continued the work and care of the household as man-head of the family. He worked in the woods, brought home lumber for baskets, and did the errands as were required of him. Annie worked hard, too, and took to manly tasks when it was required since there were only the two children. But she was more of a "tomboy" anyway, older than brother Matthew, and enjoyed playing ball, did heavy work, and could wrestle any boy who wanted to take her on. Her father had shown her and Mattie how to box and her arm muscles were strong from her pounding the boxing target or her brother Mattie or lugging buckets of water from the stream.

Annie knew hard work all her life, not for just her family but for others as well. The early years were hard on women and men and much credence was given to sharing and caring for each other in the large extended Mi'kmaq family. They helped others as was their custom and tradition. When Annie Cremo, Simon's wife and Annie's uncle's wife, became pregnant as she often was, Annie Lewis was sent by her mother to help her out. While Annie Cremo rocked in the rocking chair and spit chewing tobacco into the small opening on the front of the stove, Annie Lewis went down on her hands and knees and scrubbed the wood floorboards till they were nearly white again. She would be sent down time after time as was needed to help out her uncle and his wife.

Annie had a lot of friends and enjoyed visiting with her friends. The reserve was not large but walking from house to house at a great distance from one another often required people to find a place to sleep for the night and then head home in the morning. She often visited and slept over at her friend's house.

Young girls often did silly fun things. One night after Maltikle'wimk, or Ash Wednesday, Annie and her friends Annietina and Leste'l ate salted pancakes. They then went to bed and, as was required, they could not speak to each other until morning when they would tell their dreams. Their dream should foretell who they would marry and would prophesize the life they would have by the man who would give them a drink and by the kind of cup used to give her a drink. If it was a cup of fine china they would have a good prosperous life. If the cup was broken or chipped, they would lead a troubled, poor life.

Leste'l wanted to play, not sleep, but the girls kicked her to tell her to

172

go to sleep since they were not allowed to talk. In the morning
when they woke, Annie's mother
asked what she dreamed. "Nothing," she lied. Later when she
was with her friends she relayed
her dream. How crazy it was! The
others reported having no dream,
but Annie dreamed that her brother Mattie's best friend, John Battiste, had given her a drink. And
the cup—it was made of birch-
bark, rolled up in a cone. John
Battiste was a young boy of elev-
en or twelve at the time, much
younger than Annie, and the
thought was too funny and ridicu-
lous to imagine!

Annie had several boyfriends
in her time, but probably not one
more patient than Richard Nevins
who courted her for over five
years. Often he asked her to mar-

John and Annie in Houlton, Maine, 1953

ry him, but Annie at the age of fifteen said she was too young and had to
wait till she was eighteen. At eighteen again he asked for her to marry
him. She again said she was too young and when she was twenty-one, he
again asked and she said no. Finally, realizing that this young woman had
no plans for marriage, he told her that he had to find a wife as he was getting on in age too. They parted and soon after he found a new girlfriend
and they were married.

Annie's brother Mattie was married in 1938 to Martha Paul. He was
twenty-five years old. Martha was seventeen. One year later in 1939, Annie's mother Harriet Lewis died. Annie Lewis continued to live with her
brother and his new wife and their young daughter in the little house that
their father had fixed up.

In 1941, Annie had her first experience with sex, an event that led to
the conception and birth of her daughter Marie Eleanor. Her boyfriend at
the time left soon afterward and joined the service and was sent overseas.
When he saved a young man's life in Holland, the family offered one of
the daughters as a gift for the son's life. And he came home with a Dutch
bride.

One evening in 1943, Annie was walking down the old road of Chapel

173

Island toward the wharf during the annual mission. She met up with Mattie's old friend John Battiste who asked her if she had a date that night. Coyly, she answered no and [he] began walking with her. Such was the beginning of their romance, and that November 26th, they were married. Their only son was born on June 27, 1944, named and registered Douglas at birth, a name Annie always liked. When he was brought home, her sister-in-law and father John took him to be baptized at the nearby church. Children were baptized early in case of sickness. When they returned, Annie was informed that the baby was baptized Thomas Leo, Thomas after John's father and Leo after the priest who said that that would make him a good boy.

Centralization was a period that began in the early '40s, when the federal government decided to move all the Indians within Nova Scotia from their various locations to two locations—Eskasoni and Shubenacadie—in order to administer their own programs more efficiently. Not many Mi'kmaq could be persuaded to move from their family homelands, their farms and cleared lots, and their houses. So the governments (used) various appeal strategies on them. Some communities lost their church, or the government officials would threaten the people with loss of provisions, schooling, or total disenfranchisement if they did not move. People were being "urged" to go to Eskasoni. Tearing down the only school in the community of Barra Head was one of the means of motivating them to leave.

John and Annie lived with Mattie and Martha for a short time, but the house was small for two growing families. So John bought the lumber from the schoolhouse that was torn down during centralization for five dollars, and built his house. His father had a horse, and they dragged the lumber to the spot where they built the house near his father's house. Later that house would be sold and moved where it still stands behind Martin MacNeil's store on the shore side of Soldier's Cove. This house they sold for seventy-five dollars when John was sick and the family had to move to Eskasoni.

John had a mastoid behind his ear and was very sick. The nurse took him back and forth from Sydney by car for hospital and doctor care. This became very expensive as they couldn't afford a car and a bus was too expensive. They resolved that they had to move to Eskasoni where he could get treated by the doctor there. But first there was the operation. John had a large operation that nearly killed him. He missed the annual mission that year in 1947. Two days after arriving home from the hospital, John and Annie moved to Eskasoni with their three children—Marie Eleanor and Thomas Leo, and Geraldine Leona who was just ten days old.

John and Annie lived one year in Eskasoni. Annie's cousin Roddie

174

Gould invited them to live with him since he was not married yet and was living alone since his brother John had died. The Goulds were most well-off back then. Roddie's house was typical of the day: two-story house with a polished floor. It had been his parents' house, probably built originally by the government funds. There were three bedrooms upstairs; downstairs: a kitchen, dining room, living room, and hallway. The family also had a store when Roddie's father Simon Gould was well. Later Simon's widow remarried widower Thomas Battiste, John Battiste's father, and moved to Barra Head.

While in Eskasoni, John Battiste cut "props" or pulp wood in the woods. He and Roddie went together every day to the woods to saw trees down. Most of the men at this time did this kind of work to earn money. Other people had cows, chickens, horses, fished, and hunted. Everyone worked. They planted potatoes and turnips in their gardens in the summer. They made baskets and went by train to various towns and villages to sell them. They made axe handles, using the crude equipment that they made. Things didn't cost much and one dollar went a long way.

Women worked at home raising and caring for their families, while other women did domestic housecleaning in local non-Indian homes. They made baskets, peddled them door-to-door, bought cloth and made clothes, picked berries and made lots of pies and cakes with them. Without a freezer and with large families, they never saved the berries or canned them but ate and shared their abundance with others. And there were always [lots] of people to help each other care for their kids when one had to go anywhere.

When anyone got married, they usually made a log cabin or shanty for the newlyweds. It helped, especially since Mother's philosophy was no two women can get along in the same house. She had learned this when Mattie had come home with his wife. Martha and Annie did not see eye-to-eye on a lot of things.

On the reserve in Eskasoni was a big government store. Anyone who needed anything went to the store and charged their goods. The store was stocked by government monies to the Mi'kmaq people, but the agents sold the provisions to the Mi'kmaq and many agents, it was [said], pocketed the profits on the money sent to the Indians.

At one point John and Annie owed so much at the store that they felt they could never catch up. John decided there was only one thing to do. He would have to go to Maine to work. Annie had heard terrible stories of men leaving their wives and living with unattached women in the camps there. The prospect and rumoured stories convinced Annie that she would have to go with her husband. At first this thought did not sit well with John. How was he going to take care of children there? Where were they going to live? And the oldest, Eleanor, was now seven years old. She had already started school. They would be living in shacks behind potato houses. How could they send her to school? She would need clothes and many things that they could not imagine getting easily, including transportation to school.

Annie talked these things over with the family, the extended family, and a solution was proposed. Why not send her to Shubenacadie to school? [The Indian Residential School at Shubenacadie, Nova Scotia.] It was reported to be a good school run by religious women who loved and cared for children. They fed them, clothed them, and there were lots of kids there now and it had served John's sisters when they were young. They all had attended from as early as 1931 and learned much from it. It was reported to be a good school and why not send her there? The fact that Eleanor would need religious training soon to get her first holy communion sealed the idea. They then packed a bag, dressed Marie Eleanor in her best dress, went by train to Shubenacadie, and turned Eleanor over to the nuns at the school at the age of seven. The nuns at the school were very kind to the new visitors and to their new student. The nuns assured Annie of everything, and said she could send letters and gifts and Eleanor would receive them.

John and Annie went to Maine with their other two children, Geraldine who was now thirteen months old and Thomas who was four years old. Annie wrote often to the school, and she received letters from the school nuns, reporting that Eleanor was happy, doing well, learning well, thanking her for the gifts she had sent. These personal messages assured Annie that all was well.

Martha, Mattie's wife, later told her differently. She urged her to go to the school and get Eleanor. Her own children were there, but Martha had gone to the school at the end of each year to get her kids and then brought them back in the fall. She reported to Annie that Eleanor was not being treated well, and that she was being spanked every day. She urged her, for Eleanor's sake, to go get the child.

After hearing this, it was not long before they readied themselves to go to Shubenacadie. John and Annie packed up all the children. Another child Marie Ann had been born and was nearly two years old. They arrived [after] a long car ride from Maine. They surprised the school authorities with their desire to take Eleanor and were required to wait a very long time. John said they probably had to give her a bath. When she finally came out some hours later, she looked very pretty in a yellow dress, and bow in her hair. The nuns apologized for the delay, telling her that Eleanor had been playing in puddles outside.

She got in the car, and her brothers and sisters just looked at her in

awe. But by the time they had reached the end of the road, John and Annie realized that Eleanor did not know what the word "stop" meant nor could she read it. She could not read anything. Her head was full of lice and she couldn't speak Mi'kmaq too well. She had been forbidden to use the only language she knew and beaten when she tried to speak. No letters or gifts were ever given to her, and in all those years she felt abandoned, desperate and unloved. The nuns punished her persistently for resisting in learning English or being out of line, in their view. So she lived with daily beatings, festering her anger, fear, and resentment.

It wasn't long, however, in the family that spoke only Mi'kmaq, that Eleanor began to speak Mi'kmaq again. She was ten years old. But the problem of reading required that she be put in the first grade with her younger brother Tom. Their first school was at Longfellow School, an experience that was not pleasant for the children. The white children abused Tom and Eleanor for being "Indian" and taunted them. They were frequently in fights, so Annie put them in the Catholic school, St. Mary's School, where they were assured that no one would be allowed to call the children names. Eleanor, who had been in First Grade, was promoted to Grade Two because she was too big for Grade One. From the beginning at St. Mary's, Eleanor hated the school and the nuns. She recalled her days at Shubie and never let her guard down. She had been beaten by the nuns almost every day for minor infractions as a young child who knew no love during those three years. Eleanor had a difficult time throughout the years at this school in Houlton [Maine] because it was [run] by nuns. Finally, after much turmoil and troubled years she completed grade eight at the age of sixteen. The nuns tried to be understanding, but they had their rules, which for Eleanor were meant to be broken or to be defiantly ignored.

When Annie and John left Eskasoni [for] Linneus, Maine, they had taken very little except bare essentials, clothing, and some cooking goods. They knew they would be camping out so the bare minimum would be required. Their first house was a camp belonging to Irving Henderson. John fixed up the camp and put an addition on it to fit the growing family. John worked in the potato house for five dollars a day. The salary was so little, it hardly provided for the growing family. So John went looking for another job and found a road-paving job that offered fifteen to twenty dollars a day. Irving Henderson was not pleased with this and demanded that John take his family elsewhere.

Annie knew that this move would require her to go home. [When] she explained to her new friend Harriet Bither about her dilemma and having to return to Canada, Harriet offered them her own big farmhouse with two floor levels. It was old and cold in the winter, but it could offer them a place until they found a better place. They would only have to pay ten dollars a month rent. The house had a stove and electricity for the first time. John bought a wringer washing machine and they lived there until it started to get cold. The house was very cold, so they moved next to a house in Linneus, Mrs. Libby's house.

Harriet Bither had no children and frequently visited Annie in her camp and urged Annie to bring the children to her big house. She was a kind woman who loved children but had none of her own. When Annie became pregnant again in 1949, Harriet helped with caring for the children and gave Annie a baby shower with Harriet's friends to help her out. When Annie returned from the hospital with a new baby girl, Mrs. Bither was thrilled to greet them. The baby was a light-complexioned girl with light-coloured hair. Harriet looked at Annie's life of poverty and, being childless, she asked Annie if she might [have] this new baby. Annie was indignant. She might be poor, but she would never give her child. But she did allow Harriet to name the child, who was called Marie Ann after her niece who was named Ann Marie.

In Linneus, the Battiste family lived in a little bungalow of two bedrooms, kitchen, and sun porch. In 1952, when Annie and John had gone to town and Eleanor was home babysitting the two siblings, a fire started in the home. Eleanor was eleven years old. She got the two girls out and they stood holding a broom and basket of clothes while the house billowed with smoke. Marie was three years old and Geraldine five.

Knowing that on Saturday afternoons Tom was taken to the movies by his parents, Eleanor told one of the neighbours to [go get them]. Annie and John Battiste were informed by phone that their house was on fire. Annie asked about the children, but the caller did not have the information. When they arrived, they ran to the firemen and asked about the chil-

John Battiste in uniform. Annie with a brother-in-law, and her children:
Tommy, Eleanor, Marie, Geraldine.

dren. No one knew of any children. Complete desolation weakened Annie to tears and fear. But a neighbour soon found her to comfort her with the news [that] the children were all safe at his farmhouse nearby. The December cold did not seem so bad after that.

The town of Houlton was alerted to the news of a family in need whose house had burned and all their goods were lost. Since Christmas was fast approaching, the town's people prepared a hasty charity drive to help this family through their difficulties. They asked for anything anyone had to give. One good neighbour offered one month rent-free to live in his Nickerson Lake cottage and twenty dollars a month after that. And a truckful of goods came, including toys for all the children. The Christmas was the best they had had so far, with food, warmth, and toys.

Annie and John stayed here through two winters. Eleanor and Thomas went to Longfellow School in Houlton by bus. But Annie and John decided to move to Houlton so that they could get the religious training needed for the children.

While in the States, Annie and John continued to speak Mi'kmaq, particularly since Annie could speak very little English. She spoke in Mi'kmaq exclusively to the children. While in their Mi'kmaq community, Eleanor and Tom both learned to speak Mi'kmaq well; only when they moved and found English-speaking children with whom they played did they speak English. As the children grew up, the children had only their mother to speak Mi'kmaq with. This did not foster fluency in Mi'kmaq. As the children began switching from Mi'kmaq to English, John demanded that they either speak Mi'kmaq or English. The very sound of switching back and forth from the two languages grated on him. So when the last two girls were born and lived most of their years in Maine, they used English as did Tom and Eleanor. They always understood Mi'kmaq but rarely had a chance to use it to attain fluency, so they spoke English. Later, [when] they returned to the Mi'kmaq community, Eleanor and Tom picked up the Mi'kmaq language with some ease while Marie and Gerry struggled with learning to speak their native language.

A search for apartments found a two-story grey duplex on 122 Military Street owned by Mrs. Hannigan near the Catholic church. This family home was the home where the children lived for the better part of their childhood. They lived here for over ten years. It was an old house with three rooms downstairs and three rooms upstairs. A toilet was positioned in the back room although a blanket divider made it also another bedroom. A front-room stove and a back-kitchen stove were the only means of heat for the whole house. But this house had indoor plumbing, albeit only cold water; a flushing toilet in the house was great progress. The rooms were large, but it was still small for the family of six. Tom either got the toilet room or the hallway during those years, while the three girls slept together in twin beds. The house was old and the linoleum showed its wear, but the family frequently papered, painted and fixed it up as Annie tried to make this old house warm and accommodating.

On the other side of the duplex house lived the large family of Ruth and Woodrow Estabrook. In the house next to the duplex was a brown house rented by a Maliseet woman Eleanor Brooks. During those years John worked periodically as a labourer at the new St. Mary's Church in Houlton or on road construction building the then major highway. He worked hard in those jobs and when work was unavailable he depended on the money brought in by his wife who worked as a domestic cleaner in local white homes and various odd jobs. Annie worked hard doing housecleaning in several more well-off women's houses although made very little, only three dollars a day, but it bought the goods for the day and sometimes other things.

Many times the basic necessities of food and clothes were scarce, and Annie had to go to the town office where she asked for public assistance. Many times she was refused, but when she told her story of woe and tears came, she would be given a food order or clothing order for the family children. This dehumanizing act of begging for food or clothes was trying on Annie as was her husband's growing drinking pattern.

John was a social fellow who was called upon often to share his fiddle at weddings. An affable friendly fellow, John was a teasing and happy man, always kind with a warm smile. Everybody liked "Big John" who was a wide-shouldered tall man with strong features. No one cared to tangle with this guy, so they shared their drink with him and he shared his fiddle, his smile, and danced and partied. Unfortunately, he usually came home drunk. These events increased over the years, but when he got drunk he fell asleep, a fairly harmless pastime, it seemed. For years it did seem harmless, but as the years passed, John's drinking increased from weekend drinking to daily drinking. He would find himself without employment and a happy family. His needs of alcohol and the little money they had were often battled out, until Annie began hiding from him when he got drunk. Annie spent hours in closets, under beds, in the pantry, waiting until he fell asleep.

Annie left John several times during his drinking years to scare him into sobriety, and sometimes he would be forced into stopping, but each time he would begin drinking after a few months. Recognizing that she had limited economic skills and four children who needed her, Annie did little except work steadily where she could and raise the children with good Mi'kmaq values, with understanding of what was right and wrong, and try to offer them as good a life as was possible for poor people.

Finally when her youngest daughter Marie Ann grew up and went to college, and her son Tom had been drafted in the army and her daughter Geraldine graduated from high school and got a job in the bank and found her own apartment, Annie sought to find a life on her own, leaving John to find his own way. She found an ad in the paper for a live-in housekeeper in Revere, Massachusetts, for priests. She answered the ad, gave her references, and left for Revere. Her job was much like the others she had had, but different in many ways, too. The priests were Italian and enjoyed Italian cooking with which Annie was unfamiliar. Laura, the other housekeeper, offered her support teaching her how to make Italian sauces, pasta, and various Italian recipes. Laura did the meal planning, the food shopping, the laundry, and the household work. Annie lived at the house in her own room near the kitchen, doing the cooking and cleaning the offices and the kitchen and dining room.

The Italian priests were very formal at their meals, having several courses at the main meal, and definite patterns of what they liked. They never ate leftovers, and only pie on Saturdays. Annie observed that they wasted a lot of food, yet they would not allow her to feed any vagrants who came to the house asking for food. When she had worked for the priests in Houlton, many Indians would come to the house asking for food or money. She obliged always with a little food and more often gave some of her own money to them. In Revere, the priests discouraged her from doing this. However, Annie often found herself in the position of having to decide to whom she should give something. If the person was Native, most often she gave her own money and a small bag of food that she was

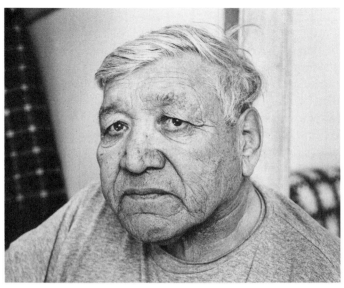

sure the priests would never miss.

Annie's daughter Eleanor had married a young man in Boston, Billy Mitchell, and had a second-story apartment in Dorchester, Mass. On her days off Annie went to Eleanor's where they visited, shopped, or went for rides. About five months later Geraldine called to ask her mother to take John away from Houlton. He had returned from Canada, was living in cars and potato houses, and sometimes came drunk to his daughter's apartment, where he ate all her goods and passed out. She asked her mother to get an apartment and take him home. Feeling sorry for both her daughter and her husband, Annie met John at the bus station and they took the apartment above daughter Eleanor and Billy.

Annie worked in Revere for ten months when one day while babysitting at her daughter's she stepped off the chair wrong and broke her ankle. She went to Eleanor's to recuperate for three weeks. When she went back to work her foot swelled up and she found it impossible to continue her work. She then quit her job and went home. John worked here and there, but never in a steady job.

Eleanor's husband Billy was an astute man who realized that Annie should have had disability insurance while she was recuperating; however, the priest had paid her without having given her any benefits such as unemployment insurance and income tax. Their return to talk to the priest about Internal Revenue and employment benefits ended in a yelling match and the end of Annie's contact with the priests. Eventually, Annie received a check from the priest for the amount he should have put to her unemployment insurance benefits, which Billy insisted was hers and need not be turned over to taxation.

John had taken all their worldly goods to Canada, which he stored in the basement of his sister Isabel's house. Some items he sold for needed living money while he was there. Meanwhile, he pushed for a house for himself and his family who, he assured the band government, would return as soon as it was built.

Meanwhile Annie found a job within walking distance of Minot Street at the Keystone Company, a factory that supposedly made cameras but behind doors actually were making missiles and bomb parts for the war in Vietnam. Annie worked all day and returned home at four p.m. John tried to find various kinds of odd jobs in the Boston area, but instead found more people to drink with and more places to drink. It was not long before the patterns began again of his drinking and harassing her for money for drink.

She found several ways to cope with this. Sometimes she stayed with her daughter downstairs, or she would take the buses to visit various friends in Boston. There were more places to go in Boston, to run away from John until he sobered up and she would go home again. Her daughter Marie had transferred to a university in Farmington, Maine, and was home frequently to help her cope with the weeks she was in misery. Annie looked forward to her daughter's coming home and she cooked her favourite meals of beans and fresh bread. And when Marie had a vacation, she cooked and cleaned and made the house agreeable when her mother came home from work. They shopped and visited and spent as much time together as they could.

Annie and John lived in Boston for four or five years in the third floor apartment on Minot Street in Dorchester. Finally John was notified that his bid for a house on the reserve in Barra Head was approved and was being built, so they packed up all their worldly possessions and headed north in summer of 1974. Marie had graduated with a master's degree in education from Harvard Graduate School of Education and she had decided to move to California with her life partner James Youngblood Henderson who had received an offer to teach at the University of California, Berkeley, after graduating from Harvard Law School.

When they returned to Chapel Island reserve, John and Annie found their house was just a shell, but it did have electricity and plumbing. It served their needs as their home while they worked each day on the house.

Annie & John Battiste's daughter, Dr. Marie Battiste

The reserve sent L.I.P. (Labour Initiative Program) workers from the reserve to their house each day, but since they were just carpenter trainees, they lacked skill, initiative or attention to their work. They arrived late each day, ate meals with Annie and John, sat around having tea and watching each other work, and finally left early or did not show up after payday for several days. Finally after several weeks, John began the work himself, doing all the finishing work in his house, and completed the house with his talents and his own funds.

The house was finally finished. John and Annie Battiste finally had returned to their "home" again among their family and friends after spending twenty-five years in the States. Solidified by their love of each other, hardened by their poverty and hard times, softened by children and grandchildren, Annie and John lived many years after in their comfortable home in Chapel Island.

Our thanks to the Battiste family for sharing their story. Regarding the children: Eleanor worked in Boston, married, and raised three boys, and is now living with her mother Annie in Chapel Island. Tommy graduated with an M.B.A. from Harvard, served in Vietnam, and is now the executive director of the North American Indian Centre in Boston. Geraldine is a banking executive in Portland, Maine. Marie got her M.A. in Education from Harvard, and her Ph.D. at Stanford. She recently finished work as curriculum coordinator with the Eskasoni School Board, and is now on the faculty of the University of Saskatchewan.

John Battiste was born October 1, 1918, at Barra Head. He married Annie Lewis on November 26, 1943, at St. Peters. He died April 18, 1990.

Horses in the Coal Mines

Patrick McNeil: I was born in Glace Bay, and of course I resided here all my life. I spent most of my life working around horses—the Veterinary Horse Hospital in the Sterling Yard. I had done some other local work for the coal company, like teaming. That would be the construction, driving horse and wagon, delivering material, before the trucks really came in. They had horses on the surface doing the work. I never worked in the mine, any more than I went down in the mine on some business connected with horses. And I was never a veterinarian. I was just an

assistant. I worked with Dr. John L. Sullivan, the first veterinarian. (*No special training?*) When you work with a vet, you learn from day to day what he's doing, and you're assisting him, and you get a pretty fair knowledge, like any other job.

If he was doing any operating or any work on a horse, I was there with the instruments, getting them prepared, and prepared the animal for him so he'd just come in and do his work. And if he was out of town, and minor things, I would do it myself. And he would prescribe treatment for this horse—"We'll do this for him this day," and that—well, I would go ahead after and do that work.

Most of the accidents they were having in the mines, the horse would run into a low boom. The horse was too high or he didn't put his head down. Well, he would scruff the top of his head, it would like scalp him. When that horse would come in, that piece of flesh would be hanging like a flap over the top of his head. Well, that would have to be removed.

185

Sometimes that would be scraped right to the bone. I saw Dr. Sullivan put a plate in there one time, and it covered right over. It was remarkable how the head of a horse seemed to heal much quicker than any other part. It was very, very interesting work.

And then, the top of the withers—that's like at your shoulder bones—call it the withers. In a low place—a big horse, they shouldn't go into a low place, fault of the mine management sometimes, they wouldn't brush the mine—and this horse would jam in there. Be going in and out, and the top of the withers would get festered—we used to call it a fistula withers. The infection would go down in between the two shoulder blades. If we would get the horse out of the mine in time, we could treat it. But if it got down too far in between the shoulder blades, it was just next to impossible.

(*How would you treat something like that?*) We used to get a lot of drugs from different veterinary pharmacies through Canada. I remember one time we got a solution, and you'd inject it in with a syringe. We'd open a hole and put it in. And you'd have to wear gloves—the stuff would burn the hands off you. Used to drive the horse foolish. There was no way to drain that out. After one or two treatments, the horse would go foolish, see you coming near him—it was that sore, painful. And you'd have to vaseline all where that stuff would overflow, because it would take the hide right off the horse. Well, that was too drastic a treatment. It was unsuccessful.

So eventually we came across some idea of trying kerosene oil—that's coal oil—and that proved very, very successful. It cured quite a few horses that otherwise we were condemning. Just a simple thing with a syringe. Put that in but once a day, and it seemed to absorb all that pus and discharge. We had very good luck on that.

Sometimes they'd get burned with that copperous water in the pit—it'd just take the hide right off of them. It's a reddish water comes out of the coal, I guess. It's the colour of copper. And that would burn in around the fetlocks, the feet, you know. We had a preparation over there. We'd clip off the hair. Oh, it would smell terrible when they got burned up with that; it would just peal the flesh right off. And with doctoring and that with the different medicines we had, we used to get them dried up and healed, and they'd go back to work.

Number 2 mine was a mine where they were very often getting lockjaw, that's tetanus. They say a horse can get that with a little scratch that you don't see. This germ gets into it, and the horse stiffens right up. His tail will come out straight. His head stiffens right up, and his jaws lock, and all the breathing he does is just through his teeth. His nostrils are protruding, trying to gasp for air, and he'll stiffen right up. We did get some

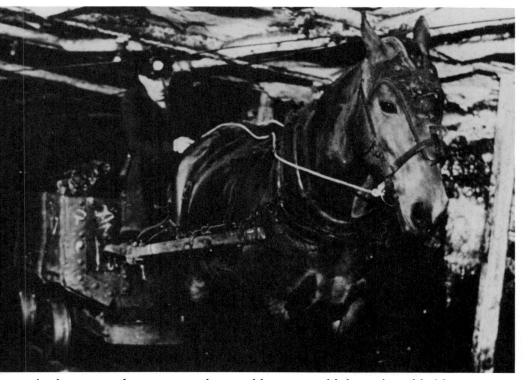

in the very early stages—a sharp stableman would detect it and he'd get the horse to the surface right away. In Dr. MacIsaac's time we treated a few of them that we got in the early stages. But Dr. Sullivan would destroy the horse right away. He said that breathing it, you could possibly catch that germ. He wouldn't let you stand in front of them. He used to take them out right away and shoot them.

So I got looking in the magazines and I saw where there was an antitoxin to prevent lockjaw. What we were using was a cure—but not a preventive. So we got this preventive serum. And we went to Number 2 colliery, and we inoculated all the horses in that mine. There were around two hundred horses at that time. We gave them an injection. We couldn't do it in a night, to get around, so much travelling too. Do a section one night— maybe a third of the colliery. And four days after, we went back and gave them the second. And you know what? They never had a lockjaw case up until the colliery closed. It was something that saved a lot of horses. There was always a fear, you know, that if a miner would get it, maybe the miners wouldn't work, they'd be that scared of it. So it was very lucky there were never any humans got it.

I would like to tell you a little more about those two veterinaries that I worked under—the late Dr John L. Sullivan, he came with the company around 1920, and Dr. MacIsaac. Before Dr. Sullivan's time there was a Dr. Jakeman. At that time the company didn't have as many horses. He'd treat the horses that came out of the mine, but there were a lot of cattle in those days, so he was out on the road. He was working for the company, and he was allowed to go out. If you had a sick cow or some other animal, he would treat it, which was very good for the public, you know. But when Dr. Sullivan came it was strictly coal company business, company horses. There was no outside practice. So he devoted all his time to the betterment of horses.

One of the best things done was, he built a horse hospital out in the Sterling Yard. And that hospital had an operating table. It was a piece of heavy hardwood, and he would tip it up straight. Then you put the horse alongside of it, and there were straps to go on the two legs, and the two girths would go around his body and draw him right in tight to the table. And then the table'd crank down, and you had him right on the table in about five minutes. And then he'd operate. Sometimes it'd be broken bones, a deep abscess that he couldn't get otherwise. They'd chloroform the horse. It was very humane.

They had a way one time, when a horse had a broken leg in the mine, they'd destroy him. Because a horse with a broken leg is no more good to the company, he's no good to anyone. The head stableman would destroy that horse. The way they were doing it, they were killing them with the axe, pounding in the head, knocking them out. So Dr. Sullivan got all the stablemen together one day. There was a horse in the hospital that was going to be destroyed. He was incurable for some reason or other, worn out, general debility. He showed them how to destroy a horse. You'd put your hand up the rectum with a knife between your fingers. And there's a big vein runs right along the inside, and you just give it a good cut. There'd be no blood would come out of the horse. He would bleed internally, and he'd just go out in a faint. Perhaps three or four minutes, and he'd drop right out. No suffering or anything. That was quite a thing, helping the horse.

And how they get a broken leg, mostly, would be—the coal was hauled on rails, the box was on rails. Well, sometimes the management in a hurry to get the coal out, they wouldn't ballast those tracks. The horse would be tramping through those sleepers, sleeper holes, and they'd get their foot caught. (*The sleepers are the blocks going across, and the rails sit on the sleepers?*) That's right. They'd just ballast it a little, but it's quite often they didn't make it smooth for the horse. And the horse's feet were going down in that, maybe a foot down, or six or eight inches, and the feet would get caught and the box would come on top and he'd break a leg. And then there were steep headways. Sometimes the driver wouldn't put enough sprags in, or the sprags wouldn't hold. The horse was kind of light, not heavy enough, and the box would come down onto him, push him down the grade, and he would turn off into the timber—it's only a

narrow space they were travelling—break his neck. Well, a horse would have to be destroyed right there.

And then Dr. Sullivan had an ambulance made, over the yard there. It was sloven, they call them; you know, a low axle, drop axle, a low heavy wooden structure. And it was drawn by two horses. Now if there was a horse injured in the mine and it was very lame or crippled up, the ambulance would be at the pithead when they'd get him to the surface, and take him into the veterinary hospital. There were a lot of horses came in that otherwise wouldn't have got in. And they had a peculiar thing—at the back of the hospital there was a big smokestack from some old colliery back of the Sterling Mine. And way back in the years, it was closed. They left the big flue up and they built an incinerator there, and any horses that were destroyed or died, they would just take them down there and hoisted up and put in this incinerator and burned. There was no need of digging holes and burying them out in the ground; just burn them right up and there'd only be an ash left. They'd burn them with old wood.

But they never took a horse's life if he would be useful to someone. If a horse kicked a fellow, he was chased out of the mine right away—they wouldn't have a horse who kicked. Now that horse would come to the surface, and we'd sell him probably to a farmer or any person buying, and that horse would never lift a leg. Whether the driver would be tormenting that horse, or what. Well, they were pretty strict on safety first in the mine, you know, there were so many people getting compensation. Get a little bump on the leg, or—well, some of them'd get hurt pretty bad, probably, from a bad horse. We always had a ready market for horses. Young fellows were always looking for a wild horse, mostly, so that they could fool around with him, tame him down. And there were a lot of horse traders in those days, Sydney and Waterford and everywhere. They were at the door over there at the hospital every day, a gang of them looking for horses. There was no problem to sell them, you know, and they would get them fairly reasonably.

As the years were going on, the mines were expanding and there were more men getting hired on, more coal production—and that increased the horses. In 1925, that was the year of the big strike, the coal company took all the horses out of the mine—they were digging in for a long strike. They loaded them in boxcars and they took them into Sydney, into the old fertilizer place there at Ashby. It's not going now. The steel company was down flat at the time, and there was a big stable down there. We had over seven hundred horses—ponies and horses. The ponies we used for the Emery seams. They were low seams, about two feet, probably three feet at the most. When the miner was loading coal, he was practically on his knees; he had kneepads on. And there was just barely enough room to get the coal in between the roof and the top of the box. And the little pony had to haul those boxes that were over about a ton. A pony is much stronger than a horse, in proportion, and a little longer than a horse. The larger seams now, they could take a five-foot horse or a little better. But a pony was only twelve hands—about three feet—to the shoulder. That's where they measure them, on the withers. And that's how they bought them, by the hands. The different collieries wanted so many horses a certain height for different places.

In those days, the horses never came out of the mine. A horse went down in the mine and stayed there year in and year out, if he lasted that long. And never saw daylight till back, I guess, in the '40s. It was sometime around that. When the miners started getting vacations, they started taking the horses up. And the horses really enjoyed it when they'd get in the fields, big pasture there. As soon as they'd hit that field when they came out of the pit, you could see them race from one end to the other and kicking their heels in the air. Really, they enjoyed it. They'd be a little, likely, snowblind when they'd come out at first, from being in the dark so long. But they wouldn't be long when they'd adapt to the daylight. I remember lots of times they'd be coming out of the pit, and there'd be a pud-

dle—they'd jump—they're not used to seeing that, you know, a little puddle on the road. That is, from the colliery to the pasture. They're skittish, because in the pit all they'd see was what was ahead of them. But they managed very well.

Bert Gouthro, Glace Bay: The men's livelihood depended on them—certainly it did—to haul their coal. That's all I could say the horse did, was just haul the coal. Oh, probably they would be hauling stone or something else, when they would be brushing—but mostly coal.

I was twenty-seven years of age when I went to

the pit. And at that time, yes, I was driving. Driving means hauling the coal from the face. The miners loaded it. You hooked your horse on and hauled it out to the landing, where the trip hauled it up the deep. You took your empty boxes and the chain dropped them in off the landing, off the deep. You'd hook onto the horse and perhaps you might have 1500 feet of a haul. You'd perhaps have two pair of men or maybe three pair of men that would be filling your boxes. They were the miners, loading it. Sometimes the driver, if his men loaded enough coal and the haul was long, would get the high rate. After 1500 feet, you got 15¢ a ton or 17¢ a ton for hauling it. I didn't qualify for the high rate until I was at least 1500 feet in. After 1000 feet you'd get what they called the middle rate. This was contract driving, travelling on rails, underground.

Sometimes the horses would have to work double shifts. Perhaps they'd work dayshift, then work nightshift. Sometimes the coal company was criticized for people working their horses double shift. But it's not as bad as it sounds. Because by the time the driver would get to the stable to get his horse out, it'd be probably 7:30 in the morning; and he'd probably have to walk half a mile or three quarters of a mile to where his horse was working. And probably his men would get done early and the horse went back in the stable again at one o'clock. And then the night shift wouldn't come for him until maybe four-thirty or five o'clock. So he actually wasn't working a real long day. See, he worked a spell in the morning and he had a good rest. Take him to the stable and give him his bellyful of grub. They probably took him out again in the evening. But they didn't do that continuously. If they were short of horses or something, probably the horse would have to take his turn working a double shift.

I often used to tell them, put up an argument that lots of horses working on a farm—a farmer's got to make hay while the sun shines. He gets out early in the morning, and probably that horse will be going till damn near dark that night. And probably got very little time for to eat his dinner. They worked long days too, sometimes. Of course then there'd be probably months in the wintertime when the farm horse wouldn't do anything. (*And that's hard on the horse, too.*) That's right. It's much better for them to be working continuously, sure.

I never had any bad accident, no. But the years I was head stableman, we had a lot of them. And that was my job, would be to destroy them. If they broke their leg or anything, you know. It happened quite frequently…. Sometimes you had a lot of drivers that were inexperienced themselves, and didn't realize what could happen. (*Did you ever have them, that miners just didn't care?*) Well, I mean, what the hell, sure.

I went down one night—they called me from home here to go out—there was a big gray horse there. A fellow who drove him left the horse on

191

the empty road. I know he did. I found out afterwards. When I went down, the horse was standing there with his leg broke off, between his fetlock and his knee. The trip came in and hit him. See, the driver left him on what's called the lower road, where the trip came in. The chain runner from the outside end, he shifted the switch. The horse, it's got to run in pretty snappy, because it drags the rope, it's fastened on to it and drags in. The trip went in a little bit farther than usual, and that horse was left standing in the dark. And of course, he couldn't see the trip coming. And he got it on the shins, bumper of the box, broke it. It was neglect, certainly. You weren't there to see what happened, and they would argue against it. Lots of time I saw that happened. But what could you do about it?

Archie MacDonald, Florence: I'll tell you a story about the horses. The horses in Florence colliery one time, and in most of the colllieries, were badly used. Now it wasn't that they were poorly fed or anything, but they were overworked. A good horse, she'd work on the dayshift. And the drivers were a contrary crowd, a lot of them, and they pretty well ran the pit. You couldn't get along without them. If they had dug their heels about something, well, they wouldn't go down; they'd stay on the surface and the pit would be idle. So they were having a problem with the horses. The good horses were overworked and the bad horses would be standing in. So the underground manager, he had a half-brother that was quite a tough character, but he loved horses, very fond of horses. He was what you might call in those days a barroom fighter—a big heavy, stocky fellow, as tall as you are, and heavier. Loved horses, and he hated the drivers. And I bet you the underground manager, his half-brother, appointed him as the road boss especially in charge of horses. And he wandered around the stables and looked over

all the horses. A horse that came in, the driver'd come with him, the way the law said; the contract said he had to take his horse in and secure him in the stable. He just didn't turn him loose, let him go in the stable. The horse would sense when he was getting handy the stable, and he'd start hurrying up, and the driver'd have to go along, take him in under control, and take his bridle off and the bit that was in his mouth, and the heavy leather piece over his head, where if he bumped his head he wouldn't knock his scalp off. It was a "cap" they called it.

In the afternoon and evening, when the horses would be coming in, this big husky fellow would watch them coming in, looking for any bruises or scrapes or anything like that. And if he did, he'd hold them up—"Just a minute, I want to have a look at that"—he'd hold them up—"How did this happen?" And the driver had to have a good reason for it, or the first thing he knew, the fellow'd have him by the throat and want to know how it happened. And he had to tell him. And there were none of the drivers tough enough to back this fellow up. And I bet you in three months, three months or less, the horses were in spic-and-span condition, no scrapes or bruises or anything like that, because they were afraid of this fellow. And they had good reason to be afraid of him, because when this fellow came, he said he hated drivers, especially a driver that was hard on his horse. That fellow, he had no quarter for them at all. He'd get him off that horse, or he had to start treating his horses better, or the other fellow'd go and beat him up. He'd do it. There'd be nobody around, and he'd get him in a corner of the stable and rough him up. So he knew he was up against his master then, the man that was looking after the horses. If he was taking a horse out, he was going to take it back in good shape. And it was a true story. That fellow lived to be an old man. He retired. But he loved horses. And he could not tolerate in any way, shape, or form a driver that abused his horse. Wouldn't put up with it. (*And he re-trained the drivers?*) He sure did. Nobody'd tackle a horse or damage a horse while this fellow was on.

Bert Gouthro: (*Bert, were some men, like yourself, close to their horses?*) Oh, very much so. Some of the drivers were, yeah. One particular case when I was driving, there was a bunch of new horses came down. And this old Mr. MacDonald—John Archie—who was a good friend of mine—he said to me this day, he said, "Bert, why don't you take one of those new horses in your section?" He said, "That mare you're getting," he said, "is getting old. You need a new horse, a young horse." He said, "There's a bay mare there, a little gray horse." So I said, "All right, I'll take him and I'll try him." So I took him in, and my God, I got attached to that little horse. He could pull like a little tractor. And he must have been about—I guess he was about five or six years old. And I took him to another section. I was what they call "hauling off from a chain." I'd haul three or four boxes at a time. And the overman used to come along and he'd say, "I'm going to watch this fellow, Bert, to see him start those four boxes coupled together." He'd get right down, and you'd see him feeling with his feet to get footing, you know. I'd just stand alongside of him, and he'd straighten out to get those four boxes moving. And the only thing I ever hit him with in my life was my glove. I'd take my glove off and I'd stand alongside of him and I'd hit him with my glove. The overman used to say to me, "Look, I never saw a horse that small do that fellow's load." Shortly after that, I went—we were running out a chain, I think—and somebody came up one evening and they told me the young fellow that had him had started down the headway with no sprags in and he broke his back. He did go to the side, he turned off, because he went over the brow of the grade, and he found out that he couldn't hold the box. So instead of crashing and going ahead of it—he would have crashed anyway—he turned sideways. And of course, he's hooked onto the box, see, and the box tipped him over, killed him. Even the loaders, the men that were loading for me, they felt bad about it. One man in particular, he met me the next day and he told me, "Boy," he said, "I came through the stable the other night," he said, "and I felt bad about your horse. He's in the stable there, and I don't think he's ever going to get better." Sure enough—he died the next day.

Oh yes, some of the drivers were very attached to their horses. And then some more of them—like everything else—you get those devil-may-care fellows who didn't give a damn.

Patrick McNeil: There was one time when they were losing a horse about every second day, the death rate was that high—four or five a week. They were buying about a carload of horses a month. At times, they were pushing for coal, great demand for coal, and the horse wasn't getting the attention in the mine. Like I said be-

fore about the tracks not ballasted, steep headways, and whatnot. And they were pushing a horse so much that he'd be gutted out—the horse would just be tired out, he'd be leg weary and stumble, and the box would go on top of him and kill him. And sometimes they were killed outright with the miners in a fall of coal. But it was very rare, hardly worthwhile mentioning it. Mostly the miners that got killed in the mine would be the man at the coal, the roof come in on him. The horses are generally on the landing, you know, waiting till there's enough boxes to haul.

But it was back in the '40s that the company started to mechanize the mines. That was great. New Waterford was the first district that went horseless. Then it gradually kept coming along, the different collieries. And then about around 1960 the last horse was out of the mine. And now there are none. They were weeding them down gradually. And it was a good thing, you know. Because it was a hard life for a horse. He was fed well and he was cared for, you might say. But when they hired a young fellow on for the pit, maybe he didn't know the front end of a horse from the back end. And that's the first job he got, was driving a horse. It was often said at the time, if they were as particular about the drivers as they were about the horses, the horses would have lasted longer and would have had a better life. A lot of accidents and maybe deaths were caused by inexperienced young fellows driving. There were lots of stories about brutality and that, but it was not much. It's a known fact—lots of times where a fellow didn't like the horse, then you'd pull the sprags out and let the box go on top of him, get clear of him. But you could never prove those things. Nobody would tell on anyone, you know, they belonged to a union and they'd stand by their member. Which is logical, I guess. But it's cruel, when you look back onto it.

Now, a good driver always looked for a horse that had some spunk about him, some temper, you know, that would be cranky and that. Because if he got a nice, pleasant easygoing horse, when that driver'd put his horse in the end of the shift, maybe some driver would come out and take that horse out and work him by night. Well then, when the driver would come out the next day, his horse would be tired and couldn't stand up to the work. Because they really worked hard. So that's why some of the good drivers looked for the horses that were cranky and that would give you a little bump. His horse would always be fresh.

I worked from, say, 1922 till the Veterinary Hospital closed. It closed in the early '60s. I took over when Dr. MacIsaac retired due to ill health in 1948. Of course, there weren't as many horses then. At that time when he left, there was a head stableman in Number 20—Jack Bennett—he took the buying part. And I did the treatment and selling them out, and looked after the records of them. And my hands were full enough with that. And then Jack Bennett got sick and couldn't work, so I had the buying and selling, the whole thing for a short time. (*So in the end you were the veterinarian?*) Well, I spent my life with it, you know, you might say, the better of my working days, but I was still only an assistant. But I carried on in the latter stages. (*You had no doctor with you in the last years?*) No, no. You know, when you spend time like that with two vets, you learn quite a bit in that line. It was very interesting work. I enjoyed every day of it.

(*And you told me it was a good healthy job.*) Yeah. When you go into a stable, did you ever notice, especially where there's horses in the morning and you open the door, you get the ammonia from the manure, it hits you right in the face. I knew a watchman wouldn't come into the stable, the ammonia, that the manure used to choke him off. But I heard several people say there's no healthier place you could work. And there's a man over there, not very far from here, he's 94, and he worked all his life as a stableman in a mine, and he's walking around, he's up in the country now in his bungalow. And he can walk to town. I know I had fairly good health through all the years I was with them. I think I got immune to diseases over there.

Bert Gouthro, with the last horse to work in a coal mine in North America

Willy Pat Fitzgerald:
"I want to know what's going on."

You know, there never was a storm, before or since, anything to compare with the great August Gale [1873]. I was married fifty-six years in August—and at the time I'm going to tell you about, I wasn't married. Father and I were in Little Bras d'Or in a vessel. And we were tied up at the live lobster factory wharf. They used to take lobsters in there and they'd spawn. When they'd grow up so much, they'd spill them out in the water. God, they had quite a set-up there once upon a time. Well, we were tied up at the hatchery wharf. We run in there in a north-easter. And the wind got so heavy that the vessel was tearing the wharf to pieces. So we let go from the wharf the next morning and we run up the harbour—bare poles, no sails on the vessel. And we had a 10-horsepower engine in her. And I had the engine going full speed astern. I believe she was making twenty-five miles an hour up the harbour before that north-easter. And we went up the harbour and there was a point came out this way, bucking in like that— there was a great cove in behind it—and father just doubled her in around

197

that point and stuck her bow in the bank. And I jumped out off of the bow-sprit and made a line fast to a tree, and Father tied it up aboard. And we just layed there against the bank. The water was deep right into the bank.

After awhile, there was an old man—well, he wasn't so terrible old. He was smart. And he came aboard. He was named Jesso or Jessome. He came down in the cabin. He and Father were talking. And he started telling about the August Gale. He rid the August Gale out in a 27-ton boat. And there was five sail of them, five vessels, fishing on a bank. The great August Gale sprung up and the other four vessels went down. He was the only one out of the five that survived. And he told Father he had nothing left, only the two masts. He said there wasn't enough canvas left on her to blow your nose. The booms and the gaffs, everything, were beat off of her. He had nothing but the two masts. But he didn't lose 'ere a man. And he rid the August Gale out.

My father was a boat builder. And he used to build vessels. Capt. J.J. Fitz-gerald, they called him. He built little schooners and he used to run them himself. Used to carry freight. Coastal schooners they called them. Ran to St. Paul's. Haul from Cape North to Sydney and back. Louisbourg and up the lakes. He used to build them out of what they called chopped timbers. Used to cut the wood crooked, like that stem I've got there. Look for the tree with a bend in it, and hew it. They used to put the frames of six-by-six—six inches thick, six inches wide—oh boy, that was an awful, awful size wood—in a vessel about sixty feet on top. The vessel would be all framed with that. And then planked with inch and three-quarter or two-inch hardwood plank. And spiked with galvanized spikes five inches long. Three-eighths square, not a round nail at all. Drive them into those hardwood frames with a big sledgehammer. I worked with Father back then, building them. I built two with him. And what I mostly build today, I learned it from Father.

Those big vessels, we'd cut every stick of it. And sawed the most of it with a whipsaw. Me and my brother were one whole day sawing oak—and the oak was four inches thick. And it had a little gradual sweep in it. And Father hewed it for a railing for a vessel. When the vessel would be built, there'd be what they called stanchions go in her on both sides, and this rail would go on top of those stanchions. He wanted this oak for that rail. Took it out and hewed it. And we had to whipsaw it the length of it. I think it was fifteen feet. He hewed it down to four and a half or five inches. One end to the other. Then he lined it, chalk line, one end to the other. Then went in an inch and a half and put another line. And after we sawed them out he laid them on their side on the top of these stanchions, and the sweep was in the stick—and it followed of the sweep that was in the side of the vessel. Fa-

Willy Pat with son Calvin and a clinker built boat he had just completed

ther had transoms for sawing—beams over a pit. Or sometimes we'd be sawing it in the woods somewhere. Then we'd limb down a tree, and we'd get two beams up using a tree and a post—so we'd have the beams even if we didn't have the pit. We shoved the stick up on the two beams with so much out over the end. And we started at the end and we sawed in.

One man would be on the ground—and that fellow on the bottom, that was me—have the whipsaw with the box on the end; and at the top of the saw there was an iron that ran down the blade and two bolts went through. Now my brother stood up on this log ahold of that top end, and I'd be down in the pit with the box on the lower end of the saw—and we used to swing her. When we swung her back she went up—and she never touched the stick when she went up. She only cut coming down. So when we'd saw, we'd both just lift it. Then coming down we'd drive her down, pushing into the wood. When one fellow'd get used to the other, you'd never know you were sawing, it was that light. Just go up like a feather. Well then, I fetched her into the wood and brought her down. He'd be helping, see, he'd be keeping her against the wood as well. And that piece of oak we were sawing, we sawed at it the whole day. From early in the morning till as late as we could see the line. That oak was hard—and when the saw hit it, it was just like a dust came down. No sawdust, just the dust. It was the heart of an oak. I told my brother when we finished in the evening, "I never want to go at that again." "Well," he said, "that's a pair of us." Yeah, all day. Oh boy, we used to work.

The first boat I remember my father building, I was fifteen or sixteen years old. And they were planked, what they called seam work. The boats I build now are lap work, they call them clinker built—but the boats Father was building had a crack between the planks that had to be caulked.

199

So one day Father was complaining all the caulking there was to be done. I said, "I'll help you." He said, "You can't caulk. Where did you learn?" Well, I didn't tell him that, because I used to make a caulking iron out of a piece of wood and caulked the cracks in the floor. There was no oilcloth on the floors then—rough boards. Father used to lay a floor out of rough boards, whipsawed, and then mother would send us to the beach with a can to bring home some fine sand.

And she'd make what she called a floor cloth—a piece of canvas—and spread the fine sand on the floor, and scrubbed it with the canvas. In other words she was sandpapering. And boy, she'd scrub that a couple or three times and it would be as smooth as that and right white, just the same as if it was planed. And with my caulking iron out of a piece of stick, I'd be sitting down on the floor, going along the cracks in the floor, caulking the cracks. I'd be at that till Mother would kick me clear of it. And I caulked every inch of that first vessel with Father—caulked more of it than he did—and the news went around then, I could caulk. And everyone had a boat to caulk came after me. And by god, I was noted as a caulker in Victoria County.

You know, the only time I was ever inside a school as a young man was to go to a show or a concert. No school to go to. And where I lived from 1929, there never was a school there—not in the history of the world. And in the early 'thirties I got a program that I was going to try for a school. There were thirty-one kids ready to go to school—five of them were my own. And I knew there were thirty-one more that would be ready in a year or two. So Jim MacKinnon in Baddeck was the school inspector. He only had one eye—but he could see more than any man I ever saw with two. And my wife used to tell me, "You can save yourself the trouble, looking for a school." But I kept at it. But when they found out I was looking for a school, the old folks—my father as well as the rest—said if I kept a-going and got a school, it would be the worst thing that ever happened. Well, I asked Father one day that he said it, "What do you mean by that? I thought it would be one of the best." Father said, "If you get a school going, they'll take everything we own for school tax." And I figured I had the biggest assessment of any man in the district. I said to Father, "Here goes it, I'm getting her going."

And by god, I think it was in 1935, there was a parish priest came to the country. And he and I became terrible good friends just after he came. I walked to his place to see him about this school. He said he could hardly believe it—eighteen families and thirty-one kids ready and no school. I said, "I've come over here to see if you'll help me." I wanted to know if he'd allow me to use his name at the head of posters I wanted to put up for a meeting. He said, "You use my name for anything that is reasonable, and I'm sure that school is quite reasonable."

The first meeting we had, that they passed the verdict, everything was sanctioned, trustees, secretary, site of the school, and everything. The priest wasn't half a mile from the house when they shifted everything. No good, the site was no good, nothing any good. Back I go again. Had another meeting at my place. I put up the posters. And when the priest came this time he had the school inspector with him—and they didn't shift it this time. And see, this school was supposed to be built voluntarily. We were going to try to do it at cost. And we started. I tell you, I did some terrible work. And the neighbours worked along with me—once we got the thing organized.

So, we carried on, and that fall we had the school ready. And we had a teacher from Margaree. And one of the old fellows—he had quite a family—and he wouldn't send his kids to school. I was one of the trustees, so I went down and asked him why. And he jumped up, and came down on the table with his fist. He said, "There was a man in here yesterday and he told me that I was the smartest man around here." "Well," I said, "there can't be very many smart ones or otherwise he's making fun of you." I said, "Listen. I didn't come here to hear that. I just came to find the reason why you're not sending your kids to school." I said, "Tomorrow morning I'm going to school, I'm going to the Education Department. I don't want to do this—but I got to do it. Because you've got a perfect right to send your kids to school and not have them to grow up like you and me." I said, "We can get along quite good now. But there's a day coming when those kids are not going to be able to get through the world without a little education." So the next morning I was there ahead of the teacher. His kids were the first ones to the school. No trouble after that. At first there were problems, yes. But once it was understood, the neighbours pitched in, and they were the finest kind.

I want to know what's going on. I reared a family of twenty-two in Victoria County—and I reared the most of them through the Depression, when the hard times were on in the 'thirties. They went through giving relief, the Liberal councillor. And he came to my place. He went in the pantry, what was in the pantry to eat and drink. I didn't hold anything against him for that. He came out of the pantry and told me I couldn't get any. "You got plenty to eat and drink and you can get it. This is only for those who haven't got it, and can't get it." I said, "Mr. MacDonald, that's not relief. That's what I call a lazy man's salary. If you work, you won't get any. But if you lay back, the county will feed you. That's a lazy man's salary." And he said, "I think you named it."

I never got five cents in my life I didn't work for. I never got relief. I never got a cent from the county or the government or anyone else I didn't work for. Always had plenty. You know, cash goes pretty quick, if you don't squeeze it tight. But the way we lived—she and I—we grew our own potatoes, our own turnips, cabbages, everything that we needed, we grew it. And in the fall—35 or 40 barrels of beautiful potatoes in the cellar. Always kept pigs. Any time we wanted fresh pork, I killed a pig. We always had two milk cows. The fall of '46, I killed two pigs—they'd weigh 250 each. I killed a yearling—I know she dressed 200 pounds. I had 700 pounds of fish, pickled fish and dried fish. I had two pork barrels salted full of fillet mackerel. I bought 35 hundred-pound bags of flour. There was a fellow went around selling beef in the fall. She bought a quarter—a hundred pounds, ten dollars. And I don't know how many deer I had. But I used to get a deer whenever I felt like it, when they were fit to eat. I don't think it's any crime to kill a deer when he's fit to eat. Middle of September till the middle of November—they're fit to eat. The first thing that'll spoil a deer is when they start eating spruce and you taste the spruce off of the meat.

And that winter of '46, there were twenty-one of us, and everyone home for the winter. And we ate four times a day—that would be eighty-four meals for one fellow. My wife worked hard. My wife baked all her own bread, cakes, and everything, and would use a hundred-pound bag every two weeks. She made all her own quilts and all the socks and mitts for twenty-two, besides doing all the wash for them in a washtub and scrubboard, hauling water from the brook. She worked hard. There's no doubt about it.

Willy Pat and Gladys Fitzgerald

I am married fifty-four years, have a good wife, and we raised a good family. We have 106 grandchildren and 26 great-grandchildren. I don't owe anyone and have enough saved to bury us both when we die.

Rod and Rheta Campbell, Marion Bridge

Rod Campbell: I was born in Big Glace Bay, 1896. I was brought up in the Presbyterian religion. I went to work at the steel works. We were on strike, a hard, hard strike, and very cold—we stood out on the picket lines. In 1925. I was communist, I thought communism was the answer. And this fellow, this Bible Student said to me, "Suppose you won everything you wanted, and still you had death and sickness and sorrow—what would you do about it?" "Well," I said, "I don't know." "Well," he said, "my knowledge of the Bible tells of a time coming when disease and death and all those things are done away with." Well, that was something new to me, because I wasn't taught that way. When that fellow spoke to me about the Kingdom, it registered in my head—that's the only remedy. Presbyterianism teaches if you die you go to Heaven, your soul goes to Heaven. But I found out from the Bible that when a person is dead, they're actually dead—they return to the dust, as the Bible states in the second chapter of Genesis. And there is no more movement from that body until the Resurrection. And when the Resurrection takes place, they have a new body but they will be the same individual, the same personality. What God preserves in the interval is the identity of the individual.

Rheta Campbell: As a Presbyterian, you're taught that if you're a good little boy, you'll go to Heaven when you die, if you're a bad little boy, you'll go to Hell—and you're tortured to eternity. But the Bible does not teach eternal torment. The Bible shows that when God created man, he told him to be fruitful and multiply and fill the earth, and not to eat from just one tree—all the others were good for food. And if he did, he would die. Didn't say, if he did, he would go to Hell. So when Adam and Eve disobeyed God, the Lord told them they were going back to the dust from which they had been created. So they have gone back to nothingness. But see, Christ came and died for mankind, for Adam's children—so that they could have a resurrection. See, Jesus said, "Marvel not at this, the hour is coming when all in their graves will hear his voice and come forth."

Rod: And the good and the bad people are coming. The just and the unjust. See, in Romans 6, when a man dies, his sin is canceled. And Jesus is going to give that soul a new body—but he'll be the same individual. And he's going to live on this earth. This earth is going to be a paradise. (*Not Heaven?*) No. There is a Heaven, but the Bible says there are only 144,000 going to Heaven. (*The rest will live on earth?*) Yes.

Rheta: That is, those that are willing and obedient will live on earth. But the Bible says, all the wicked, God will destroy. If people are wicked, they are not going to be permitted to go on living, because they would only do the same as they've done to this earth.

Rod: The earth will survive. The earth abides forever. One generation cometh and passeth away, but the earth will never die out.

Rheta: I was brought up a Baptist, and their teachings were pretty much the same as the Presbyterians, only they believe in immersion for baptism, not sprinkling. See, there's nothing in the Bible that says anybody should be sprinkled. One should be immersed. There is a meaning to it. It's not just formalism.

Rod: See, Jesus was immersed. So any follower of him would do the same.

Rheta: Nothing in the Bible says to sprinkle children. He sent the disciples out to teach the people and baptize them. (*So they have to be teachable?*) Yes. (*Wouldn't a child be baptized?*) No.

Rod: Not until they understand what baptism is, at any age.

Rheta: Twelve or fourteen. There's not many children at twelve who have knowledge enough to dedicate their lives to do Jehovah's will. (*So you weren't born Jehovah's Witnesses?*) No. To be a Witness you have to study and get information that you can give to others. It's not something

These rough but rare snapshots show the Pioneer troop camped out, 1932; and two views of the housecar. When the housecar stuck in the sand in 1929, oxen pulled it out.

to join. It's something to study—to find out what God's word, the Bible, teaches—and then to help others.

Rod: There's nothing to join. It's a matter of dedicating your life to do Jehovah's will. And be immersed in water, and being a witness.

Rheta: Look, we're giving you a Bible lecture. (*Oh, that's all right. I want to know about you, and that's been your life.*) See, they weren't called Jehovah's Witnesses fifty years ago. They were called Bible Students and Russellites, because Pastor Russell was really the greatest Bible Student of his day. He's the one who straightened out the hellfire business—showing people the Greek and Hebrew words from which the English word hell was taken, how it merely meant a hole in the ground. And the hellfire—Jesus used the garbage dump Gehenna outside Jerusalem to show the utter destruction of the wicked. You didn't throw something in the garbage dump to keep it burning eternally. You threw it there to dispose of it, get rid of it.

My father was a shoemaker and he had a shop, and Mr. Marchant came there with the first three volumes of Pastor Russell's books—way back probably in 1902 or somewhere along there. I was just a youngster. My father had read Ingersoll and Tom Paine and religious books—and he had come to the conclusion that there was something radically wrong. The doctrine of hellfire and trinity and all—he couldn't accept them. Marchant convinced him to read these books, and he hadn't read very far before he knew that this was the truth. You got sense to what you were reading and the Bible was being made plain. So he became a Bible Student. My mother still took us kids to the Baptist church for years. But my father got the *Watchtower*, and it carried the international Sunday School lesson at that

205

time—and we got that too. My mother taught Sunday School in the Baptist church. (*Did she disagree with your father?*) Yes. Nevertheless, she entertained what we spoke of as the Pilgrims at that time. They were traveling speakers, traveling ministers—all Bible Students. And she started reading the books to show my father where he was wrong. The more she read, the more she saw that she was the one who was wrong. (*She became a Jehovah's Witness?*) Indeed she did.

Rod and I were married in 1930. We met in this work. Then I took up the Pioneer Service—the regular work, going from house to house—and Rod was already in that. He went in in 1928 and I went in in 1929. And we were in the same town, Yarmouth.

(*Were you doing anything else to earn a living?*) No. (*When you were doing this work, how were you supported?*) We were not supported by the society. We never took up collections. We never solicited money. But we always had enough to eat and wear and what-not.

(*You were a full-time Pioneer?*) **Rod**: That's it.

Rheta: You can work part-time, a little on the side, in order to buy your bread and butter, pay for your room. What they call Special Pioneers—they get a very small allowance from the society. **Rod**: Today they get fifty dollars a month. Way back then, it was thirty dollars. But we weren't supported by the society, and we never solicited money. **Rheta**: But we were able to keep going. We lived very frugally. We got along very nicely, always managed. Some of us have relatives who are Jehovah's Witnesses, and they certainly wouldn't see us wanting. And some of us had a little income on the side. As far as Pioneer work is concerned, a lot of young people do housecleaning and office cleaning—enough work to keep them in clothing. And some of us don't require as much clothing. And sometimes other people's clothing fits us very well.

(*Rheta, would you call it hardship?*) Well, we got along with a lot less than other people would. A woman said today, "You wouldn't leave enough to feed the squirrels." People throwing away things, it always bothers me. We weren't wasteful. We were very careful. (*But you are both bright attractive people. It seems to me, if you had decided to put your energies into earning money, you'd have succeeded.*) I worked for the C.N.R. railway for years as a private secretary, and I gave that up because I believe that this is the most important thing on earth.

We lived in one room mostly. We had a housecar, and we lived in that in the summertime. But it caused a whole lot of work trying to keep that on the road, because it would give out. In Montreal we had a room with a day bed in it and a little kitchen off where you put a quarter in and got gas to get your meals. We lived very frugally, but we always had lots to eat. Got along very nicely.

(*My sense of Witnesses has been someone who works, earns a living, and then goes door-to-door, perhaps one day a week.*) Yes, and they have children; we would have had to go to work in order to support them. The income we got would certainly not have kept a family going, but it did very well for the two of us.

Rod: I ran this farm for years. We kept as high as six cows, and we always had a garden.

Rheta: That's one thing that supplied some of our food those days.

When Rod's mother was living, he wanted to be handy her, so we've just worked on the island of Cape Breton for a number of years now. We worked up all around the North Shore and up to Meat Cove, Capstick. We had a panel truck then and the road then was shale and I said, if it rains we'll never get back—the cliffs were steep right down to the ocean. Got as far as we could with the truck and Rod walked from there on to these families. And it started to rain. And I wrote a little note telling our names and where to send our bodies and put it in the glove compartment. Nobody knew us up there and the truck was licensed in Ontario. (*This is the 1930's.*) Yes. But we weren't the first down north. I don't know how far Mr. Marchant went, the man who had called on my father. He was an old bachelor. He had a bicycle and he went up over those hills.

Now that's another thing, many people opened their homes to us, had us sleep at their home. Even when we had the housecar, they would insist that we come in, give us our breakfast. Oh yes, people were kind to us.

(*You never found any anger?*) Oh yes, we did. Sometimes—one house in Cheticamp, it was way off the road and I had walked up to it and oh, the man was wild, he told me to get. And he walked down to the road with me. And every so often he'd start to give me a push. I told him if he put a finger on me, I'd have him arrested. And he'd stop and then he'd swear. Kept on with me to the gate. And different places, they'd yell at you to keep away from there, they didn't want you. But within the last few years, we've found a great change.

Rod: I know in North Ingonish, we would have difficulty in getting a hall or schoolhouse to give a talk. But after it smoothed over, there wasn't trouble there.

Rheta: I came to a door and a woman said, "What do you have in that bag?" "Well," I said, "even if I had snakes in it, wouldn't you invite me in?" She started to laugh and said, "Sure, come on in." Different times people would say they didn't want us in the house, and many times they would phone ahead and tell people we were on the way, not to let us in.

(*Was there ever really any danger for you?*) I know in Inverness, the time we were arrested, the mayor there said I should stop because they might take sort of mob action. But he was just trying to frighten us. Only once in a while would you find people really vicious. One man told me, if I came back again he would shoot me. Well, I just wouldn't go back again, I didn't want to get shot. Some would say, "Get! Get!" and once they set a dog on me—and I just got through the gate in time. As a general thing, I found people kind and good.

We were arrested in Inverness. There were ten of us Pioneers working. I was picked up first and was in talking to the mayor and the town clerk—said I would have to have a license. That was ten dollars a day. I told him we didn't take licenses out—this was benevolent work and we were allowed to do it. That's when the mayor told me not to do it. I told him, "I'll have to be like the apostles, whether it's right in the sight of God to listen to you or to God. Judge for yourself, but as for me, I'll listen to God's ways." So I went out and I started again. Then Ellen MacDonald was picked up by the Mountie, said she sold him a book. They had a trial and sentenced her to ten days in jail and a fine of six dollars and a half.

Then they got Rod and me, took us in. They started a trial on me. I asked that the case be postponed, to get in touch with our headquarters in Toronto. The magistrate said, "Well, is your God in Ontario?" I said, "No, but the head of God's organization for Canada is." So he said, "Get back here tomorrow morning." So I said, "If Mrs. MacDonald is going to jail, I'm going with her." He said, "She can go home with you." I said, "All right, and you can come along too, if you like." He said, "You'd talk my ear off if I went with you." Imagine! This, a magistrate.

Anyway, we landed there next morning at nine o'clock. Town policeman said, "I was hoping we'd never see you again." They really thought we'd just keep on going. "Oh," I said, "we always keep our word." "Oh yes," he said, "you're very good people"—just disgusted with us. In the meantime I had typed off a couple of pages on our work, and the society had told us what to do in case of arrest—because there were lots of arrests those days. I started to read this, that this is what had happened to the disciples, and we're not surprised, and we intended to keep on with the work. He said, "We don't want to hear any sermon from you." I told him that I understood under the British law, we had authority to plead our own cases, and this is my defense. "Yes, yes, go on, go on." And I started reading again. And he said, "Will you shut up! The glibness—I never heard the like of it. God help the man that has to put up with you."

He went to the back of the building. It was an old barn. The courthouse had burned down. And he and a priest stood back there smoking cigarettes. Then he came up and said, "Are you through?" "No," I said, "I'd like to read the charter of our organization." And he snatched it out of my hand and said, "Well, you won't read it." And I snatched it back and I did read it. And I showed that I had not sold books. But the magistrate didn't care,

208

and I was fined five dollars, and a dollar and a half costs—that was it. Or ten days in jail. I said, "We'll go to jail." Well, if you had thrown a bucket of whitewash at him, he couldn't have looked sicker. They never dreamed of us going to jail.

They were taking us to the jail in Port Hood. And I said to them, "Now drive as fast as you can. I've never had a drive fast enough to suit me. I'd be arrested if I did." Anyway, he drove pretty fast. The Mountie said, "I think you people are getting a real kick out of this." And I said, "If you think I'm doing this for fun—to carry a bag of books and a phonograph and walk up to the top of these Cape Breton hills and then probably find nothing but a police dog—people don't do that for fun. The trouble is that your priests and ministers don't want you people to know that Hell is not a place of torment, there's no such a place as Purgatory." And I talked from then on into Port Hood, telling them about Hell and Purgatory. So when we got to Port Hood, they went into the courthouse first and explained about it. When we went in the sheriff said, "I understand you ladies are not criminals, we're not going to put you in the jail." They kept us in the jury room. Nice room. I can't remember whether we were there two nights or just one.

[Rod was free and went for papers to appeal the case. The two women were released pending the appeal. The case came up a long time afterward in Port Hawkesbury, and even a longer time passed before they learned that they had to go back to jail and complete the last eight days of the sentence. Their lawyer got in touch with the sheriff in Port Hood, and he said, "Don't send women up here this time of the year, it's too cold. You wait until spring." So in the spring Ellen and Rheta went back to Port Hood and presented themselves to complete their sentence. They were told to "go home and forget about it."]

(*But this was before the Second World War. With the war, did things get even rougher for Jehovah's Witnesses?*) **Rheta**: We were under ban. If I came in your house and you said, "Are you one of Jehovah's Witnesses," and I said, "Yes"—well, you could call up and have me arrested and

209

A baptism in the Mira River

put in jail. (*Why?*) Because our books were supposed to be seditious. That they were telling people not to fight—which wasn't true. (*Would a Witness join the army and fight?*) No. Because the Bible says not to. It says Christ's followers would be known by the fact that they have love for each other. Love is the fulfilling of God's law. So a Witness would not join an army. But I would not tell you not to join—that's your business. We knew a lot of young boys put in the concentration camp at Chalk River, Ontario. The ban said that I could not go to a home and talk about one of our books. But I could go with my Bible and talk all day. (*Were a lot of Witnesses arrested then?*) Yes, quite a number. And R.C.M.P. in plain clothes were here and searched the house. If they had found any quantity of books, they would have had us arrested and fined or a jail sentence. And we were also under ban in Germany, and persecuted right to the death there—put into concentration camps. They got the same treatment practically as the Jews.

But we didn't stop our work. We had a booklet, *The End of Nazism*—and we rolled them with an elastic. We would take sacks of them and four would go in a car and we'd sling them out in the driveways in the country. And in the cities you'd just walk along the street and distribute them. One night we did it after midnight. Dozens of Jehovah's Witnesses were out in Sydney, Glace Bay—all over. It was hectic. But you did it because you believed that it was going to mean life to others as well as yourself.

(*But you don't seem all that angry, looking back.*) No. Because we expect that treatment. What did they do with the apostles? Didn't they do everything terrible to them, even to stoning Stephen to death? And if you'll read that account of Stephen in the Bible, it's marvelous the discourse he gave those Jews about what they should have been doing and what they had done. And they hated him for it. See, people hate the truth. They don't want the truth. They want, like Paul said, to have their ears tickled. Like in Jeremiah's day, when he told them Jerusalem was going to fall and there would be such a terrible slaughter, they said, Prophesy unto us smooth things, don't tell us all that stuff. Well, that's how they have felt about Jehovah's Witnesses.

And there were many times we'd sort of feel we had guidance from above, that the angels were sort of directing us. (*You feel you've had*

210

that?) Oh my, yes. Many times we've been in pretty strange circumstances and things would clear up. So we've learned to do what Jesus said: Take no anxious thought of tomorrow. Each day has its own anxiety. I've often said I'd love to live my life over again. I'd love to be young and able to do the work again.

Jack Yazer, Citizen

Jack Yazer has very few memories of his childhood. When you ask about himself, he tells you about his current ideas, his plans. His mind is on a new hospital—some scheme for worker-ownership of an industry—or an idea that will give young people incentive to drive safely and to live drug-free. His ideas are rooted in today's problems. And, implemented or not, they have always made us argue and think. None of his ideas bring any return to Jack. He is proud of his ideas and works fiercely to see them through—but they are not his living, only his daily life.

So when you ask him about Jack Yazer, it is hard to get him to focus on Jack. Still, we wanted to know, where did he come from? Is it possible to get a hint of what made him an extraordinary combination of a proud and selfless man?

In the following conversation, Jack Yazer struggles to recapture his childhood in Europe—a terrible time that has left only fragments of memory. Then, with no difficulty, he tells us of his years as a peddler in rural Cape Breton—clearly happy memories. But we haven't got a full portrait of Jack Yazer. We may not have even come close. If what follows doesn't satisfy you, you can try for yourself. Jack will talk to you. But you may have to chase him down the street on his way to meet with high school kids to tell them about his latest plan to encourage less driving accidents, less drugs.

Jack, where were you born?...

Jack Yazer, Sydney: I was born in Poland. Suprasl, near Bialystok. It's a small shtetl. (*By shtetl, what do we mean?*) A small little village—small country place. Mostly Polish. But then during the [war] it was changing hands a lot—the Polish, then the Germans, and the Russians. You know, it was a spot where it was changing hands. But when I was there it was just Polish, in my time.

(*Did you think of yourself as a Pole?*) No, I always [was] Jewish. Because the Poles didn't let you forget that you were Jewish. It was very, very hard to be a Jew in Poland. It was mostly Poles. And there were I don't know how many Jews. I don't remember too much. But mostly it wasn't Jewish, you know. I can't tell you how many. But now, you see, I

212

don't remember too much of my life when I was young. See, my mother died when I was five—I saw her dying.

And I remember, like, I was telling my wife, Zelda, I was telling her the other day—I saw somebody walking on stilts. I said, "Gee, I remember now, when we were kids, we used to walk on [stilts], and then we used to go in the firemen's place to get an apple from the tree." You know, I remember that, how we used to walk. But I don't know much more about it. I just happened to see that—yeah, that just hit me.

I used to play soccer, when I was a kid. But all I remember [is] one particular game. Because it was Rosh Hashana, and I was supposed to be home. My father was alone, and I was supposed to be helping home, whatever it was. But the game was on, you know. And then it was time for me home. And I remember the kids saying, "There comes your father." And I remember running home. And we had, like, in the porch there was a stairway. And I hid myself in the stairway. And I—kicked me, you know, took me. I remember that part—I remember the game. But I don't remember any other games.

Like school, I don't remember very much. I remember we had a high-peaked cap—navy blue with white stripe, and the grade school [name written] on it. And I can just see that. But I don't remember a thing about my class. I remember there was a high fence, maybe twelve feet or fourteen feet, right around the school. And you had to go to this gate you were going through, and they gave us an opening. And as soon as you get out there, they throw the stones at you, you know. "You damn Jew, you!" you know.

So I remember things like that. Those are things just—you know. But I don't remember much. Why don't I remember more? There's more than that....

Then I remember, like, I was working for a butcher, as a kid, trying to get something to eat. And this field I'm talking [about]—there was like a gate. And you'd come in this fellow's back yard. And then there was like a butcher, you know—his tables and the whole thing, and his house was there. And I remember once—my father didn't want me to drive the horses. He knew that I was driving too fast. So, what I used to do with that field. I used to drive so fast so you couldn't tell who was on the horse. But this particular time he was at the gate. And the horse comes to a gate, slows down. I went over; the horse went over me. Nothing happened. But I remember that scene, you see.

Then I remember this butcher. And we used to go feed the horses in the morning. You had no breakfast. So you went, you fed the horses. Then you came back at noontime, you watered them. And then you came in the house for dinner. They were having a dinner. And I remember a room as big as this, I guess, and a huge table. They'd eat, and I'd sit against a wall

213

or on a chair. And I can still see them with a big plate—everything was on their plate. Whoever left something, was put [on] my plate. You know, I remember—those scenes are still there....

And then, you can come back after school. You clean the stable and oh, you were getting something to eat.

And I remember once going in, sneaked in, from the barn to the back yard. I remember stealing some money, some change. And that always bothered me—you know, stole some money. (*From the butcher.*) Yeah, the butcher....

Then I remember when my mother died. They had her on the floor on straw, and candles on top of the—you know—in the wake, whatever. I remember that. Those are scenes. She was going to buy fish for our Shabbat [Sabbath]. And she came to this house. And I was outside, looking in the window—I didn't go in. But the door, let's say, was here, and the window was here. And I was looking in there, and then she.... She said she wasn't feeling too well. And she went in, the woman gave her some milk. And she had taken the milk like this [like drinking it], bent over—and she was dead. I happened to look in the window. So I remember that.

Then I—there's certain things. And I remember I used to always hang onto her skirts. You know, wouldn't let go of her. And she told me she was going to put me in jail. So she took me once to the police station—you know, not in jail, the police station. Then I promised, you know, I wouldn't do it any more. (*Hang on the skirt.*) Yeah. So after that—and if I saw a policeman on this side, I was on this side! But if I were on that side, and he was coming that way, I was already on this side!

So, those are the scenes that I remember. But much more, I don't....

I don't remember very much of my father—I wouldn't know what he looked like....

(*Do you have any idea how you came to decide—how you learned about America?*) Well, years ago, my mother's brother, Mr. Spinner, he ran away—he was in Russia at that time, that part—he ran away and he came to Canada. Then he brought his sister over—my mother's sister. Then my mother died. And after she died, my aunt brought my sister over. My sister was married to Nate David—used to be David's Market here years ago. And she died at childbirth.....

My aunt brought my brother [Mendel] over. Then he brought me over—either my aunt or my brother—I never found out yet who paid for it. But they got me.

So, they had a little store where the Vogue Theatre is now, used to be a little store there—Mrs. Cohen. And finally, she owned the store that [is] Ike's now....

(*Your memories—they're like little bits of dreams, though, aren't they?*)

Yeah, it's like a dream, you see. But those are the things that I remember.

The biggest thing, I think, at that time, was, you had no vision of what's ahead of you, the future. You had no dreams of coming anywhere else but there. And you had no—you didn't do too much thinking. You were thinking mostly just of your existence from day to day. That's what you were going by. You didn't have much.

(*And what was your name when you were in Poland?*) Yazernicki—Yona Yazernicki. And then when they came here, like, they changed it—into Yazer.

I remember from the time when I came here [to Cape Breton], from the time I went peddling, incidents that happened. All of those things. Why was everything [before that] shut out? I can remember coming in the boat, going to

Yona Yazernicki's passport photo—
Jack Yazer

Danzig. And coming with a boat—*Empress of France*, from Liverpool. I remember all of those things. I remember on the boat how they used to chase me—the stewards....

I got in Quebec City and I couldn't stay still. And I had, I think, $2.50 in my pocket. And we wore those knickerbocker pants. And I was wandering around, and I saw this little store there, and I bought a pair of golf socks for 85¢—you know, to match. And then I was wandering around and I got lost. I couldn't find my boat, back. And I was panicking. And then, I kept on showing—we had buttons [we wore]—so they took me back to the boat.

Then they took us on the train—put us on a train in Quebec City. And—I don't know —between Boisdale and Montreal, wherever it was—there was a fellow sitting right across from me. He was going: [Jack made a chomping sound, smacking his lips]. And it was bothering me. He was chewing gum. You know, I never saw gum. So I asked him.... He said, "Gum." So then he gave me a piece. And I took it and I swallowed it. He said, "No, no." So I learned from him. So I remember that particular scene.

And then, we were told not to talk to just anybody. And this lady came in past Boisdale. She started talking to me, and I just ignored her. She kept going, and she came back again. It was my aunt. She met me in Boisdale.

She picked me out on the train. And then we came here, and there was my uncle, my aunt, my sister, my brother. And they made me welcome.

I started school in Central School here. I was going on fifteen, went with kids six years old. That wasn't for me. That's when I was ready to go home. And I wanted to go home. And I quit there, and then I went peddling....

My uncle [Morris Spinner] had Spinner's store at that time. But he also did a little bit of peddling, which he did originally. And my aunt, Mrs. Cohen, she had a little grocery store, candy store, whatever you call it. And my brother [Mendel] was already peddling. He peddled two years ahead of me....

Another thing just hit me, when I was still in Poland—you know, certain things stick out. I remember breaking into a place to—in the orchard, to steal apples. It wasn't because I wanted an apple, it's just that—you know, it was food. And I remember getting caught. You see, I went in, like, over the fence, and I got caught. But the owner that caught me had two big dogs. I don't remember what kind of dogs. And I had the apples. And he took the apples back from me, he led me—showed me where the gate was. And he sicked the dogs after me. He sicked his two dogs after me. And to this day, when a dog chases me, my hair stands up. I can still see the two dogs, like, over my shoulders, you know, jumping, jumping on me. And me running out.

And I remember when I was peddling in Cape North, Sunrise Valley, I think it was, or, no, it was on the other side. And I remember that I picked up a stone—there was a dog chasing me or coming towards me—and I picked up, like this—I remember the dog jumping on the back of my pack. As I said, my hair just—even now, I've had dogs, I pet with them, and everything else. But sometimes, they come out of nowhere in a hurry, I can just feel my hair stand up. And I remember this, when this guy was throwing the apples at me and sicked the dogs on me.

(*Tell me about starting to peddle.*) See, my brother [Mendel] peddled before, so that he knew what I had to have. We used to have in the bottom of the pack, like, pair of jeans, overalls. Then the next thing was underwear. Then you'd have sweaters, and dress shirts, you know. Few pair of pants—build up the pants. Maybe the pack was as big as this, you know, from the floor. This high. Maybe a fraction wider than that. (*So it's about two feet high. And maybe two and a half feet wide.*) Yeah. Could be a little bit smaller than that. It's a regular pack. But it used to be like a mattress— the blue stripes, you know, burlap like—that used to be the pack. Then you'd have like four sides. You know, tie it up this way, that way. And then you had leather belts you'd put over you. And in the front you had a little black case—it was a wooden case. You had [in there], like, jewel-

216

lery, small stuff, socks, to balance you. (*You wore that in front.*) In the front, you'd hook on the belt.

So, this is what we had.

This was pretty heavy for a kid. It was a pretty heavy pack. I don't know exactly what the weight would be, but it wasn't easy. And I remember a lot of times in the summertime, your shoulders were eaten, you know, from the straps. It used to irritate you.

(*Where would you start out?*) Well, the first start—there used to be a ferry go across from Sydney to Westmount. And you'd go to Westmount. You weren't allowed to peddle in [Sydney]. So we took a boat across the [harbour] called the *Mary*. And she'd end up pretty well where the [Dobson] Yacht Club is. Then you'd peddle back to Sydney, to the city limits—you know, walking.

Then, when you got braver, you went to North Sydney, in the city limits, and you started peddling. Come the way of Westmount, you'd stay in different places—whether it's in Rudderham's Road or wherever it is. You've got people—people were glad to see you. And then [my brother] Mendel already had broke the road, made it a lot easier for me. So you'd stay there, then you'd come back to Sydney.

Then I went to Boisdale—you know, peddle back. Then you go to Grand Narrows, and peddle back. And the trains used to be very plentiful there. There were a lot of freight trains. And a lot of this, from Boisdale, it was all near the tracks. And the train would come, and they'd stop and pick me up, take me from place to place! Stop the whole train, just to take me wherever I was going. (*Not at the station.*) No, no, just if I happened to be walking on the road, they used to do it.

Then I went to Bay St. Lawrence. *Aspy* [a coastal boat] used to go to Bay St. Lawrence. But it wouldn't go to Meat Cove. So in Meat Cove they had a smack. You know what a smack is—it's like a fishing boat, but it's a bigger boat [used for gathering the catch from several fishing boats]. So you'd get off of [the *Aspy*] and you'd go on the smack, and take you into Meat Cove....

(*Now, could you get refills? More things to sell?*) Yeah, when I need it. Because the *Aspy* would go into Ingonish. And if I need it—my brother would send it up. I'd have it there. But most of them you'd try to sell what you had. Then you came back [to Sydney] and replenished. And you kept going farther. And [when] you came back, the next time, you brought the things they were looking for.

See, that time, the only business they had, the only connections they had, was Eaton's. Eaton's catalogue was used as a carpetting for the floors. It was used in the kitchen as carpet, tearing the pages. If you go in the bathroom—not the bathroom, in the outhouse—it was Eaton's catalogue. See, the only thing they had—it was order it.

But when a guy came to [the house]—I was news. You know, different people. They were so glad to see you. Somebody coming out from the other side of the world. Because they didn't have buses, they didn't have cars to come in. People from Bay St. Lawrence didn't know what Sydney looked like. People from Sydney didn't know what Bay St. Lawrence looked like. So when you came there—they were glad to see you. Half the time they didn't want to charge you for staying the night. Though we always made a point—Mendel made it clear—you know, pay them. But half the time, now, they'll do anything in the world for you.

So you were doing a service—you were selling them things. At the same time, they were happy to see you more as a—not as a movie—but just to see you.... (*No—"as a movie" is interesting. Go on.*) You know, you were there, you just saw them, then you brought the store to them. And if they happened to need something, it was a big thing. They didn't have to go looking for it. Didn't have to send away to the Eaton's catalogue for it. So when you were there, you were more—it's a guest. If they liked you. If they didn't like you, you had no chance. If they liked you, there's nothing in the world they wouldn't give you, or wouldn't do for you.

(*You used the word, "like a movie." By that do you mean you were like entertainment for them?*) It would be entertainment. Somebody's coming in, you know—entertainment. Not their next-door neighbour coming in to play cards or chop wood with them. You came in, you were a little different. You brought something different to their life.

(*I take it your English had improved by then.*) Oh, yeah. When I first came, I learned to speak more Gaelic than I learned English, when I went peddling. I used to be able to sort of pick a few words, put together, in Gaelic. Especially in North Shore.

I remember there used to be—she had two boys—Angus was a minister. And she had Tommy—oh, I think he got blind, there—he lived in Skir Dhu. He was a MacDonald. His brother Angus MacDonald used to be a minister. Just at the bridge there in Skir Dhu. Well, their mother—his mother—I can picture her. I've told that story a million times—when I first came there—she just thought I was God. And she had no English. And she always used to wear black dress, you know, black gown. And I remember I was eating porridge in the morning, and I had my spoon in my hand like this. And she put her arms around me like this way—and then she'd pick [up] my hand this way, to put the spoon in my mouth. She wouldn't take the spoon, but she moved my hand—you know, like she was feeding me. And she used to go like this. Look me in the face and say this, "You are pack too." "You are pack too." "You little black Jew." When she said, "You are pack too"—but you could see the love—"You are pack too." (*She'd want to feed you.*) Feed you, yeah. But she didn't take the spoon. But she'd move my hand. And she had her arm right around my neck, the one side. And she's bent over me on the table. You could see the whole family—they liked you so much....

So when you came there, you actually brought them something, you know. Something to look forward to. Like, you'd go, let's say, in the wintertime, when we had the stove, and it was really cold. And we'd open the stove door. And you'd put chairs—you know, you were just sitting almost in each other's lap, trying to put your feet on this door. And they'd keep on asking you questions and all this stuff. They asked me where I came from, and where did I come from today, and who did I stay with. You know, what's Sydney like, sometimes they would ask. (*Did they know about Europe at all?*) No. (*They wouldn't ask about that.*) No, no. (*But to know about Sydney.*) Yeah.

(*Were they interested in world news?*) Not too much, no. See, those times, everybody was wrapped up in this one little part of the world. For instance in the summertime they used to get enough highway work to pay the taxes. At that time they used to get 35¢ an hour.... People that had the fish plants, they used to buy the fish from you—[and] they had the [local] store. And then they gave you, if you wanted a shirt, and what account [you had, it] was charged up against that account. I don't know how often or how much money you ever got. But you didn't know where you were [that is, how much money you actually had in your account]. You know, they took their word for it, there was so much fish. And this is the type of life they lived.

You know, they didn't go too much past there because they didn't come in too much to Sydney at that time. You see, to come into Sydney

A rough but rare photograph: Jack Yazer with his horse and packed cart, peddling down north.

was an ordeal. Years ago, it used to be an ordeal to come in from Glace Bay to Sydney. The roads were just narrow roads. In places, even with a horse-and-wagon, there was just enough [space for] one way, one path. It wasn't like two car or horses could pass by....

The first time I took my horse in to Meat Cove. But I had a big heavy express wagon. It's not like those driving wagons. And I remember coming around this turn like this. But it wasn't wide enough for the wagon to make the turn. And I was only a youngster. And I remember laying on the ground and pulling the wheels away from the rock. Then move the horse ahead, and move the wagon just enough. And then I remember, as soon as you made a turn, there was a downhill and a little bridge, to go up there. See, I remember—then coming up, I had a lot of trouble with coming up. And I allowed myself more, to be further away from the rock. Because this was the first time. So [on the way] back, I already figured out a little bit, it was a lot easier. This is how the roads were.

Then I remember going from Meat Cove to the place they call Lowlands. There was at that time, I think, four houses. And I was going there, and two young fellows were going to help me to carry the pack. And I remember they threw me down—they wanted me to drink that screech and I wouldn't do it—and they threw me down. I guess they were going to rob me, whatever it was. And they were pouring it, and I wouldn't swallow it, and it was pouring out here. And finally they gave up. You know.

So this was a road that you had.

But it's all experiences. Another time I was sitting like this in a chair, and the pack was here. You know, like this. And I see a shirt going disappearing here. I see a housedress going there. And I look. Geez, not very much of my pack left. I couldn't hardly speak English. I said to myself, "Geez, am I going to have anything left? I can't accuse anybody of stealing." So it hit me, an idea. I took out a piece of paper, and a pencil. When I saw the shirt going that way, then I knew who it was. "Shirt." I didn't point to anybody in particular. "A dress." I kept on pointing. As much as I could remember, you see. So, they paid for some of it, and some, well, they gave me back. But, you know, I didn't accuse anybody. All I understood [was] that they were buying it.... But they were actually, you know, grabbing and stealing it.

(*But were you ever actually robbed?*) No. (*Never.*) No. (*They threw you down and they tried to make you drink....*) Well, that's youngsters—you know, they thought they were—you know, do something.... Oh, I was scared, don't get me wrong.

Another time I remember I was with a girl—just fooling around—and I remember she was trying her darnedest to get my money from the billfold.

Oh yeah, another time I remember, I was sleeping with a fellow in a place—same bed. And I had, like, my money in the pocket here. In a shirt. But it had a safety pin on the inside. At that time I guess they had no other beds, and I slept with him. I sort of woke up. I didn't open my eyes or anything. And I felt—he was at—money. So he was bothering me. So I kept on, like, twisting. And then he'd try again. And finally I turned myself around—in my sleep, of course—and I put my arms around him, over him. You know, just—I was snoring—sleeping. And then when he'd turn around, you know, my arm would move with him.... So I just kept him in control for the best part of the night. And in the morning I got up early. He said, "You usually get up early?" I said, "Yeah, I always get up early in the morning," you know. I never let on. But I never went to that house again. I've had my lessons.

(*How do you work? You come to a person's home.*) First thing I ask them if they want to buy. (*Are you walking?*) Oh, yeah. (*At first there's no horse-and-wagon.*) Oh, no, just walk.

(*So, you come to a door, and what do you do?*) Well, "Would you like to buy something?" You know. It's the first question you ask them, "Like to buy something?" And they don't say, "No." Next thing we do is come on in. "Do you want to look at the goods?" Sometimes say, "No, but...." You'll show it to [them]. They'll see a pair of shoelaces, and a pair of socks, or a tie, or housedress, a pair of stockings. Sometimes a work shirt or underwear he wants. The next time you knew what they needed. You came back, they'd ask you for it....

Then if you like the people, or if you already knew—like, Mendel already told me in what places to stay. Because he already stayed there, you see. So when I ask, can I stay there for the night—"Sure." And when I kept going, the longer I went there, they kept on fighting for me, where I want to stay. This one, "Why don't you come stay here tonight? Why don't you?" You know, they just—"Come and stay here. We'll go someplace and play cards." "Might as well stay here tonight—you can go back there tomorrow." If they liked you, there is nothing they wouldn't do for you. If they don't like you, there is no use in you going there. And I was very fortunate that I got along with them over the years.

Even when we started the store [in Sydney Mines]. I remember, this man and his son came in—he got this girl in trouble. And then the mother came in with the girl that was in trouble. And like, in my store I have two doors. The mother came in first—they wanted to see a lawyer. So I gave them the name of a lawyer; they told me the whole story. It's the boy's fault, of course. They walked out the door, and the other one came in the other door. They told me the exact same thing. You know, it's the girl's fault, and all that. They want a lawyer. So I had to—you know, just balance it. I didn't know anything about it, of course. But those were the things.

And then, when I stopped peddling, when we had this store—Mendel took me in as a partner. He started the store in 1930.

(*I want to know so much about peddling, though. Being in the homes like that. Would there be any entertainment? Would they sing, when you were there? Was that part of it?*) Yeah, among themselves, they used to sing. The most of them always said Grace before you had your meal. They were always a very close family. And a lot of it—don't forget, they spoke [Gaelic]—which I didn't understand enough. But then I remember they used to have what you call milling frolics a lot. Or they used to go like in the church groups, have affairs. And you go in different homes, playing cards, and teas.

I remember one [milling frolic] very well in Ingonish. I was learning to speak English. And I thought what the word was, but I didn't think it would come out in my mouth. There was a woman, a Mrs. Hussey. She had—whatever it was, she dropped it. Then she had tea, and she dropped that. There were a lot of people around there, you know. She said, "What sign is that?" (*As in, "What does it mean when you drop something?"*) And my word came with "clumsiness," and I said it—you know—"Clumsiness." It came into my mind; I was just trying to learn to speak English. So she started up, she said, "Johnny Yazer," she said, "you're not going to sleep with me tonight!" And everybody else, "Oh, I see, so Johnny Yazer's sleeping with you, eh?" You know, they just kept on, you know, teasing her. And Johnny Yazer.

Then another milling frolic. There was a minister—what was his name—MacDonald—I think it was Nelson MacDonald. He was a very strong NDPer, I think. And he used to tell jokes in Gaelic. And he was telling a story there about Hughie Mary Peggy. You know, like, out the windows—just trying to force the couple to marry, like matchmaking. And everybody was just jumping out of their seats. I can still remember seeing it—he was trying to explain to me, you know, what he was translating. And I used to enjoy those things.

And they used to dance in square dances. They used to love to do that. And they treated me as though I was part of the family, wherever I went. And it was really—I don't know, I felt part of them. I'd say the happiest days of my life were when I went peddling. The people were so genuine.

(*Would they know you were a Jew?*) Oh, yes. I always made it a point—a Jew. And then, I always said my prayers in the morning and night, with my skullcap on.... To this day. Morning and night, before I go to bed. (*You would do this in the homes of Catholics.*) Didn't make any difference. (*Protestants.*) Like, I wouldn't eat pork. They knew, you know—and I would say, "I can't eat pork."

See, I learned to speak a lot of English. We used to have the silent movies here. And they used to have the captions underneath. And to go to the movie that time was 25¢. So I used to go to the movies. And in between [peddling] seasons I worked for Mason's Wholesale. I used to get, like, $6 a week. And $5 a week I paid for board and room. The other dollar, I used to go to silent movies. (*How did you learn to speak English from the silent movie?*) Well, see, I could read. I had enough education home. You know, put together the alphabet. And then you try to put words together, what they were saying—in the captions, from English. So that helped me a lot....

(*Now, when you were peddling, were you able to keep the Jewish Sabbath?*) No, I didn't keep the Sabbath. (*But did you work on Sunday?*) No, they didn't—no. (*So you'd go door-to-door on Saturday.*) Yeah. (*But on Sunday....*) I would rest. And if they would come in, if they wanted something, you know, I'd sell it to them. But it was up to them. If they say fine, you'd sell it to them. But you didn't dare [peddle]....

Talking about Sunday, I remember I tipped over the horse-and-wagon, I smashed my wagon in Tarbot. Then I went to Petrie Beach in Cape North and they made me a new box, you know, woodwork. But I had to go to a blacksmith to do the old ironworks. So I went to that fellow, it was around the last of July or August sometime. And his name was Angus MacDonald—he used to be the blacksmith in Cape North. But he was also—when they had no minister—he used to be the elder, he used to do the preaching and all that stuff. So I went to him and I asked him to do it.

He said, "Go away, Jack, go away." He said, "We've got to work in the hay. The weather is fine, we've got to finish the hay first." And I said, "Mr. MacDonald, what about tomorrow?" And he said, "Tomorrow, if it's a fine day," he said, "we're going to have to do the hay." I said, "Mr. Mac-Donald, if it rains tomorrow, will you do the wagon?" He said, "Yeah." "Well," I said, "I'm going home and pray that it'll rain."

Next morning, it rained. I came down. There was a bunch of people in the forge. He looked at me, he said, "Here I am, a good strong Christian and an elder in the church." He said, "I pray to God," he said, "for fine weather," he said, "and you pray for rain," he said, "and God listened to you. He wouldn't listen to me." For a long time you heard him talking about it: "The Lord listened to you and wouldn't listen to me. It rained." So they all knew. I never—in all my life since, I never made it a point to deny I was a Jew.

Once I didn't say [I was a Jew], in which I should have. I was in the army. And I know we were working at night, I was there, and about four desks from me, there was a major there. And this chap walked by. You know, I just saw him walking by—you know, fellow in uniform. And I heard him say, "I can't do it." And, "I can't do it." So I turned around, I looked at him. But I didn't see anybody else, you know. I said, "You can't

223

do what?" He said, "I can't recommend him for a commission." And I said, "Why?" I don't think he even realized—he was just talking, you know. And he said, "He's a Jew." This was a sergeant, and he didn't want to recommend him. And I didn't say I was a Jew. It bothered me for a long time after. But he didn't want to recommend him because he was a Jew....

But those times when I [make a speech]—sometimes I'll go in there, "I want to wish you a Happy Jewish New Year." There's certain people, they don't like Jews, and I know it. There's certain people that I know would ask me to go to their house, I'm not too fussy. The next one, I'll go. But you know it. And I knew my spot, my place, all those years—where I'm wanted and where I'm not wanted. You know, I'm just—my makeup is that I can smell it or feel it. And this is a way of living. And I've always been proud of being a Jew....

Then—there was a MacLeod fellow and a Morrison fellow. Couple of times they helped me carry the pack on Smokey, they felt so sorry for me. You know, so hot....

I made very, very close friends. When I first started there—I'm not going to mention the name, I'll just say the place. It's on this side of Bay St. Lawrence. I was there, and a man gave me $7000 to put in the bank. And I said, "Look, you don't know me, nothing...." "Look," he said, "I want to give you the money." He said, "I don't want to put it in the bank." So I brought it and I had it I don't know for how long. It was driving me crazy, and I wanted to put it in a bank. (*Take it to Sydney?*) Yeah. So I had the $7000, hiding it in my shoes and the mattress, and the whole thing. Every day it was just like my prayers. So, a few years back—oh, quite a few years back—he was in the hospital in Neil's Harbour. So my wife and I went to see him. So he was [reminded] about this. It took me I don't know how many years, I got him to put the money in the Bank of Nova Scotia [in Ingonish], to open up an account. He was sick in the hospital, and he was still telling my wife, he'd rather trust me than trust a bank. After I don't know how many years....

Another time—who was it? I sold the fellow a suit. And he had no money. He gave me a piece of paper, to give me like $32.50, to go to the bank, and his bankbook. He signed his name. So I went to the bank. And I remember the boy, the fellow at the bank said, "I'll mail it to him"—[bank]book. I said, "No. You give me $32.50. And write it in." I didn't want to give it to him. But he just trusted me with the bank account, just go there.

Another time—some places religion was very big, too. You know, like, Catholics and Protestants, there was still a certain amount of—in places. I remember this fellow in Middle River. His daughter married a Catholic. And oh, he didn't want to have anything to do with her. And I had to try to tell him—I said, "Look, she's still your daughter," and all that stuff.

But they—a lot of them, they'd come and tell me things that I don't think they'd tell anybody else. But they just trusted me, tell me their troubles. And that continued when I was in the store. People would come in, confide [in] me.

(*Did you peddle in the wintertime as well...?*) I did some in the winter, but most of it in the summer and the fall. But the first winter I carried the pack was very rough. I remember I think it was on Boisdale, it was so slippery. And I was going up two feet and come back ten, you know. And I was ready to commit suicide....

And I remember going into this house, and they wanted to buy a pair of braces, I think, for 75¢. And they offered me 50¢ for it. After me carrying the pack way up the hill—and I didn't want to sell it to them! I just didn't sell it to them. But then, a lot of days you went, you didn't sell a single thing. The next time you would....

A lot of things that happened there. But in general they would give you the shirt off of their back if they liked you. They'd go away fishing—three, four o'clock in the morning. They'd leave you with their wives, their daughters. There was no—there was never any question of anything there....

But this was experiences I had. You can't buy it for money. In places—kids wouldn't go to school, they'd come with me in the wagon. There was a Kerr fellow in Cape North. And the young fellow wouldn't go to school when I was there. Pete Kerr's son, yeah....

I carried the pack mostly, then I went to the horse-and-wagon. And then my brother started the business [a store in Sydney Mines], and I still went with the horse. And then I gave up the horse and I went to work with him in the store. Yazer Brothers. He took me as a partner; he started at it....

We had a nice Jewish community. Then, the Pier was fairly big. Glace Bay had a big Jewish community. I went to Sydney Mines with my brother—we were just batching, you know, we were boarding. But see, I found it hard here. Like, you'd ask for a Jewish girl to go out: "I'm busy"—I'm this and this and that, you see. So naturally you went with [girls that were not Jewish]. At that time you were considered a greenhorn. Today you're a European—you're not called a greenhorn. You haven't got that title. It's a big difference than it was then. (*You mean among the people of the Jewish community?*) Yeah. You were more like a greenhorn—you know, just came over, you don't know anything. But then after awhile you get in with them, then you're okay....

I think I'm satisfied with my life, you know, what I've had. I can see difference in our thinking here. But I think our values, I think, have gone down, from when I peddled. It meant—going to church was a big thing. You know, there were a certain amount didn't, but it meant good. A lot of places you never ate until somebody said Grace. If a policeman came into the house—you know, say, "Hi, sit down, have a cup of coffee." Today if he comes in the house—"Aw...."—the neighbours: "He had it coming to him." You know, "What's going on?"

And I remember many a time when a priest or a minister used to come into the house. Nobody got excited if it was lunchtime. The mother would say, "Pull over. Put a chair in there for Fr. So-and-so," or whatever it is. He sat down, there was no excitement, nothing—just squeeze yourself in another chair. Nobody touched anything till Grace was said. Today if a priest or a minister comes down to the house, somebody's sick or somebody's dying.

Teachers. I remember taking a young girl around the Cabot Trail—I was young. I wanted so much to make a pass at her—kiss her. But how do you do it—a teacher! How can you do a thing like this? You know? Today, you know....

I mean, those are just the things that I can see.

The list of causes and organizations for which Jack Yazer has volunteered is long. It includes the Canadian Cancer Society, Red Cross, United Jewish Appeal, Nova Scotia Family & Child Welfare Association, and the Cape Breton Island Regional Hospital Foundation, of which he was the founding chairman. In recognition of service to his community, he received an Honourary Doctor of Law degree from St. Francis Xavier University in 1978.

Gordie MacDougall, Boxer: My Life

Gordie MacDougall of South Bar was a boxer. He had sixty-seven fights, four losses, three draws. He was also a seaman, and a man who spent some time down on his luck. He always fought his way back up.

When we talked with Gordie, he was living under what he called "a death sentence." He had ALS, a disease doctors call Ameotrophic Lateral Sclerosis but which most of us know as "Lou Gehrig's disease." Gordie was born June 16, 1934.

We visited with Gordie and Shirley MacDougall. We asked Gordie, "How did you get started boxing?"

Gordie MacDougall: I got started mainly through a good friend of mine, went to high school together—Ernie MacKinnon. He was a heck of a good fighter. He was fighting at the time. So he used to ask me to go down to—they had a hall down by his place, down Low Point.

So the two of us would go in the hall, we'd put an old alarm clock on the chair. Only two of us in the hall. We'd set the alarm clock to go off in maybe three [minutes], some rounds would be five. And we'd box. He kept after me, "Come on. Come on to the gym with me." So then I final-

GORDIE McDOUGALL IS ANOTHER EXAMPLE OF THE MANY GREAT FIGHTERS SPAWNED IN CAPE BRETON DURING THE POST WAR ERA...

...GORDIE'S STYLE IS TO COME OUT FAST AND GET IT DONE QUICKLY!

SORRY BUT I GOT AN EARLY DATE!

2 K.O.

LEATHER IS NOT THE ONLY THING WE THROW EH!

AN ALL-AROUND ATHLETE - GORDIE ALSO THROWS BASEBALLS FOR THE MARITIME CHAMPIONS - THE 1959 NEW WATERFORD GIANTS!

KARL MARSH 88

ly—"Yeah," I said, "okay, I'll go in the gym with you."

John Nemis had the Police Club then. When they weren't working out there, I could go down to the Strand Gym. Then from there, next, you know, they'd coax me, "Come on"—fighting. So I did, and I started boxing. So poor Ernie got killed in the meantime, in a car accident. Coming home from work one night from the pit—killed in a single-car accident—rolled the car on a turn coming home. That kind of set us, me and Johnny Nemis, back quite a bit, because I lost one of the best friends I ever had in Ernie MacKinnon.

So I laid off boxing for six months or so. Then I started her up again real sincere, more or less on Ernie's behalf, you know. So, things steamrolled from there.

(*Gordie, how did you train? Did you take vitamins?*) No, there was no such thing as vitamins. You had your mother's good home cooking, that's what you did. Gosh, you worked hard. I worked on the railway, old S & L Railway. I was a fireman there, shovelling coal. Walked to work. Ran back in the morning from work—worked nightshift on the railroad shovelling coal. I'd run home in the morning—my roadwork. Go to bed. And go that evening to the gym. I was working out with some pretty good boys. There were a lot of fighters around here then. There was Mitzi Krszwda, Gordon "Gramps" Kiley, Tommy "Gun" Spencer, Charlie Pyle, Archie "Bear" Hannigan, and his brother Ernie "Champ" Hannigan, New Waterford. And Al Hogan. "Diapers" Gillis—he's a policeman in New Waterford now. Bobby Moore from the Northside. Buddy Greer. A lot of the local lads here. Tyrone Gardiner [Lightweight Champion of Canada]. Later, Rocky MacDougall came in [Featherweight Champion of Canada].

There was quite a crowd of us around boxing. I mean, there was no shortage of sparring partners at that time. Now, we haven't even got one pro fighter. I think we've got maybe six in Nova Scotia today. There's nobody of any recognition. Whereas one time, there was no shortage in the Maritimes....

Now, you know—they have a few amateur clubs going now, which is

"MacDougall's body attack. Gordie MacDougall of South Bar, right, is shown above, ready to deliver a left to the body of Doug Odo of Thorburn in the main event of the Sydney Police Boxing Club card at Sydney Forum last night. MacDougall won by a technical knockout when Odo was unable to...start the 9th round due to rib injuries." **Gordie**: Oh, yeah, he was all red, too. Blood was coming right out of his ribs. I was only about 5-foot-10, you know. Could punch like hell though. Oh, I loved—I could pound the body out of you, you know what I mean? I was stocky and powerful, as you can see. Lots of upper-body stretch.

good. But even they don't fight often enough. That's what holds a young fellow's interest. If he's kept busy. You're not training all the time in the gym for maybe a fight every three months or a fight every two months. To me, I think a young kid should be fighting every two weeks. That's the only way of keeping him sharp, for him to learn his trade. If you're a carpenter, you have to be in the building trade constantly. You work with some older carpenters that show you the tricks of the trade. Well, it's the same with boxers. You box often, you keep yourself sharp. You're around better fighters or you fight better fighters, and you keep your eyes open, you learn off them. At the end of my career, after ten or eleven years at it, I was still learning....

I worked in the woods. I was a lumberjack. When I lived out in East Bay there, I cut timber, hauled timber. And I boxed, in the meantime. Kind of toughened you up [on the] job, you know. We had punching bags.

I used to spar at least five or six rounds a day, say five days a week. And then when I went to the States, boxing there, I used to spar up to six, seven rounds a day for six days a week sometimes. You took more punishment in training than you did sometimes in an actual fight....

But I was very dedicated. First seven or eight years I was, you know, gung-ho, as they say. And worked hard, trained hard. Well, I just loved the sport. I loved to fight. The tougher the fights were, the better I loved it. Harder they were, yeah. Some of them were real wars, they were real tough. God, you went home after a fight, your face was pretty sore. I remember one time I fought a fellow—I'm sure he must have kicked me, because I was sore from my head to my feet. Holy smoke, I was sore all over. But those things, after a few days, a week, everything heals over and you forgot about that one, you move on to the next fellow, that's all. You had cut eyes or stuff like that. Well, the old doc stitches you up. And in about seven days time, you're raring to go again. The cuts are starting to heal and you're wanting to get back in the swing of things.

Your nose, after every fight, looks a little different, gets a little flatter. Seems that's the focal point of all the punches. If they land, four out of five land on the nose. Just gets to be a piece of rubber after awhile. I had mine busted four or five times.

You don't bother fixing them after the first time because you just keep the doctor in business then. Just leave them, they'd grow back crooked....

Things like that never bothered me, no. While I was in the ring I had eyes closed and cut eyes. But you see some of the fighters now, they come back [to their corner]—see them with a slight cut or there's blood dripping. "Oh, my, how bad is the cut?" They worry about their facial features. God Almighty, I came back, I couldn't see, I couldn't see anybody in the corner. Eye'd be closed, right level over, you couldn't even see my nose. Referees I know a couple of times wanted to stop the fight, but I said, "No, no. Let it go. Let it go for another round, I'll knock the guy out in another round or two." Sometimes that happened, sometimes it didn't. They'd have to stop it [sometimes]. Pretty bad. Long as you could get off the canvas, you know, and crawl on your feet, put your hands up, they'd let you [go on]. Tough days, you know....

(*When you went to the States, did you make a living in fighting or did you have to have another job?*) Worked a little on the side. Because you never make a living off boxing, no. So there was one place there, I hustled in a nightclub. Then another job, I worked in a plant, down in Boston. Out in the Midwest, in Minneapolis and places, this promoter had a nightclub he owned. So I used to get work in there. That kept me in pocket money.

I stayed in a Y.M.C.A. down there. Twelve dollars a week. I used to pay thirteen dollars. If you paid the extra dollar, you had the use of all

Y.M.C.A. facilities—the swimming pool, their gym—any activity you wanted to use—bowling alleys. They had racquetball places, stuff like that. The gym was just around the corner down the main drag, so that's where we worked out.

I was based there [in Minneapolis]. But then I'd fight over in St. Paul, which was the twin city. Then I'd go down to Kansas City and Missouri and St. Louis, South Dakota; Butte, Montana; Omaha, Nebraska; and those places. Boxing. California. I was really out there a couple of years. I really loved it out there in Minneapolis. It was beautiful. The people were lovely. And I loved the countryside there.

My God, it was cold there in the wintertime though. I used to run and do roadwork around this lake.... And you couldn't take deep breaths, you know, or else you'd freeze your lungs. God Almighty. Nostrils'd be all icicles. My eyebrows'd be all full of ice. Coming back after running and you'd be all froze up. But you didn't mind; it was kind of a dry cold, like our Out West in our country, prairies.

But, I really loved it. And a lot of fine people. It was a real adventure for me, and I loved it. I guess I was twenty years old out there. So, did a lot of kicking around, met a lot of fine people. Pleasure meeting, like, you know, Jack Dempsey. Down in Harlem, Sugar Ray Robinson. Many famous fighters in the gym I met. Had the occasion to spar with some. Others I just met. Saw a couple of big fights there. Archie Moore and [Floyd] Patterson, for the title—was at their training camp. I went to see Rocky Marciano training.

So all in all, it was good to me. I really enjoyed it.

My daily schedule—I was up at six in the morning. I'd go down to the cafeteria. Or, if the cafeteria wasn't open in the Y I was staying, I'd get all my heavy boots on and turtleneck sweater and toque on my head, long underwear on and everything else, your mitts. And I'd carry the two-pound iron weights in each hand. So then I'd walk down—there used to be these all-night places—they were built like a little castle. All they served was hamburgers and coffee and that, you know. It's a chain. So I'd stop in one of them. It was about a half a mile to the place where I ran at this park, I'd have a black coffee, and they'd give me a little cup of—like you see ketchup in, those little cups—of honey. I'd put that in my black coffee. Drink my coffee and have my toast.

I'd walk to the park, and then I'd do three to five miles of roadwork around the park. So then I'd jog home to the Y, change out of my clothes, shower up and that. Take all my wet clothes down to the laundromat, wash them and dry them, hang them up. Then I'd go down and have my breakfast in the cafeteria downstairs. I'd have a big grapefruit cut in half—I love grapefruit. And then I'd have my black coffee and maybe I'd

231

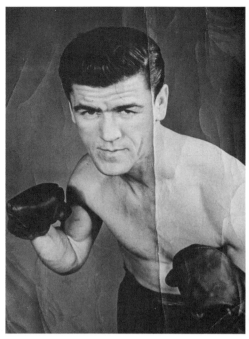
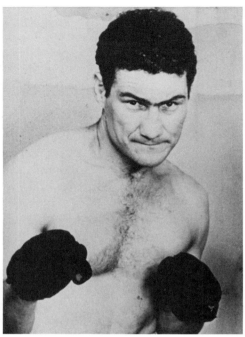

A mini-gallery of only a very few of the Cape Breton boxers who have made a name in the sport. Left: Tommy "Gun" Spencer, Welterweight Champion of the Maritimes; right: Archie "Bear" Hannigan, Maritime Light Heavyweight Champion.

have a couple of poached eggs and a piece of dry toast and another bit of honey in my coffee.

So I'd go up then and I'd lay back and relax. Lay down. Had a little radio—turn the radio on and go to sleep. And then get up, oh, maybe twelve, one o'clock—have a coffee. Grab my gear, walk down the main drag there in Minneapolis City. Go up to the gym. Get ready to work out around two o'clock.

So we sparred, like I said, anywhere from five to seven rounds a day. We warmed up. We got in the ring. First we'd have to get dressed—taped your own hands and that—and I'd get in the ring and I'd shadowbox— you know, to break a sweat, loosen up, do some bending exercises. Get all the kinks out of you. Then they'd come put the gloves on you and you'd spar. Some of those sparring sessions were pretty wild.

So then when you finished sparring, they'd put you on the heavy bag, you'd do a round or two on the big bag. Then they'd put you on the trainer—you know, you'd have the big palm gloves. He'd get you firing combinations. His hands'd be moving, tell you to hook, jab, hook, straight right hand, one-two punch. Then you skipped rope. Then you did calisthenics. You had to do a special lot for your stomach. Because your stomach, it'd absorb a lot of punches and your stomach's got to be hard as a table.

So when you finished all that up, then you had a shower, got dressed.

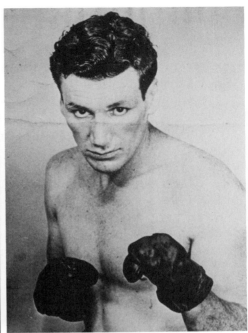

Tyrone Gardiner, undefeated Lightweight Champion of Canada, and Donald "Red" Mac-Pherson. Though he never won a title, "Red" defeated some of the best in his class.

Then I'd head to supper. I'd have my supper. I'd relax. Maybe later took in a movie or something like that. You weren't out late. Ten o'clock you'd be in bed. Be up early in the morning, six o'clock, be on the road again.

(Where did you find the time to work?) When I did get a job—I didn't have to be down to the nightclub till nine o'clock. I'd work there till about 11:30. So I worked there; well, I ate there, too. Fellow who owned the nightclub, he was the guy that sponsored me up there—he was a millionaire—Tommy Anderson. And he was a fight promoter. So it was very easy to get time off. Once one o'clock came he'd say, "Okay, Gordon, time for the gym." So I just punched in about five hours a day, that's all, four hours a day. That's all I did. So that made it a convenience.

Other times. Like when I was boxing home here [in Cape Breton] I'd work nightshift—work anywhere—like on the railroad. I'd go to work usually ten o'clock till midnight. And work to six, seven in the morning. Like I said, I'd run home—that'd be my roadwork. Well then I'd shower up and then go to bed, then I'd get up after dinner sometime—two o'clock or something like that. Well, there's supper at four. After supper, into the gym I'd go.

I was playing ball that time, too. So I'd go up to the Pier playground with my ball gear in a bag with my boxing gear. After the ballgame, I just switched into my streetclothes, put my ball gear in with my boxing gear, jumped on a bus and I went over to town, over to Sydney. Worked out.

Then I got a bus back to Broadway, down to the Pier, and I walked home from Broadway. It was about two, two and a half miles I'd walk home.

Get home, and then right back out to work. Before midnight I'd have to go to work. That's before I had a car. Then when I got a car, made it a little easier. You'd drive, and never lost so much time. But then eventually I had to give that up because you were burning the candle at both ends, as they say then, you know. Starting to take its toll. So, you know, you couldn't give your all to it.

I remember one time I fought Saturday night in Glace Bay. And this fellow butted me in—I don't know—second or third round or something. Broke my nose. Gee whiz, I knocked him out in five or six. But by that time I could hardly see out of both eyes. So I went home, on a Saturday night. And I woke up Sunday morning. I couldn't open an eye. My eyes were closed tight as a drum. So I had to get my mother to bring me up some ice in a towel. And one eye I could get open with my fingers, you know. So I put the ice on that eye. I got a slit in that eye open, you know. And at one o'clock the bus came for me—I was playing Junior Baseball— I was pitching then. So they came and picked me up for ball; we were playing ball in Waterford. So I went down and I pitched, and won a game four-to-three that day, only looking through one eye.

Like I said, you know, you were clean-living at that time. You weren't running around spending all hours of the night. You just never had time for that. Dances—if you went—a girl or something like that—you went out Saturday night, that's all—Saturday and Sunday, that's all. Because the rest of the nights you were working or you were in the gym....

So that's the way it was. It all worked out. So I gave her a good shot for—like I said—about seven years I gave her a real good shot. Then I had disappointments. Between promoters and Boxing Commission. (What kind of disappointments?) Well, you were promised fights. If you fought this fellow and you won, they'd promise you a shot at the Canadian champion. So you fought the guy. Then you were waiting for that big shot. Then they'd give you a runaround, the promoter or the manager of the other fighter'd give you the runaround. Instead of signing to fight you he'd sign to fight somebody else. Sidestepped you. You know, you got kicked around a lot....

Then the latter [years], I'd get discouraged and I'd quit. I'd go sailing, and then I'd come back and I'd make comebacks. And everything'd be going good, and then I'd throw in the towel again, you know, get discouraged or get a runaround. You wouldn't be getting enough money for the fight or.... What used to get me: they wouldn't fight me often enough. I was a guy that—keep me busy. That's the way I was. I was a guy who wanted to be kept busy, you know. This here working out in the gym all the time—that was no good to me. I want to fight every two weeks. That's the way I am.

So, when you get dogged like that, you know. And then, promoters would gyp you out of money and everything else. Pretty discouraging when you work hard at something. That's the way it went in those days.

(When you were young, before you started boxing, what did you think that you'd become?) Well, I'll tell you the truth, I thought I'd always be a fighter. I remember as a small fellow, eleven or twelve years old, I had a pair of boxing gloves. And I used to take

the neighbourhood kids my age—maybe a year older or a year younger—and we'd all go down to my father's barn. My father hated boxing, he would never let me box or anything like that. So I'd get the kids to [go] there. I'd send them home with black eyes, bloody noses, and everything else! Used to be terrible! Beat up the kids, and then I'd have to give them candy or something like that to get them back in the next day, so I could do the same thing to them! [Gordie laughs.]

So then I used to beg my father to let me listen to the Friday night fights on the radio at eleven o'clock. Well, that was late to stay up then. So he let me stay up. I listened to Joe Louis fighting all those guys, fighting in the '40s, late '40s, early '50s then. And I'd idolize some of those fighters, you know. I'd be delivering papers, you know. I'd be delivering papers, I'd fantasize that I was a fighter—big-time guy fighting in Madison Square Garden. Little did I know, a few years down the road, that I would be up in those places....

But I always said that, you know, I was kind of a bad kid when I was going to school, I was full of the devil. It's a wonder I wasn't killed or punchdrunk. Because all the kids used to pound me. You know, I'd be always in trouble and fights. The older kids'd pound me. I was right mischievous and saucy. So it's a wonder I survived, because I used to get some awful poundings in school....

(But your father didn't like boxing?) Oh, God. He never went to one of my fights. That was one of the hard points of my career. And I tried so

hard, and I tried to be the best I could. Which I was. I was no punk, you know. But he wouldn't go. He wouldn't go to a fight. He wouldn't let my mother go. My sister went to every one of them around here. And then my aunts and uncles, and my grandfather—my father's father—oh, yeah, they all went to see them. My mother's sisters. That was the one disappointment, that he—I mean, if it was my son, I'd say, "Hey!"—I'd be so proud, have my chest out, bust all the buttons on it. You know, I had some big fights, and I won them.

I can see if it was just a ham-and-egg or getting beat up all the time. But, you know, I was well-trained....

So, like I said, that was my biggest disappointment was that he never came to see me, then he could evaluate me himself, you know what I mean. So that when you look down in the audience and see all your relatives there, and your father's not there, you know what I mean. And give you a bit of encouragement. He even went, when I first started—he found all my gear in a bag down in the basement and he threw it in the furnace, bag and all, the whole thing. I went down that night to get my bag to go to the gym. I said, "Mom, where's my bag at?" "I hate to tell you," she said. "Your father threw it in the furnace and burned it." I said, "Did he? Well, that's all right." I went and I started gathering up junk—beer bottles and everything else—and I bought it all back. It was only secondhand, but I bought it all back, boy. I used to hide it out in the barn and everything, so he wouldn't get it. Oh yeah.

I was a quiet guy. But when somebody came up to me and said, "Hey, move over. Get out of my way," I'd say, "If you can't walk through me, you'd better get out of the way. Because I'm going to beat your brains out." That's the way I was....

(*Do you feel you were bad?*) No, I was just—I was mischievous, bad, like, you know. I had a tough mind.... I was scared of nothing, when I was a kid....

And you know what? I used to get more beatings—I should have been punchdrunk before I got out of Grade Six. The older kids used to pound me. And you know what? They'd beat me, you know, down in the school-yard. And I used to go—we'd get out at 3:30—I'd say to the teacher, "I've got to use the bathroom"—quarter after three. So I'd go out and use [the outhouse]. So I'd run across the street—it was all woods then. And I'd gather a whole pile of rocks as big as that chair. When those two guys that beat me came out of school, I'd pelt them with rocks, till they'd lumps on their head, boy, going home. And the next day they'd beat me. And the next day they'd get rocks. Oh, I'm telling you, I was some tough kid....

Shirley MacDougall, Gordie's wife: A little note on that. No matter

236

who you ask today about Gordie: "Gordie was always a gentleman." **Gordie**: Yeah. I wouldn't go out of my way, you know, to do any harm. **Shirley**: But Gordie was a gentleman. He treated women—always, whether they were ten years old or a hundred years old—no matter who you talk to, they'll tell you that—Gordie would always treat you with respect. And he was a fantastic person to visit his old friends—oh, real old men who were in their seventies when Gordie was only forty. **Gordie**: Yeah, they'd be in the hospital, I'd always go to the hospitals.

Shirley: He was wonderful to go visit, bring them little gifts. He just— a wonderful gentleman. Everyone loved Gordie. Everyone.

Gordie: But they were part of my experiences, you know.... I loved it. When I was [a kid] getting in trouble, that's how I got my mark. (*Because you were getting into trouble?*) Well, I was getting in trouble, and the cops and the Mounties were kind of picking me up and keeping an eye on me. And then the Police Club had a boxing club and Johnny Nemis was there. I was in with Ernie MacKinnon.

Of course, the cops told Johnny Nemis about me. He told me, he said, "Look. What I teach you in here, it's in here, and that's as far as it goes." He said, "I don't want to catch you," he said, "or the cops never tell me that you used this stuff on the street. And," he said, "if you do...." And I got to like coming to the gym. You know, this was an outlet, I guess. I

Gordie MacDougall: I'm boxing at the same time, and I'm running a lot of road races. I used to run for that Broadway Club. And I ran here in the Cape Breton championship at the Sports Centre. And one night there in the Cape Breton championships I won two gold and a bronze on the same night. I won the mile, junior mile, and junior half-mile. And I came third in the senior miles.... I ran the 24th of May Legion road races at Whitney Pier. And the guy next to me I think is Joey Mullins, who was one of the greatest runners to ever come out of Canada at the time. He raced in Arizona State University, and ran in the British Empire games in Scotland. And also ran, I think, in B.C., for Canada. Him and I ran head-to-head in three or four races. I think I only beat him once, which must have been a fluke, because he was quite a runner, you know. [Gordie is fifth from right, back row.]

Johnny Nemis came from a boxing family. In nearly three hundred professional fights, he met and defeated some of the best in North America. He trained such boxers as Richardson, MacDougall, MacKinnon, and MacPhail.

don't know. And he said, "If you do," he said, "you're out of this gym," he said, "and don't you come back."

That guy had an impact on me. That guy had a good impact on me. So then I gave up that kind of life, and then I just strictly stuck to boxing. I was dedicated to it. I just gave up that kind of life. All the time I was—for about eight years, you know, when I was going good, I never bothered anybody. I'd walk away if somebody got smart. Ordinarily, I'd put a belt on him. Wouldn't have thought twice about it. But I just used to walk away.

But it changed my life. Johnny Nemis changed my life. Canadian Welterweight Champion. Oh, yeah, good fighter. Two-hundred-and-some fights.... Johnny Nemis, he came from Fourteen Yard. That was the hardest section of New Waterford....

And I'll say this—I've said it many's the time to people: No one ever taught me more than Johnny Nemis did about boxing. But, he was a bad manager. He was a good trainer but a bad manager. You understand what I mean?

See, Johnny fought in the '20s and '30s. He fought for wristwatches and suits of clothes, twenty or thirty dollars, and maybe a meal. You understand what I mean? In those days, when I could be getting $1000, $200 was okay—long as we got a scalp on our belt—that's what he used to call it. "We got another scalp. Never mind about the money." Geez, you know, you fight your guts out—$200. Then you're back in two weeks later again, you know, for maybe $100.

Geez, I fought a top-rank contender—he was the tenth rank middleweight in the world. I fought him and beat him for $100. Gave him a ten-round decision.

But it just rolled off, you know what I mean.

But it didn't always roll off. In other conversations, Gordie told of low periods in his life. Tough as he was, sometimes Gordie could not handle his

238

disappointments, on boxing and in other ways. He talked about some of his roughest days.

We drank everything. I drank old bay rum. I drank 78 records. I've got more Bing Crosby tunes in me than Bing Crosby. I was on the streets. I was on the skids. And I drank. And I used to hang around with the skid row boys. And we used to drink down on the railroad tracks, the old coal trestle here in Sydney. And we used to sleep in the Stephens lumber shacks.

Then I got straightened away. And then another time I went on the skids after I'd fought in Minneapolis, Minnesota, and I went back there. And I went on a drunk, and I couldn't get off it, one time. Off a ship. I'm the only guy that ever missed a ship in Minneapolis, where there's no water!... Because I got off a ship in Duluth, Minnesota, flew down to Minneapolis, Minnesota, to visit some friends that I hadn't seen for thirteen years. I used to box up there.

So I got down, then I got into the sauce and parties. And I forgot—and I missed my ship and everything else. So I was down there for two and a half months. So I was on skid row down there, and I was sleeping in mission houses, fifty cents a night—250 flops, and oh, geez. On a street corner five o'clock in the morning, trying to get a job. Enough work for— like, you know, a furniture guy came along and he wanted to move furniture. You know what I mean? They went and they'd hire you for the day. And then at the end of the day they'd give you ten or fifteen dollars. Well, that was good. So you paid three days ahead in rent to the mission house, and then you got the rest in wine.

(*I don't understand about the 78 records.*) Oh, we used to melt them down. See, we used to go to garbage—see, garbage day—around the city. This is years ago, when the old 78 records were on the go. So there's people had broken records. So they'd throw them out in the garbage. So we used to pick them all up. There's alcohol in records. So we used to go, and we'd take a pot, and we'd go down by the railroad tracks. And we'd boil the records—78 records—we'd boil them down. And we'd strain them through cheesecloth into a pot. And we'd drink it out of a pot....

But jesus, it gave you a hell of a bang after you drank so many of those records. And then you went like loony tunes down the street.

(*Was it because you were an alcoholic or was it because of your life?*) No. My life.... I got discouraged, I was having a bad down time, you know, in life. And everything. And so, I got in with kind of a bad crowd. And then I drifted into the skid row crowd.

See, I'd known them.... When I was a young fighter, I used to see all the skid row guys by the old coal haulers' depot on George Street. So I used to go by—"Hi, Gord"—all these skid row bums. "How you doing,

Gord? Geez, that was a great fight you had," you know—like, that's the night before.... And I was too young then to go in the liquor store. So I used to give them six dollars—and they could buy wine for eighty cents a bottle then. So I'd give them six bucks and they'd go in and, gee, they'd come out with about seven bottles of wine. And then they'd go down back of the Sydney Rink—the old Sydney Forum—down by the railroad tracks, there used to be a coal trestle there. And J.W. Stephens had shacks down there, construction shacks. Well, that's where they used to drink it.

So then after—oh, maybe eight or nine years later—you know, I had some hard times, and I just happened to drift into that life. (*Is it fair to ask you what hard times are?*) Well, discouragements and—in a boxing game, and I was having discouragement on a job. It was a number of different things. You know, I just thought—everybody thinks the world is tumbling down on you, you know what I mean. And I said, "Aw, jesus." And you think out of the mouth of a bottle, it solves everything. You know what I mean. And the more you drank, the more carefree you got. And you forgot all your troubles, see. So of course you drank more to forget all your troubles. So then, when there was nothing around for us to drink, well, we drank anything.

We were walking up Charlotte Street one day. And this guy—it was his turn to go in the Metropolitan [store] to steal some shoe polish. (*Shoe polish?*) Oh, yeah, we used to drink shoe polish. The paste shoe polish. You'd melt that down.

And [one fellow] said, "Geez," he said, "get anything but that Nugget [colour]," he said. "That goddamn Nugget gives me heartburn!" Imagine!....

And vanilla extract—geez, we used to drink that by the bottle. And shaving lotion, we used to drink that. And perfume. Oh, you'd drink all that stuff. Oh, geez, that was great. You know, we were the only smelly guys in Sydney.

(*How did you get out of it, then? Clearly, you did.*) Yeah, I got out of it. (*But how?*) Well, it took awhile. I guess—you've got to hit the rock bottom, you know what I mean? You hit the pits, and you're right down and you're out. And you're sick and you're degraded. Well, you humiliate your family—my family had nothing, wanted to do with me. Not even some of my friends, want to associate with you, you know what I mean? And then you pick yourself up by the bootstraps. And I got up, and I....) Okay, then. So then I went away. (*Is this when your family fell apart?*) Yeah. That was part of the whole thing, see.

So then I went away—you know, change of scenery. I wasn't happy in the situation. But it's a situation where you wake up every day and you say you're going to change it. And then a guy's got a bottle there. And

Above, left to right: Joe Jackson, Blair Richardson, Johnny Nemis, promoter Gussie MacLellan, Jack Dempsey (World Heavywieght Champion 1914-27), Gordie MacDougall. Right: Blair Richardson, Middleweight Champion of Canada and Middleweight Champion of the British Empire, who held a high world rank.

Gordie MacDougall: "Blair Richardson was a terrific kid. And he used to come and—he boxed when he was around twelve in a Golden Gloves, and he was a very shy kid, and that's the only time he fought. And then he started coming to the gym with me, carrying my bags. And then he'd come in the gym when I'd work out in the afternoon to spar with me. He was shy in front of a crowd. And then I got him coming at night, and he kept coming. Then he kept training with me and then—God, he trained with me for about five years, until he went away to sea. He trained with me till he was about seventeen, eighteen, I guess. He used to fight six-rounders on my main event.

"Well then he went away to the States and he fought some of the top-notch fighters in the States. Good fighters. He fought in Madison Square Garden. He fought Joey Archer, who was around the seventh-rank middleweight in the world, and he lost to him in Madison Square Gardens. So, he fought some good boys.

"He died of a brain tumour when he was thirty-three. He collapsed and died. He was a teacher at Boston University, teaching theology. He put himself through college in Boston. He was married—married a beautiful girl from Sydney Mines. And she was pregnant. He died in February, and she had the baby in May.

"He was a terrific guy. He was a very religious person, very religious."

---

you're so happy to grab that bottle....

I slept shoulder-to-shoulder in mission houses in the States. When I was in Minneapolis. And there were doctors, lawyers, and everything else, slept in the bunk next to me. And they were rich men at one time. And there they were, the same as me, out on the street with raggedy clothes, panhandling for a handout. And geez, you ate out of garbage cans....

(*Where in your life does this fit? Is this before you became a boxer?*) Oh, no, no. This was about the middle part. And then there was another time. And then I made comebacks. And then after I became a fighter, then it happened to me again. After I retired from fighting, see, it became a part of me again. And thank God it only lasted about three months the last time.

I had a very good friend of mine, this Fr. Murphy, in Minneapolis. Who kind of practically picked me up off the street. He got me straightened away and pointed me in the right direction. And I was very thankful for him afterwards. So I got back, and then I got—he got me to get ahold of my father, which I didn't want to do. Send me some money, you know, to get back to Canada, eh?

So what we did.... See, it's easy to get in the States, and work if you want it—you know what I mean? So what I did: see, I'm on the row—I'm on the skids down there. So I went and I got a guy that was on the skids with me. He's got a social security card—an unemployment number. And I said to him, "Here's ten bucks. I'll buy your social security card off you, see." For ten bucks—that was big money. So he gave it to me.... "Listen. When I get a job, and I make some money, and I get out of the country, within six months time, or I quit my job—I'll give you the social security number back, card back, and you can go and collect unemployment." You understand what I mean? And that guy is a bum, see, and he never works. Street smart, see?

So that's how I used to work it. So I went to work, and I got a few shifts. So then I went and I gave the guy the [social security] card, you know, the number back. He got unemployment. I took off out of the country. See, there's angles in everything, you know what I mean?... It's really survival, you know.

I met a lot of fine people in my travels down there [in the States]. When I was out in California, through other people, I met the Rat Pack, you know—Frank Sinatra, Peter Lawford, Shirley McLaine, Sammy Davis Jr. The Rat Pack, they called them at that time. See, they were all fight fans, all those people. And I was only fighting, like, six-rounders out there.... But I was over with guys like Del Flanagan, Al Andrews, those guys. They were fighting main events—top fighters in the world. And I was out with them, sparring partner. They'd get a six-round fight for me, you know.

And afterwards, there was a party at this big country club, see, and that's how I met them. All these celebrities were there. Here I was a dumb cluck from Cape Breton out there, waltzing around the floor. And I got a dance with this—Diane Dors was her name. She was an English girl. She was like a Marilyn Monroe at the time....

So, anyway, like I was only young, I was only nineteen when I was out there. So, from there I came back home and fought around the Maritimes. I went away to Boston again and fought. And then I came back. Then I went to sea. I quit boxing, I went to sea. And then I made comebacks, like, you know.

And this funny incident—I was maybe a year and a half out of boxing. I was living out the country, East Bay way, and I was working in the woods out there. I had two small children, living in a small bungalow. And fifty dollars a week I was getting, working in the woods. So this promoter from Sydney, Benny Gaum, he came out. Big Cadillac car, pulled up at my door and came in. Well, I'd fought for Benny before. And he said he wanted me to fight. The other card—Blair Richardson was going to make his first ten-round fight here in the Glace Bay Forum. And he wanted a name semi-final fighter, you know. So my wife said, "Oh, no way—he's through. I don't want him fighting any more." So I hadn't had a glove on for about seventeen or eighteen months.

So anyway, a couple of days later, back he came again. So he threw a whole bunch of money on the table, you know. Ooo, you know, your eyes light up. When you're working for fifty bucks a week, and you see a bunch of money on the table. So, he said, "That's yours, Gordie, if you'll sign for the fight." She said, "No." So I called her in the bedroom. I said, "Hey, we could use some bucks, you know." Baby was only six months old, and an older fellow. So, finally agreed. And I never asked who I was fighting or anything like that. All I remember saying was, "Well, when is the fight?" I figured I had a month, you know, when I'd get ready. He said, "In ten days." Imagine—ten days!

So all I did was run back and forth through the woods. And I put a punching bag up in the barn, and I punched that. I had no car, so I couldn't get to Sydney, do any sparring or anything.

So, isn't it funny? When I was going good, you had people around you all the time. Take you here. Gee whiz, they'd shovel your driveway—which I didn't want, you know. And I had a car of my own. My heavens, that night—how easy fame is forgotten, eh? Here I am, out on the road, hitchhiking from East Bay to the Glace Bay Miners Forum. (*You had to hitchhike to the fight.*) Yeah. Nobody came. See, that's what I say: fame is fleeting, you know what I mean. When you're on top, everybody wants you or wants to be around you. But when you're nothing, you're down on the bottom—I'm making a comeback now. So, here we go.

So I got to the Esplanade, and I got a bus up to Ashby.... I'm hitchhiking now from Ashby to Glace Bay. So finally this car stops and I got in. My bag on the floor, driving along. I said, "How far are you going?" "Oh," he said, "I'm going to Glace Bay." He said, "Are you?" I said, "Yes." So we got driving along. And he said, "I'm going to the fights tonight. I'm from New Glasgow. I'm coming down to see that MacDougall fight," he said. "He's fought in New Glasgow and Stellarton. Terrific

243

fighter." You know this was in past years. And he said, "He always gives you a good fight." So I never let on who I was all this time.

So we got down, before you turn up on the Forum. I said, "I'll get off in the parking lot." So he pulled in the parking lot, shut off the car. And I opened the door, the bag—and that was the first time he noticed the bag. So when I got out he said, "Hey, by the way," he said, "are you fighting tonight?" I said, "Yeah, I am." He said, "What's your name?" I said. "Oh, my God," he said, "I've been driving the last fourteen miles...!" He said, "You're the guy I came all the way from New Glasgow to see fight...!"

So anyway, I went. And I put on quite a show that night. I fought the guy to a draw—me with ten days. Tore the house down. I've got a write-up in the paper about it, you know. Those are some of the experiences I had.

And then I drifted into sailing. [Gordie sailed for over 20 years.] And, oh God, been all over around the world. I went on the Lakes, and sailed there. Then I'd get a little restless like that, and then I went deep sea. I went to Europe, and down to Africa. I was in England, Germany, Rotterdam. I spent a lot of time in the Caribbean, South America, southern part of the States and that. And I loved the sea. And especially the deep-sea aspect. Because you were always going to new countries, mostly new cities, new towns. Meeting different cultures, different people. And that was terrific, you know. I loved it....

(*What were you transporting?*) Oh, we were general cargo, like coal, iron ore, grain, salt, gypsum. Anything, general cargo, you know what I mean. And it was terrific. Oh, I just loved it.

See, it was a great experience for a young fellow to go away, and see the other leaf of the page. Because here you don't see any line-ups for food. And you can go and buy what you want as long as you've got a buck in your pocket. But over there the people don't have the bucks. And if they do, they've got to stand in line. I used to tell people you'd see them standing in line for bread or—they'd tell me I was crazy, you know.

It was terrific for me. I was always learning, you know. You should never—like my fight career. I was in it ten or eleven years as a pro. And I never stopped learning. Even the last fight, I was learning, you see. Life is the same way. You should always be on the lookout to pick up something new, to learn something new. Broaden your mind, you know. And I'm no scholar—don't get me wrong. Because I've got no edumacation! But that's the way I am. That made me a scholar that way, you know, through travelling....

And then, my heavens, I got a call. Had a friend down in the unemployment office. He said, "I recommended you for the Coast Guard." So I went down and I applied, and I was taken right away. And I sailed with

Mooney Clarke on the receiving end of Benny Delorenzo. Delorenzo won Golden Glove Featherweight amateur titles, and then turned pro. Right: Gordon "Gramps" Kiley, another winner of several Golden Gloves and Maritime amateur titles.

them for a little over five years.

And then I developed this disease. [Gordie has ALS—Lou Gehrig's Disease.] Oh, I guess, the last year I sailed with them. I went to the Arctic. I noticed my back was bothering me. Went away in the summer—went away in July, and my back was bothering me. And then I noticed my leg was flopping. It would give out, me going downstairs and stuff like that. God, by the time I got back, in around the first of November, the pain in my back, across the bottom of my back, was terrible, and down my leg. It was almost unbearable. Had to transfer to another ship because mine was going on drydock. Finally it came December, I said I have to go to the doctor, see what's going on here. In the meantime, on the ship we had a nurse while we were in the Arctic. So she was treating me for arthritis. She gave me all these pills for arthritis. Which weren't helping me at all.

So he started treating me for arthritis. So every month I was coming back, I was worse. I was working Search-and-Rescue—I was twenty-eight days on a ship and then twenty-eight off. So then we got in Sydney the end of May. And we were five days at sea, fired around, quite choppy weather. And I had a hard time, you know, when you're keeping your balance. I worked down below in the engine room. So, we got to Sydney here. Shirley saw me coming down the gangway one day she came to get me. She thought I was half loaded or something, you know—the way I was walking or limping. "No," I said, "my back is just killing me, you know. I can hardly walk." So, same thing home. The next day I went back, and I got a slip. And I haven't worked since. And that's—well, that would be—that was three years out in May.

So then I took quite awhile. They were going to operate on my back, and I said, "No." They wanted to operate here in Sydney. I said, "No, I'll go away to Halifax," you know. Pretty sensitive part, to start cutting into your back. So I went away up there. They were going to do the same. But, oh, day before the operation—the doctor that I had up there, he brought in a couple of other doctors, and they examined me. Said, "Gee, we're not going to operate on him." They cancelled the operation. Neurologists, you know. The nerve doctor. So anyway, it ended up, about six or seven months later, after I spent—the last time in the V.G. they kept me in for over three weeks. They finally found it. I was being examined by ten doctors a day. And the tests I went through. They finally found it. ALS [Ameotrophic Lateral Sclerosis], which is Lou Gehrig's Disease, you know.

I remember that day, the doctor came in, the neurosurgeon—the head guy that was looking after me. And he was sitting up on the bed. I was walking with a cane. And he said, "Gordie," he said, "I've got good news and bad news for you. I want to give you the good news first. You're going home tomorrow." "Oh," I said to myself, "gee, here I am going home. I still don't know what the hell's wrong with me," you know. He said, "You've got ALS." All I can say is ALS—I can't pronounce the words. "It's Lou Gehrig's Disease." He said, "Do you understand that?" I said, "Oh, yes." Because I read about Lou Gehrig the ballplayer died of it.

"So," he said, "it's a terminal disease, Gordie. It's a disease of the nerve endings in your body. Which, as they die, they kill the muscles in your body. And it's the only disease of this kind. Like, MS and all them are diseases of the muscle. Yours is the only one that's terminal. The others may last ten or twenty years. But you have a life span of only three to five years to live. There's no cure for it, there's no medication. There's nothing." He said, "I want you to go home and make out your will." And he said, "Get your insurance and pensions in place, and that's it." He sat back.

And—which may be only about thirty seconds—he said, "Gee, Gordie," he said, "I'm surprised at your reaction, you know." Because usually people fall off the bed, you know, or deep panic. You know, you get a death sentence, you know what I mean. So I said, "No," I said, "because when I came back in February from seeing you, I said to the wife, I said, 'There's more wrong to me than a disc in my back,' I said. 'I think'—I was doing a little reading, you know. I said, 'I think I've got Parkinson's Disease.'" "Well," he said, "you weren't far off. It's a cousin, you know. But yours is the only one that's fatal."

So here I am, I'm home. So, all in all, a year before I was diagnosed, I

246

had it—like I said, when I was in the Arctic. So I got it four years out this summer. And I'm still going, stronger than ever.

Gordie visited Sugar Ray Leonard (left)
Middleweight Champion of the World

(*Do you know how it starts, what are the causes of ALS?*) No. They don't know—no causes, no cure.... And in the meantime, I've had four friends of mine die of it, and they've only lasted two or two and a half years. I'm a very positive thinker. And I never even look on it as a disease, you know what I mean? I have a very positive attitude.... I take things in stride. And every day's a good day for me, you know what I mean. But I don't harp on my disease. I don't think about it.... Oh, I did one time, got depressed maybe three years ago. I never even think about that now. One thing you learn about this: you never look about tomorrow, you worry about today.

And—teaches you a lot. At one time, I used to drive in the fast lane. And never had time to look each side of the road. Now when I drive down, I stop and smell the roses. Didn't do that before. But, I'm coping with it very well. We try to make it a normal life as is possible. I have a lot of help from Muscular Dystrophy [Association], they're really, really tremendous with me. I also have now the Homemaker Program come in four times a week. And I have a great woman that comes—she's like part of the family now. She's been here almost a year now. So she's very good, and she's comforting with us, and it's very good. We laugh and we have a few jokes, all of us. And it's tremendous.

And the people—our friends come and visit. And it's funny, too, there's a lot of friends really—close friends that we know—they don't—they say to Shirley, "God, how's Gordie?" "Oh, same old Gordie, you know." Like, even sailor friends of mine that haven't seen me for awhile. Say, "How's Gordie?" "Oh, good." You know, "Gee whiz, how is he?" "Oh, good. Same old Gordie." "Gee, I'd like to go visit, but I don't know how to talk to him." Like they think I'm shrivelled up. See, they don't know what to say to Shirley. And Shirley tells them, "Oh, God Almighty, if you called him an old so-and-so on the ship, he's the same—come down—he's the same guy, you know."

And of course, my wife is bearing up to this tremendous because it's a big burden on her. Like they ask, how's her husband getting along, how's he coping with it. But nobody asks her how's she coping with it. You know what I mean? Because it's kind of a burn-out program for her. Because she's got to live this thing side by side with me every day. She's got to cope with all the problems that people on the outside don't see, you know what I mean. These are inner things, like, you know.

Shirley: Sometimes I—we have a lot of cries together, too, you know. Sometimes when—Gordie, when you were so frustrated.... **Gordie**: Frustration with this disease. **Shirley**: And then we'd say a prayer, and I'd read off the prayer, and both of us would be crying. But then we had a lot of laughs. You know, we have a lot of laughs here.... **Gordie**: Little anecdotes that happened. **Shirley**: And then we sit and we're watching TV, and he's—like you say, he's a little bit under my feet. And what do we say, Gordie? "Aren't we lucky, to be here?" First good luck was this place [their apartment in the Senior Citizens' Complex]. Because we had to leave our house. It was my parents' house. And his mother has a nice house down there, down in South Bar, that was supposed to be his. But we couldn't get up the steps or anything. Thank God for this place.

Gordie: Oh, we have a lot to be thankful for. **Shirley**: When we look at TV and see all of these homeless people. And Gordie feels sorry for the suffering of kids. Or pain.... He has pain, but.... You feel so sorry for the kids. **Gordie**: God Almighty, I don't go anywhere near with the pain and suffering. People I hear them in the hospitals, suffering with cancer, screaming with the pain. **Shirley**: And we know the worst is yet to come. We know. **Gordie**: I know what's going to happen to me.

Shirley: We talk about death. He talks about death like he's going on a little trip. **Gordie**: But it doesn't bother me. **Shirley**: But we were talking to someone else who had cancer, and has the same attitude as Gordie. She's only a woman of forty, with four small children. But, we talk about it. She said, "Are you afraid...?" And I used to say, "Gordie, are you afraid?" But when you talk about death, like, Gordie says, "Well, what's to say?" He said, "I know, I've got a sentence, they say... Terminal illness. But who's to say that I'm not going to go to my car and...." **Gordie**: Get killed, you know. **Shirley**: Or have a heart attack through the night. Or my young son, three years ago—my twenty-seven-year-old son. Who was coming home from work, and so excited—you know, he called his wife, he said, "We're going to do our Christmas shopping." Never got home.

So death is going to come to everyone, right. And we never know. Gordie's terminal, but he doesn't know when. And we're all—and we don't know when.

Gordie: And I'm the happiest guy in the world, because I was telling you—I live for today.... It's my last day on earth. Every day. I have a good time. I meet people, I enjoy, I smile, I laugh. I do what I want today. Because just like it was my last day—that's the way I am. But I'm not down—I never ever think of being down, depressed.

Shirley: I'm just going to read this little paper. I'm a terrible one for diaries, like the daily diary. But I keep this—it's called "Thoughts and Special Moments"—just mine. But this is one that my daughter had in a book. And Gordie liked it. And he said, "That's me."

And it says: "And in my life, I'll experience everything. So on the journey to my death, my nights will not be haunted by regrets." And it's so true. You know?... Gordie, remember we wrote this one: "For Gordie MacDougall: While alive, he lived!" [Gordie and Shirley laugh.]

Gordie: And I'm still living. I'm still living. The guys can't get over. All this summer I was going from here, down to the Steel City Tavern in this thing [the wheelchair]. Every day. Down to the tavern, come back half drunk, all over the road. But I made her. And you know, the guys couldn't get over me. And all I can move is—my angle was even better this summer—was that finger and thumb, see. But it's getting worse now....

I always lived in the fast lane. As you can tell by some of my stories. I went down the road, never looked on either side of the road. Now, since I've been sick, I go down the road and I look at both sides of the road, and I stop to smell the roses. Something I never did before.

But that's pretty much my life. And there's nothing I haven't done or tried.... Who I feel sorry for is young children, anywhere from seven or eight—any child—up to maybe their teens, that never had a chance in life, and never experienced anything in the world. To them, I feel really bad for, you know what I mean. But me, I've done everything and I've fulfilled my life. But see, He doesn't want me up there yet, and He's keeping me down here. And the devil doesn't want me. And I've got too many people around here I want to see yet before I go. So nobody wants me, so they're keeping me around.

Gordie MacDougall died on April 17, 1992. This article is edited from interviews by John Cochrane and *Cape Breton's Magazine*.

A Visit with Steve Whitty, Ingonish Beach

I was born here in Ingonish, 1897. My father was born here. He fished mostly all his life. Farmed a little, but didn't do very much farming. Just what we needed to eat, stuff like that. My mother was born in Margaree. Came here with her parents at the age of a year and a half. She died at the age of 99. My father was going on 88 when he died. They had their sixty-fourth wedding anniversary in their house. All of their children but one that died as a child were there. And Mike MacDougall's mother, Mary Ann, was the only girl of the nine that lived. And I think three at that anniversary were drawing the old age pension at that time.

Used to go to the Bird Islands. Used to go up there to get bait, to bait our trawl gear. We'd stay there in the night. (*What kind of bait?*) Squid. Thousands and thousands of them. And there'd be as high as twenty-one and twenty-three boats up there. The large boats, now. Not like those boats here. They were the sailboats. Those times, there were no gasoline engines. Everything went by sail. That's a long while ago. We used to go out from Ingonish here to the Bird Islands, and there used to be a lot of Newfoundland boats come over—that's where the Newfoundland boats used to get their bait. And the most of them took their fish into North Sydney. But we used to split our fish and salt them aboard of our boats. Probably we'd stay up there four or five days before we'd come down home and sell them to Robin Jones or Capt. MacCuish. There were two buyers here at that time. But, my dear, that went on for years.

(*Do you use bait to get squid?*) [Steve laughs.] No, dear. You catch them with squid jigs. You've seen squid jigs. All the little pins in it. You're liable to get as high as four and five on that jig at one time. (*But how do you know they're there?*) You know. They were out to the Bird Islands—that was the home of it. That's why we used to always fish up there. The darker it is, the better they'll jig. That's how we used to get so many in the nighttime. It was just like that, as fast as you could ever take them up with your jig. The least thing will take them up, but when they come up, boy, watch out. If that stuff ever went in your eyes, you won't do any more jigging for a long while. My son, I'm telling you right here. Some call it "ink." That's not what we called it. It's usually not so nice of a name. Especially when it went in your eyes, I can tell you that. (*Did you ever have it happen?*) Yes, thousands of times.

After you jig your squid, you start baiting your gear. And then probably an hour or an hour and a half before daylight, you'd sail off down a piece to set your gear. Well, the way you used to set them, you'd have a torch. I don't know if you ever saw one. It was like a lamp, but the wick was about two inches, around that. The cylinder on the torch would be about four or five inches high, and then there was a ring on the side of the torch—and that went down over your trawl tub to show you how to set your gear. See, your trawl—seven lines of gear—was down into a flour barrel. The flour barrel had a piece of it cut off, and you made a "trawl tub," we called it. And then there were three holes went in that tub. There were two on one side and one on the other. And the rope went in this and you spliced it, and then you brought the rope over the other side and went in and tied it.

Well, all right now. When you went to put your gear in the dory, a man in the boat passed you the trawls and you fixed them in your dory—the five tubs. The other man was already on his oars, to row. When he'd pass you the five tubs to your dory, you were clear of the boat altogether. And then you start to rowing. Both dories were heading the same way, but you were probably five hundred feet apart. Well, you'd go off then to the distance—whatever your five tubs of gear would be—there'd be seven lines to a tub. Took you out almost a mile. Then, when you go to set your gear—you never saw it? (*No.*)

All right, before you start to set, you tie your trawl onto an anchor—on the fluke of the anchor—and then the stock part with the ring into it, your

251

buoy line was tied to that. Well, your buoy line, you had a little over the depth of the water. And then you had a trawl keg, a five-gallon keg, and the first thing you did was fire that over. You put your high flyer in that—we used to call it a black ball—and you'd fire that over first. Then you'd fire your buoy line, then you came to your anchor. And you'd let your trawl go little by little, you know, right slow. Till you got down to the bottom. Well then, as fast as the fellow could row, you could fire the gear. That's it. There's nothing to it. (*One fellow rowed.*) And the other kept setting the gear till you came to the end of the tub. Then you held onto the end of the tub [the trawl line], and you hooked it onto the next tub, and you did the same with that tub and with every tub. You hook one back-line onto the next back-line. Then when you got to the outside, your last tub, then you had to do the same with your anchor—you had to tie your anchor on first, then your buoy line, then your keg was the last thing. Then, after both dories were done, the man in the big boat, the schooner, would pick us up and sail back for the kegs.

You come back to your inside end, we call it. And you start hauling; the first tub you set is the first one you haul. If it's a fine day, you leave that first tub down around two hours before you start to haul it. You'd have a lunch on your way in—bite to eat—then probably stay an hour, hour and a half, before you'd start to haul. When you haul, you start at the first tub you started to set—the inside end. First thing you do is get your keg and pull your keg in, then you coil your buoy line down—pull that up and coil it down—and then you come to your anchor with your trawl onto it—understand now? Well, your anchor now went into the stern of your dory. And your buoy line and your keg—that went right aft in your dory. Then you untied your trawl, and you were in the forward part of the dory—one fellow was hauling with a roller in the dory. You had the trawl gear in this roller—and you pull the trawl over that. Only for that roller, you wouldn't get your trawl gear. Because it would be hooking in everything. You take trawl gear when it hooks in the bottom, you've got a hard break out, you'd never break it out of a dory.

Oh, dear man, that roller's as good as two men on the trawl. The lobster fishermen today have rollers on the side of the boat. And when you'd pull it in, the codfish would be on your gangen. The gangen would be about two and a half feet long; from your nose to the end of your arm—that's the length. And when there'd be a fish, you'd just slap him in your dory and keep on hauling. You never had to look back, you were so used to doing it. If you lost the fish, all you had to was reach for the gaff and hook your fish. I was so used to that. Not me alone, but all. Everyone was fishing. Then the fellow right behind you, with this trawl tub, he was piling your gear as fast as you were pulling it in. (*Was he baiting it?*) No, no. You had

to bait it fresh again, the next day.

Now if there's any good fishing, every seven lines [one tub] you lighten your dory. The boat comes up alongside of you—we call it "lightening." She takes that tub that you hauled in aboard the boat, and your fish, and then you start on the second tub. After she leaves you, she goes down to the other dory, to do the same thing. Then she comes back here to you. She waits there till you get to the end of the second tub, gets your fish and your tub. It takes you an hour to haul a tub of gear in good fishing. (*And one tub of gear might give you a dory load?*) It could. In good fishing, it would. In the fall of the year, you generally always lighten out a tub, anyway. You never want your dory too heavy. These dories used to take a thousand pounds of fish, round fish—they could take more than that, but that's all you'd put in them. For safety. A fine calm day, you'd take more than that—fourteen hundred.

The man aboard the boat always had something for you to eat when you went aboard—meat and potatoes or fish and potatoes. And tea and everything. But sometimes you had a hard haul in the fall. You'd get a load of fish to every tub—probably you'd have five loads of fish to each dory—that'd be around ten thousand pounds. I've often seen the skippers of the boats—I didn't fish all the time with my father—but I often saw the skippers of the boats come and fire you a bun of bread in. Just get it like that and tear it in two halves, and one fellow take one half and the other, the other—take a bite and lay it down like that and start pulling again, boy.

At night, after you'd clean your fish, after you've hauled in the five tubs of gear, you'd start in, say, and there'd probably be no wind—little or no wind—and if there was no wind, you had to get in your dory and tow that big boat, the two dories. But there'd be generally a little draft of wind, and they were great sailors, you know. And as the years went by, they started getting the gasoline engines in their boats. The sixth man came in the boat—a man to run the engine. But I fished in a boat for two or three years before the gasoline engines came here. If you were out in the bay

253

you were okay, but if you got off of Smokey and there wasn't an air of wind, well, you had to jump in your dory and tow your boat to get in. And you'd be surprised how two dories could tow that boat. Good oarsmen.

The hulls of those boats would take—well, you could salt twelve or fourteen thousand pounds, that's split fish. Fire the head overboard and the bone you would fire overboard. You had your tub to put your fish in, and your splitting table. The way it was there, one fellow splitting and the other fellow the head and the other fellow the gut—the other fellow'd fork the fish into the tub, and the other fellow probably'd get something for you to eat down forward. It was a great life, the best life in the world. I loved it. You were your own boss. There was nobody boss over you. The captain of the boat, well, he'd never say anything to you. Everyone did their work right; well, he didn't have a chance to say anything. My father owned the boat, he owned the *Whittier*—*T. J. W. Whittier*. There were three brothers owned her: Tim, Walter, and Jed. When I fished in the boat at the Bird Islands, they were all aboard of her—my father, Uncle Jed, and Uncle Walter, and my oldest brother, Pius, and myself. That's the way it was all around here. It was generally all a family affair.

I can point you out twenty-two of those sailboats were owned here in the harbour. All right, now. This place was getting along great at that time. Up until 19-and-23. God-darned plaster started up here [quarrying plaster in Ingonish]. It worked here for five years. It started in 19-and-22—we built the trestle. In 19-and-23 they started shipping. And in 1927 it ended. All right, that was five years. And all the fishermen, the poor fellows gave up fishing and sold their boats for little or nothing. Most of them went to Newfoundland. They thought the plaster was going to last forever. They got clear of their boats. Their trawl gears went to hell, rotted and all of that. And they worked for five years, and it went down just like that. There were all the fishermen left on their behind. Had to start all over again, trying to get boats. But they never got those kind of boats. They couldn't afford it. Those kind of boats—all the stuff was taken out of the woods, way back in the country. The plank of those boats was all built out of hardwood. All that beautiful hardwood, inch thick. And that was all sawed with whip-saws—a pit—one above and one below—boy, I've done enough of that in my life. So, they couldn't get vessels like that again. And you see them now with their bent timbers in the boats, but the timbers that went in those boats were all grown timbers—they found crooked sticks, the shape for your boat. An awful lot of work to them, but they were great boats, my God almighty.

The boats were just called fishing boats. And you got the salt from the fish buyers—you know, Robin Jones and Whitman—and there'd be steamers coming here to take the fish away. You see, that fish they'd get from you or me, whoever was fishing—was Robin Jones's—they owned all that beach. Well, it was three times as big as it is now because it was washed away. They had flakes all over the beach, and faggots, barracks that came down over their pile of dry fish. They used to make all their fish on the beach. They'd take them and wash them out, and then they'd dry them along the beach and spread them. Spread them generally first on the stones, till the years we got the wire flakes. I'm safe in saying I worked there for three years for Robin Jones—five cents an hour. And my sister worked there—five cents an hour. We were carrying in fish and out-spreading them, turning them over and packing them up in little faggots, you know, things like that. You'd never stop, my boy—ten hours. Take your grub with you.

Now, I often tell the young race of people—and I know they don't believe me—that I've seen the Whitty boat, the boat my father owned at that time—and he had her hired to Robin Jones—and he went into her, carrying the haddock, from down at Middle Head (from the traps) into Robin Jones's. And there'd be as high as seventy men working there. Not all from Ingonish. The most of them were from Newfoundland. And those poor men came from Newfoundland to work for thirty to thirty-five dollars a month. But I tell this as I've told lots of young fellows: I've seen my father going down to that beach—Nate and him and Pius and the Whitty boat—took her down to the wharf for carrying haddock—so he got thirty-five dollars a month. He'd bring a load of haddock in, and when he came to the wharf and tied her on, he had to jump on the wharf and grab the splitting knife, start splitting. The young fellows jumped in the boat, pitched the fish up. Well, all right now: he got thirty-five dollars a month. Pius got twenty dollars a month for what we call heading the fish, taking the head off of the haddock. I'd reach in the tub and pull the guts out and pass them to my father to split them. And I got fifteen, and the boat got ten. Add that up, that's eighty dollars. But how long did you work for that? Two months—160 dollars for a whole spring.

Well, people ask, how'd you live? I'll tell you how we lived. A hell of a lot better than people are living today. The first thing my father did with that 160 dollars—he went to George Hines's factory down there—he was packing lobsters—and he got his winter's flour. Probably he bought twelve or fourteen barrels. All he had to buy, clear of that, was tea, molasses, sugar, and tobacco, if you used it. A little clothes, but that's all. Everything else was grown. You had your vegetables, everything. Lots of meat, piles of meat, piles of potatoes, cabbage, turnips—all kinds of stuff to eat, the very best of stuff. We're not eating that today. We're eating God-darned stuff, half of it coming in cans. That's what's causing cancer today. Because we're not getting the right kind of food—and that's the whole truth of it.

We were brought up in the hardest kind of a way. We didn't have everything perfect. We had what everyone else had. You had burning wood. When you went to bed, the fire went out. You had your kindlings in to make your fire in the morning. Probably the water'd be frozen in the kettle on the stove. That happened.

(*If the haddock was in the spring, when did you do the trawling?*) Late in the fall. (*Is that what you call the winter fishing?*) Yeah. We started probably in November, the first of November. Fished November and December. I've seen us quit on the 20th of January. (*Must have been cold.*) Yeah, but you'd never mind out there. Wouldn't mind that at all. You had your winter clothes on you—and once you put your oilclothes on, brother, there's no way water can go through them. And generally, under the oil-clothes what you'd wear was your underwear and your outside clothes and a sweater—to get in the dory. Good rubber boots and good socks and mitts—you never were cold, never. You had to strip off bare-handed to coil the gear. You'd coil, then you'd slap your hand to get them warm, feeling would come back in them in a minute. I never heard a fellow saying yet he was cold. And I know I fished thirty-five years.

See, the way we used to do it, we used to haul a tub about. Well, you'd go in the bow of the dory and you'd haul like the first tub. You'd come back, and I'd haul the second. Then on the fifth tub, the man there would haul three and a half lines, and you would haul the balance. Sometimes when it was cold—what you call cold—your hands would get cold—my father would haul like three or four lines and give the other fellow a chance to warm up, you know. But hauling gear, you had to haul with a great big pair of woollen mitts on. You never were cold that way, no way in the world. You had a wonderful sou'wester buttoned underneath your chin and man, dear! (*You didn't haul bare-handed?*) You couldn't, dear. You'd coil in the tub bare-handed, but you couldn't haul the gear bare-handed. Some people would coil with mitts on, but I couldn't because the hook would stick in the mitt.

(*How did you avoid the hooks when hauling?*) You got used to it just like everything else, boy. (*And you didn't get caught on hooks?*) Never in my life, never. The only time that ever I got a hook stuck into me was in that finger right there, setting trawl gear fair off of the Bird Islands. I was in MacIntyre's then. And my old uncle was rowing the dory—Tom Donovan. And there was a great big square-rigger going into Englishtown. And there was a big sea on, a big roll, you know. But I was setting, anyway, and he was rowing. And on the roll of the sea, like, if you're rowing you've got to kind of back water—don't let your dory go ahead too fast. Because some time the trawl gear will go too fast for you. And boy, the hook got me there. Well, I'll tell you how bad the pain was: I was going to jump overboard. Split that finger right open. And went out and split that and got a chew of tobacco into and tied it up—that's all. After a week or so, it was all right. I never stopped fishing. No, sir. Dangerous, dangerous. One fellow, he was sitting like that, and there was quite a sea on—and the hook came up, poor fellow, and went right in his nostril. Had to take him to North Sydney to get the hook cut out.

But I loved it. Because it's the healthiest life on earth. People often ask me, if you had your life to live over again, what kind of life would you live? I'll tell you the kind of life I'd live. I'd like to get into one of those boats, fishing.

I saw us one time—I was fishing with this fellow and my father. She was only a one-dory boat; she was smaller than others. But we fished until the 16th of January. And it was on a Saturday. The harbour was frozen, you could go onto it with tractors for weeks before that. I was only eighteen. We were coming in pretty well where the buoy is at there, off of Smokey. I said to my father, "I ain't going out tomorrow." He said, "Why?" I said, "Because I'm getting sick of this. I've been fishing now since the first day of May. I'm only a kid and I want a little recreation somewhere." All he said was, "Okay, me son, you quit, I'll quit." It was Saturday. When we got in, Papa said, "Steve is not going to fish any more." And we had the boat loaded with fish. "And if he quits, I'm going to quit." "Well, well, well," he said, "we should fish a week longer yet." But we said we were quitting. So he said he'd get out with the other fellows Monday. They had two dories. Greedy, that's what it was.

So he went in with them. And instead of five tubs to a dory, they'd have six. They went out two days later [a Monday] and they set the twelve tubs of gear—and all they got was nine fish. The fish left just that quick. We knew they were going to leave because of the great big fish we got. You see, there's no haddock or anything in the fall, the last fish. First going off, you get mostly haddock—probably two or three weeks you get more haddock than you do cod—then you start getting the cod. Then the last going off, well, there's fish, my son, it takes two with a gaff to get in the dory. And there's very big sores on the side of them—and that's the sign of the last school of fish. You knew then the drift ice wasn't far away. That day coming in, I told my father, "That's the last of the fish." And he said, "I don't doubt you." So those fellows didn't make very much out of those tubs of gear.

(*Sometimes it must have been snowing out there.*) Snowing? You couldn't see your hand before you. I'm telling. I've seen us out there, my dear, in the *Beatrice*, after my father sold the Whitty boat. Robin Jones had two boats with lovely engines in them—one was the *Reliance* and the other was the *Beatrice*. And in 1917, that was the time of the explosion in

Halifax. Well, we were fishing fair off of Neil's Harbour buoy that day. And we heard that explosion just the same as if we were ten miles from Halifax. We could hear it as plain as if you went out there and fired a gun against the house. It was calm on the water. Just after the explosion, the water all started to tremble. And my uncle said to me—we were in the dory—he said, "Sydney Mines must be blown up." The steel works were there then. We didn't know what it was till we came in that day. A man that was bookkeeping for Robin Jones—his name was Albert Ozone—he had two children going to school in Halifax, and he couldn't get word, whether they were dead or alive or what. The lines were torn up.

And the next day we went out fishing, went down to the same place— and the snowstorm started. Well, there was snow on the ground, lots of snow, the day of the explosion; but we were down there fishing, and the wind struck from the northeast, and snow—you couldn't see anything. We had a wonderful boat, she was a bit boat, bit engine into her, too. Now we were down north, we were running this way, we were running south— we had fair wind, you know. Anyway, when my father came down to lighten Tom Shea and I—we were in the dory, and Uncle Jed and Pius were in the other dory. He said to me, "When you come to the fourth knot, don't go any further till I come for you and pick you up"—because you couldn't see from one dory to another, couldn't see anywhere. But he had his course with the compass, running back and forth. We came to the fourth knot. We stopped. And she was as close as that post when we saw her. He hollered to us, "Cut the gear." We had to drag the anchor, put it on the buoy line and chuck the keg—then he picked us up.

When I came down forward, there was none of them had any watches. And we had a clock sticking up on the foremast. They asked me what time it was. And we had all the sails off her, all but the foresail and the riding sail—that's all she could carry. And there was ten thousand pounds of fish in her. We had one dory on deck and one dory astern. So Tom Shea and Pius and myself went up forward, and we were watching for seas to break on the shore—we didn't know how handy we were to it. But she was taking those awful deep rollings, you know. Pius said, "We're pretty close to the gut"—the entrance coming in the harbour—"because I know the water's shoal." And then we saw the shore. We were pretty near up to the church, up North Bay. He'd hauled her up too quick. He hauled her up at 55 minutes, and he should have let her run one hour. Would have cleared Middle Head to come in, but she went up on the other side.

And then you couldn't see fifty feet—no way in the world—but we could see the sea. Then we argued it both ways. Some said we were above Smokey, and my father said, "No, we're in North Ingonish." So anyway, he swung up and back to find out for sure. As soon as he saw the sea break on the shore, he knew where he was at—but you couldn't see the land at all. And that engine was taking that boat out against that storm. Then we got over there to The Point, Allister Mac-Leod's, and we stayed there all night. And the way it was snowing, God Almighty help us. But we didn't eat a bite—just jumped down, got a cup of tea, something like that. Really truly, I wasn't frightened, but I thought we were going to be drowned.

We got her tied to the wharf, and it was as smooth at that wharf as it is on this floor. See, the sea was coming from the northeast, the wind was rearing around the island there. Uncle Jed and I walked from there, from The Point clean up to the end of the Whitty Intervale that night. Great big pair of rubber boots on us and our oilclothes—walked over eight miles. And every step was to our knees.

The next morning my uncle and I went down and saw that boat coming around Middle Head, and you'd swear she was one of those great big slabs of drift ice—she looked that white. But the storm was pretty well over then. That was about the worst experience that ever I had on the water.

Still, you always looked out for that, for the winter, your fall fish—

which they don't do at all today. They sit home and draw unemployment. And they've got better boats now than we had then, to fish. We used to fish up until the 18th and the 17th of January. We fished till the drift ice stopped us—all the young people. But my dear, there's an awful difference. I'm not running down the younger people at all. The younger are just as good today as when I was young. People are all bellyaching about them. First thing, they say they're no good to work. Well, the reason why is, they weren't learned to work, same way as rearing a child.

Not blowing or bragging about it, I was reared, and all my brothers beside me, were brought up the toughest kind of way. We had to get out and saw with whip-saws, learn to chop wood, split wood. Plant potatoes, hill potatoes, and all of that. Put out manure. You can't get young fellows today to go in the barn and hitch a horse for you. Not their fault. They weren't taught. That's as far as I can see into it. They don't get a chance. Why, they don't stop going to school until they're about nineteen.

I stopped when I was twelve, going on thirteen. My father said, "Now you've got as much education as I have—now you're ready to come on the oars and row." I could row at that time great. I thought it was wonderful to get clear of school. But I can see today it wasn't wonderful at all. If I had my life to live over, I'd like to have a little more schooling, but I'd like to live on a farm.

When I was married in 19-and-22, my first wife—from above the post office on the right side going up, there was a house on the right side—it's still there yet. Tim John Donovan owned it. And the next house to him was Frank Doucette's home. Then Jim Doucette owned a home. And the next home to that was where Bill Donovan's was. And today you can count seventy in that distance. A lot more people today, but as far as my part, there's not a quarter of the company. There wasn't none of that television stuff, there were no radios—and all your company was people coming to the house and playing cards and telling stories and singing songs—and if they didn't do that, get the hell out. That was the way it was. And you had a lot of fun. Had more fun then in one night than I have now in two years.

Joe Delaney & His Scarecrows, St. Joseph du Moine

I was born in 1916, the 12th of July. And about in 1922—in those days times were getting pretty good in the States, where down here the times weren't that good. So a lot of people from this area, from St. Joseph du Moine and Cheticamp and the Margaree area—well, as far as we could say, Cape Bretoners—a lot of them went to the United States. A lot of them landed in Massachusetts.

So we were there for ten years. We went there in '22, because we came back in 1932. I was only fifteen or sixteen years old. Well, I was the oldest of the family of seven. And my father says, "The others are going to go to school, but you'll have to stay home and help me." Because when he came home from the States, he landed here, no home. Everybody had a barn, you know, doing a little farming. So, no house, no barn, no nothing. So he had to start all over from scratch, like we say.

Probably some of you people are probably asking yourself, "Well, how come did he come home?" Well now, that was what they call at the time of the Crash—1929. That was when the Depression struck. And then up until—well, till 1932 a lot of people were having a hard time on—we'd

call it welfare. They were going to the city for an order in order to be able to eat and all that.

And then from there on, well, I stayed home with my father. Then we started, we worked in the pulp wood. I did labouring, a little bit of fishing, a little bit of everything. I'm not a jack-of-all-trades, like they say, but do this, do that, in order to make a dollar. As the oldtimers will remember, from 1932 on till the war broke out, times were pretty hard. And then after that, it picked up.

I was a school janitor for twenty-seven years. I started in 1958, retired in 1984. St. Joseph du Moine Consolidated School down here. I quit in '84. The school only went for about three or four years after that.

But anyway, in '84, not knowing what to do. I had a piece of land over at Cap LeMoine, and it was getting to be—not bushy, or bushland, but pretty close to it. There were all kinds of spruce trees and rubbish, trucks. And it was right along the Cabot Trail. So I said to myself, "Look, Joe boy, the first thing you know, you're going to have a woodlot over there on that piece of land." And there was about twelve acres, you know, of frontage there.

So, my two boys had come home from Toronto. I knew I'd have to feed them. They were home on vacation for a month. So, seeing as I'd have to feed them, I said to myself, I'd better put them to work. Because at night they'll be out timing—go here and go there, you know, parties and all that. Instead of sleeping in the daytime, I wanted them to give me a help over there in cutting the trees and all that, plowing the land and pick up the rocks and all that, in order to cultivate that land. It would be a better appearance, you know.

Anyway, so we did. But we didn't clear it all, you know, in the one year. We just cleaned out a certain patch the first year. And we put vegetables at one end and potatoes at the other: 150 yards—450 feet long, 30 feet wide. And every year we broke a strip, you know. Clearing another 30 feet and another 30 feet. It took us quite a few years to clear it out open, you know, to have a nice field.

Anyway, once we got all the gardening in, the potatoes and everything—we were living two miles from there. I'm talking about Cap Le-Moine, and our home is in St. Joseph du Moine. Not being able to supervise the area, the neighbours said, "Joe, we hate to see you doing this, because we tried it. And the foxes, the deer, the seagulls, and the crows—you name it—they ate up everything on us."

And then one fellow says, "I don't know—maybe if you put up a scarecrow." So that gave me an idea. So we came home. And with the boys, we made three of them—three scarecrows. And in the olden days the farmers—they'd put up a scarecrow. All they'd do is drive a post about four feet high that it would remain, and then they'd nail a board across. Throw an old jacket around the board. And then the arms—the sleeves, you know—they would flap in the wind....

But we came home, and we said to ourselves, We're going to make three scarecrows and we're going to make them almost real. We made them the height of basketball players—six feet, six-feet-two, six-feet-four inches high. And well-dressed. You know, suits, necktie, white shirt, gloves. Oh, they were better dressed than we were! Once we got through with them.

And then we put these plastic flappers—strips of plastic around the waist. And some of those strips, we tied them in their hands. So that also, in the wind, would make noise. Keep the animals away.

Okay, we made the three of them. And we put them up at night so that nobody would see us. We put them up at a quarter to ten that night. Full moon. One at each end and one in the middle of the field.

And the next morning, when we got there, you know, at the garden, there was a chartered bus parked on the side of the road. And there were about ten cars behind that bus. And everybody was in the field. The bus had about thirty-five to forty passengers. And some of them had white shoes. It had rained during the night. So those white shoes that the ladies had, once they left the field, the garden, they were black!

But no fooling—about thirty-five. And then there was about another twenty with the cars that were parked behind. Everybody was in the field with cameras. And they wanted a close-up shot of the scarecrows. They wanted to get as close as possible. And when we arrived there—I'll never forget this. There was an elderly couple from California in the group. They had a camper. And the lady—we introduced ourselves, you know—and she said, "Joe, for the love of God, never mind your garden. Put up more scarecrows. That's what we want to see. If you can make those three, you can make more. And that's what people want to see. Instead of these gift shops and museums and all that."

And that's how it sort of got off the ground—the scarecrows. That's how we sort of got started, eh? (*You sort of stumbled upon something.*) Yeah, it was by accident.

But then—down in this area here—in a way as an accident. But not in another. Because in this Acadian region, from Margaree all the way down to the entrance of Cape Breton Highlands National Park, well, the majority is French. And in this Acadian region, we have an old custom, an old tradition. And what is it called? It's called the mid-Lent, sort of the mid-Lent break—mid-Lent festivities. But in French, the real name for it is La Mi-Carême.

Well, this old Acadian tradition has been going on for over 125 years. Some say that it's older.... We'd dress up. You've got to disguise yourself. Everybody was looking forward to that—the festivities—the old tradition. Why? Because in Lent, in those days, no sweets, you know—no candy, no cake. Meat once a week. No dancing, no parties of any kind. (*Lots of prayers.*) Oh, yes, yes, prayer. The people used to go to church—oh, my God—a lot of people'd go every day of the week of the forty days of Lent.

And then on Friday afternoon at three o'clock, we had what you call the Way of the Cross. At that time of the year, when Lent took place—that was March and April. Forty days, you know. Well, we used to take out firewood for fuel, to heat ourselves. And then the idea was to saw it up and split it up and everything—that would be done during Lent. But on Friday afternoon at two o'clock, everybody would stop sawing wood or splitting wood—whatever they were doing—and everybody'd go to church for the Way of the Cross at three o'clock in the afternoon. Unbelievable.

And some were walking three and a half miles to go to church for the Way of the Cross. Sacrifices!

And that's—why did we look forward to [La Mi-Carême]? You were kept so strict. You know—none of this, none of that. Well, my God, were we ever glad when the mid-Lent period came around. That was only for three days—Wednesday, Thursday, and Friday. Boy, were we glad to dress up and get out and go among people, you know, and have fun.

Sometimes your father would hitch up the horse and take you for about a mile and a half, down the road. And then you would get off there. And then with this tradition of the mid-Lent festivities, you dressed up something like a scarecrow. Well, you've got to disguise yourself, right? You've got to change your voice, you've got to change your walk. That's to fool the people so that they won't know who you are. So once your father'd take you down for about a mile and a half, two miles, then he'd drop off a bunch there. We weren't only the family. If he came, there's about seven or eight, nine, ten kids get in the sleigh, and down we'd go. And then we'd start from there back home, going from house to house, you know. And the idea for the people at home was to try and guess who was under that outfit, the mask.

(*In your childhood years, where did you get the clothes and the mask?*) Well, a lot of people—clothing that had been abandoned, that was of no more use, but it could still be worn, like, you know. But it hadn't been cleaned since quite awhile. But another thing. Where we were very fortunate. The people that were [still] in the States. They had relatives down here, friends and all that. And they used to go to rummage sales up there in Waltham, Mass. And they'd get a barrel of clothing—a barrel full. Well, they'd probably pay three dollars for that. In the barrel there was about half a dozen pair of shoes, two or three suits, a coat, half a dozen shirts, sweaters. You know? And they'd mail that barrel of clothing to their relatives—whoever they had down here. And then some of that clothing, well, the people weren't used to that kind of clothing. So they'd put it aside, and that would do for the mid-Lent festivities.

And when somebody got a barrel—there wasn't only one barrel coming in. There was about—oh, my God—ten, fifteen, twenty families getting these barrels of clothing. So when the mid-Lent festivities came around, you went to see some of these kids. They'd only loan it to us. You had to give it.... (*You would exchange it?*) Right, right. Because you had to have clothing for three days. So if you'd have gone around with the same outfit the three days, you'd have been known. So you had to change. Make sure that you would swap uniforms.

And the people down here are good for that. Some of them are better than detectives. If they see one of your ears showing! You'd got to hide everything. You've got to sort of have a cloth-like over, before you put on your mask—hide all your hair, your ears, the side of the face. So that once you put the mask on, there's no skin showing. Because some of them, they can guess—if they happen to see one eye, end of the nose, an ear—right away they've got you. Oh yeah, it's unbelievable. (*But it's a lot of fun.*) Yeah. Oh, fun!

Did we ever look forward to that, you know, in those days. Why? Because you were kept so strict compared to today....

I remember my grandmother leaving home at Cap LeMoine in 1935, let's say—'34, '35. And walking to church. Two below zero. The Mass was at eight o'clock in the morning. Walking two and a half miles to church, with a sandwich—she had made herself a sandwich the night before—she had that in her pocket, so that after Mass she'd be able to eat that. You weren't allowed to eat after midnight. You were fasting from midnight until the next morning after you'd go to communion. You could only eat after that. So that sandwich, when she took it out of her pocket, it was something like the ice that are coming in on the shore here on the Gulf of St. Lawrence. That sandwich was frozen. It wasn't soft bread any more.

That's what I say, the sacrifices that were made in those days compared to now—the teenagers and the younger children. My God, now during Lent they even have dances. Parties of some kind, and all that. And this mid-Lent festivity affair, compared to those days—now you go by car....

Like I was saying a little while ago, the scarecrows. When we had put up the three scarecrows, and that busload that was in the field, and people from about ten other cars that were parked there. So we're going to take it from there, where that woman had told me, "Joe, never mind your gardening. Put up more scarecrows—that's what we want to see."

Well, the first year we finished off, I think we had around a dozen. It was in '84. In '85 we were somewheres around thirty. And '86, I had—I think I was up to forty-six. And the people were coming, and they were coming. The first two years. The third year, at the end of the season I got vandalism. And every one of them was demolished with the exception of one. The forty-five were demolished; there was only one left. Well, it was sort of discouraging, after having worked that hard.

And the people, it's unbelievable. Unbelievable the way that in three years—well, in 1986, it was somewheres around eighteen thousand that had come through the field. Visitors. They came from all over. All over Canada, almost every state of the U. S. A. And then you'd get them from about twelve to twenty other countries. You know, England, France, Italy. You name it. Germany, Australia, New Zealand. They were coming from all over, visiting. And they just couldn't get over it. They couldn't get over it. To them it was out of this world. Those scarecrows. Imagine! I was finding that nuts. Crazy. And people thought I was an artist! "Mr. Delaney" here and "Mr. Delaney" there. And where did I learn my trade as an artist, you know, and all that! And I had quit school in Grade Eight. Art! I didn't know anything and I still don't know anything about art and artists and all that....

But anyway. When this happened, I called it The 1986 Massacre—Le Massacre. When all these scarecrows had been demolished. They had been demolished on the eve of Armistice Day, around the 9th or the 10th of November. Everything was demolished—all broken up. The arms, the heads, the legs, their clothing cut up and everything with knives. There was only one left. I baptized him "Rory—the Lone Survivor of the 1986 Massacre."

And what did I do? I sat down like we're doing here today, and I wrote an article about the dirty job that had been done, and all that. But I couldn't use dirty words, you know—you've got to watch your language. But anyway, I started the massacre, and it was the same as if Rory had been doing the talking, not me. Rory was doing the talking. And Rory was telling the people, "It's too bad you weren't here. I wish you had been here to see the way my brothers and sisters have been demolished. It was pure cruelty." You know, and all that. And it was only scarecrows, eh? There was no flesh involved. "How they suffered," and all that. "It was heartbreaking for me to see that." But he was the guy that was doing the talking.

And the story went on. He was saying, "I talked to Joe, to try to get him to put them up again." The scarecrows. "But the way Joe answered, I don't believe that he's going to do it. Maybe if he got a little help from the people. Seeing that he put everything he had into it. He's there with nothing now. Got to start all over again from scratch. Maybe if some of you people wanted to, we'd get together, you people and I, and we'd probably get Joe to put them up again." He was doing the talking.

My God, the telephone started. I put that out in the *Oran*. The *Oran* sold copies. And then I had some put through the mimeographing machine.

Then the telephone calls started to come in. "Joe, put them up!" They sent money—five dollars, ten dollars—cheques, twenty dollars. People sending old clothing. The overalls, old suits, jackets, shirts, pants. Sending it down by trucks. Got some from Halifax, New Brunswick, Sydney—all over. In Inverness County, unbelievable the people that sent clothing. From around here, I'll tell you. Not only outside, the people here—local people. (*You had local support from the community.*) Yeah, yeah, yeah. Got local support, I mustn't forget that. Not only outside.

And people getting in here from New York, Baltimore—you name the place—New Jersey. Any state of the U.S.A. Toronto, Ontario, Saskatchewan, B.C. And getting in there in the field and saying, "Where's Joe?" Somebody'd tell them, "There's Joe over there." "Where's Rory? We want to see Rory, the lone survivor of the 1986 massacre." They had read the story in the *Oran*, and they wanted to see Rory, and they'd get their picture taken with him. Go back home and say, "We had our picture taken with Rory, the lone survivor of the 1986 massacre."

It's unbelievable the way the people got there—you'd have sworn that they were asking for their father-in-law! "Where's Rory...?"

Another fellow—he was born in Richmond County, schoolteacher, teaching out in the Northwest Territories. Married; they had a couple of children. Anyway, he received that *Oran*. He was a teacher at the high school level—Grade Ten. What did he do? He put on a play to raise money, on Joe's scarecrows. He telephoned; he called me up here, if it was okay, if he could use the story of my scarecrows to put on a play out there in the Northwest Territories. And they had the CBC-TV of the Northwest Territories filming the play. He sent me the tape....

Coming back to the scarecrows. We put them up again. And last year—let's say the year before, I was up to a hundred and seven scarecrows. This year I only had about ninety-eight. There's some again that had been damaged, demolished. Not as bad as the massacre. I still have about ninety-eight out there. That takes in the children in the sandbox, on the swings. You name it: the married couple, the fishermen, the farmers.

(*Where do you get your ideas?*) I don't know. To tell you the truth, like I told tourists—a lot of tourists ask me the same question. I tell them, I can't answer. When I start—where an artist, he knows what he's going to make. You know, a guy that has arts in him. Me, when I start, I don't know what it's going to look like when I'll be through. I get the surprise of my life when I see that it's done. You know what I mean? Yeah! Oh, God. And that's what I tell the tourists. I don't know what they're going to look like. I get a surprise. Sometimes I'm ashamed. I've got to change it over again. Nobody sees it, you know.

For us people down here, where we have this mid-Lent celebration, it's

not crazy. I can use the word "crazy," yeah, but it's not crazy for us. But what I want to bring out is, we celebrate this mid-Lent festivity, and we dress up like these scarecrows that are seen in the field, that I have there for five months in the summertime. Well, local people going by and having a look at those scarecrows, well, they just say, "Oh well, it's all right, but we do that in the wintertime. You know, in the month of March. The mid-Lent festivities."

But now let's come back to the outside world. Not quite the outside world. Beginning at the Northeast Margaree, Southwest Margaree, Inverness. West, you know. All the way down to California, Europe, Asia. And the people that come there—well, you've got to be there yourself to experience yourself how it's appreciated by them. They leave their comments. We have—one guy, he put his comment, "Dear Joe, I have travelled the world over. Have never seen anything like this." Others: "We have travelled 2000 miles just to come to see your scarecrows—to make sure we saw the scarecrows." Travelled 2000 miles! I wouldn't walk ten miles, you know—ten steps! You know what I mean? It's unbelievable, the comments that you get there from the people. "Good boy, Joe. Keep it up." "We were here in 1984, '85, '86. We saw you grow. Keep it up—put up more. Might see you next year."

A schoolteacher from Spain—him and his wife, coming at the scarecrow with a movie camera. Wanting to get the story, the same as what I'm telling you today. Teachers from New Jersey. The same thing, with movie cameras. They're in the teaching profession. Filming me and all the scarecrows and all that. Telling me, "That's going to help us with our program

269

of studies, once we get back with our students." No wonder that education is not going far today!

In 1990 we had 119 buses. And we're not on the tourist agenda.

(*Joe, what made you do this?*) The wife says I'm crazy, Number One. We were interviewed once by a reporter. He was asking me questions the same as what you're doing. Once he got through with me—my wife, Bella, was alongside, sitting down. So he says, "And you, Mrs. Delaney, how do you find that?" Meaning to say, the work that Joe's doing. And Bella answered, "I was looking forward to the day when he would retire. At that time he was a school janitor. I was looking forward to the day when he would retire. But now, I see that he's both retired and retarded!" And the reporter says, "Am I going to put that on the paper like that?" I said, "Don't you leave out one word. Put it down exactly as she said it."

Edited from Joe Delaney's conversations with Rosie Aucoin Grace.

With Hilda Mleczko, Glace Bay

I love Cape Breton. It's beautiful. I love Cape Breton. People'll say to me, "If your old man died, you'd go back to England, wouldn't you?" I said, "No, I wouldn't. I'd stay right here. This is my country now." Not that I'd turn my back on the country of my birth. Anybody who does that isn't very much. It's like a thumbprint. I'll be English till I die. You can't erase that. But I'd prefer to live in Cape Breton, and I want to stay here all the rest of my life. I love it here. I think the people are salt of the earth. I haven't made an enemy. As far as I know, anyway. I like people and they like me.

I tried so hard to talk like the Cape Bretoners when I came here. I'd say, "I'll leave you now...." And, "Where is it at?" Hmm—it still came out English twang, so I quit.

And of course, I married into a Polish family. Now, I tried to learn Polish. Well, that really cracked up my Polish family. Not my faltering attempts at Polish. But the fact that I was speaking Polish with an English accent apparently was very funny.

So I said to myself, "Before I learn Polish, I'll have to learn to speak English a little bit." Because I do fracture the Queen's English, I know I do. I mean, don't think all English people talk like me, for God's sake. I mean, in fact, they don't talk that fast. Can you follow me? (*Every word.*)

My Polish father-in-law, he'd say, "Hilda, you nice woman"—like broken English—"you nice woman, but you talk too fast, too fast." But you know—when I'm excited, when I'm happy, when I'm anything—except sad....

I can be quiet. Now, don't laugh! I can be quiet, really. And I can be a good listener on occasions. I used to visit the sick when I was younger, and sit by many a bedside of a person that was dying. They used to think I belonged to some group or organization—religious group. I did it on my own. And I'd sit for hours listening to their secrets and their little admissions—just sit there listening to them, while they died. So I can be quiet. But it's—not very easy.

[Hilda shows a photo of her husband Henry, and one of herself.] It just shows you what the ravages of time can do to a person! (*I don't know—time wasn't too hard on you.*) He's mostly bald now. He's got a pot belly—although, I guess it's gone now. I mean, he lost about 25 pounds. But he's still the soldier boy I married. He's still the soldier boy. He'll never be nothing else to me....

(*Now, when were those two photographs taken?*) 1945. (*Just before you were married?*) I'll tell you. I met Henry—oh, that's a long story—you haven't got all day. Finally when I met Henry—he knew me a long time. He'd been [following] me for months. I didn't know. But he wanted to meet this English girl who was wandering through his life. And he got to meet me at a show.

The first time that he got to talk to me, he asked me for a date and I said, "Well, I can't come with you because I've got an appointment with a photographer." And I think he thought I was—you know, pushing him off. So just to show him that I really wasn't doing that I said, "Come with me, Henry." And when I had the photograph taken, they took Henry as well, at the same time. But that was our first date, really. I mean, it wasn't a date, because I'd already had an appointment with a photographer. But that was the first time. But that was really funny the way Henry met me.

(*So you have no regrets that you spent the last almost forty-five years here in Cape Breton.*) Not one day of it, no. I had a hard time here, of course I did, after the war. It wasn't like it is today, now. For instance, those houses going up there. We never thought we'd live to see the day that houses would come up here. We were on this hill all by ourselves. Now, I'm watching them. The way they bring up complete sides of houses, and clap them together with—I don't know—staples or glue. I mean, a few days there's a house. But we did it all, all plank by plank, board by board, nail by nail. And it took us longer.

(*You say "we." Did you participate in building your home?*) Oh, yes.

Hilda Tipper and Henry Mleczko in England during World War Two

Of course I did. I learned how to shingle, and how to saw on the line. And I learned how to paint without covering myself with paint. When I came from England, I didn't know a shingle from a nail from a 2-by-4, but I'm telling you, I soon learned.... We built on a shoestring, because we didn't have much money. Henry left [England]—we were married in 1945. And he came over in December—back home [to Cape Breton]—December 1945. We were only married a little time. And then I followed him in a war brides' boat, April 1946. So in that time, we didn't have much time to save money. I was getting a Canadian allowance—army allowance. I was working in a factory at the same time. So I never touched the army allowance, only to cash it and put it in the bank. So that helped start our home.

Now, we knew we'd have to do it ourselves—with the help of a few kind neighbours. And his brother helped him, in between shifts in the pit. This was all going on while the men were working hard in the pit—eight hours a day. Come home and have their supper. And then have a little rest. Instead of put their feet up and drink a six-pack of beer watching television—none of that.

You see this road? You see it coming all the way up from there. Right from the corner of the road here to this house, we built our own—dug for our own water line—nine hundred feet.

They were just in shifts then [in the mines]. They had dayshift, nightshift, backshift. Any shift that they were on, they'd come home, have a

273

bite to eat. A little nap in the chair maybe a half hour. And they'd be out in there. My Henry went to bed, more times and enough, with mud still clinging to his hair and his ears, from the ditch he was digging in, because he was too tired to wash himself properly....

When I was in England, Henry would tell me about the place where he wanted to build the house—which was here. He wanted to be next to his parents. And it was still for sale when we came here. But they upped the price, double. When they knew we were going to buy it. But would you believe, it was still only three hundred dollars for two acres. See, no water.

Well, people were coming up to us, when we started putting the stakes in to build. Oh, I loved that day. I sat in the middle of my magical stakes, and I planned where all my rooms would go.... So people would say, "Henry's a nice fellow and you're a good woman, but you're crazy building up here. It's silly. You'll never get nothing to grow. It's awful up here." My husband's had better stuff in that garden—he's coaxed it and pleaded with it—he's got a green thumb, you know. And people now— especially in the summer—they'll come up and ask us if we'll sell our land. "Oh, it's beautiful up here. We'd love to live up here."

See the difference? When I first came here, we were crazy building up here. But Henry had to move rocks and boulders and trees and shrubs— great big trees. And [as] I said, all that from when he was working in the pit. In fact, when we built our home, he just built the foundation—he dug the foundation, where the box had to go. And left in the middle all still humped up, you know. It wasn't levelled off.... We just did around like that, where the box for pouring the cement had to go. And for years after- wards, when he had the time and the energy, and he wasn't working, he'd open the cellar window and do a bit of digging, and throw the stuff out the window. Until he got the [basement] floor all flat. And then got it cemented.

No, everything we did was the hard way.... There's not enough money in the world to buy the memories in these walls. I'd never, never part with it. As long as I've got the strength to maintain it adequately, I'm going to live here. Even if my husband died—God forbid—but if he was to go be- fore me, I'd still try to keep this house up. Because I love it. It's my home, it's my castle—it's all we own. I mean, everything we own is under this roof. It's ours. And like I said, every nail, every board, every splinter and cobweb—we did it ourselves. Everything.

Now, when I was putting in the basement, helping build the basement, I was pregnant. I didn't know it at the time, but I was. I was wanting a baby so bad in England. And Henry said, "No. The rationing here and every- thing...." Still on starvation rations. So we put it off until I came to Canada. But I wouldn't put it off any longer. And I was only here about a month. I knew—well, I missed a period—in those days you had to go three months before they were reasonably sure that you were pregnant. Today, well, five minutes after they tell you you're okay—urine tests or whatever.

Anyway, I wasn't sure that I was pregnant, but I was. And I worked hard with the men, shovelling—you know, getting the wheelbarrows, and running around on our little platform we got made there, and tipping the cement in. We didn't have these great big cement mixers. We could have had them, but it was the money, see. We were working on a shoestring. And I was working hard with the men, tipping the cement in with the wheelbarrow and everything.

And then I miscarried the baby—which I didn't know I was carrying at the time. But that's what happened then. So I mean, it was, you know, pretty tough....

The other thing—I wanted a bungalow. And Henry stuck out for me. He said, "No, I want a house where you go to sleep upstairs." But I still wish we had bungalow, especially now we're getting older. But that's all right, I can still climb stairs, I can still walk around good. I have an exercise bike; I use that. And I've got a rowing machine, I use that. And I walk everywhere I possibly can.

I always walk to town. Unless it's dark. And then I don't walk because I'm scared, you know. All kind of screwballs around now. They crawl from under rocks at night and [Hilda claps her hands!] I've lost my nerve. That's funny, too. In the war, I'd walk home from a show—maybe there'd be a raid. And after the raid I'd pick my way around the rubble and the devastation, stepping over unexploded bombs where I could have had my leg blown off—thinking nothing of that. Wasn't even scared. But today, I'm more scared now. I would never walk home from, say, the Savoy Theatre—I was there last night—to home. I'd never do it. I'd be too frightened.

It's not that I think I'm so beautiful. It's just that these people—whatever they are—you know, they'd slit your throat for fifty cents, you know. They must support their habits.

(*Have you actually had an encounter like that or is it just that you know that these things can happen?*) Oh, no. Although once—just once—I was coming from the show. It was when they had—the taxi stand was still there at the post office, and they used to operate at night. They don't do that now. They quit about five o'clock; you'd never get a taxi now. And I was standing waiting for a taxi to come—it was quite late. And these kids—they seemed up in their teens—they got in a circle. And they were sort of dancing around me—their eyes were right glassy. They didn't touch me. But I had a feeling, "Oh, my God." And the taxi driver drove up, and he knew me well. And he came straight up to me—Hector Gillard—I don't know if you know him. He's an old man now; he's quit. And he said,

"Come on, Mrs., jump in." And when I got in the back seat, I said, "Oh, my God. I don't know if I was supposed to be frightened at that. But," I said, "it got me, kind of struck a nerve—something weird about that." "Oh," he said, "they're on something." They didn't hurt me, they didn't touch me. They just—they were chanting, and they held hands, and they did a circle around me, and they were chanting, like witches. Oh, geez.

I don't know if that was an encounter or not. It wasn't very pleasant, because if he hadn't come when he did, maybe—I don't know what would have happened. But then again, maybe they'd have run away.

(*But in England during the war, you don't think you were feeling much of what you would call fear.*) Honey, when the war was on you didn't have time to be frightened. It happened so sudden. You were only glad to get a few hours rest between each bombing raid. If you could only have a little bit of rest, that's all you asked for. And then you'd sleep, it's kind of a desperate sleep; you'd go, sort of almost drugged sleep. And then you'd wake up to face another day, and another bombing. And hopefully you'd see the end of that day.

Some of my friends didn't. Like I said, I must have had a charmed life. God was intending me for other things. But of course, I know now—I'm here, aren't I? But God was good to me. As I said, I'm not as religious as I should be. In fact, I don't attend church regularly. But God knows I believe in him and I love him, and I thank him every day of my life, for being right here, now, talking to you. It's only for his grace, I wouldn't be doing that, I know.

I'm telling you, there's so many miracles that I've seen in that war, you'd never believe. I wouldn't even try and tell you. (*Well, try and tell me.*) There's no words—you just can't.... (*What do you mean by miracle?*) Well now, I'll tell you, for instance.... This is just a little thing. I was coming home from a show, and sirens went. And you could see the ack-ack guns started up—blue sparks flying down as the shells kept hitting the sidewalk. And you could see the searchlights trying to catch the bombers. And you could see the bombers—waves of bombers. And of course they'd fire up at the bombers and try and bring them down. But it's harder to fire up at something than down. So we used to get the worst of it. They just dropped their bombs on us, clobbered the poor guys with their guns and silenced them, and that was it.

Well, I was on a piece of ground that had been once a housing development, and it had been bombed. And they'd razed it to the ground, they'd made it flat again, because it was no use, it was only rubble. And there was no protection for me at all. It's in the summer, and I had a thin summer dress on, and sandals—no tin hat. Just carrying my gas mask with me, which you always did—you had to do that—it was regulations. And I didn't know where I could run. Because when the sirens went—especially when you saw it was action, you saw the planes coming over—you were always told to dive under something, get under shelter, under cover. There was no air-raid shelter there. There were plenty of them around, but not there, because they'd just razed it all around. So I didn't know what to do.

So I saw this one brick wall—a retaining wall that had been left standing—maybe about three or four feet high—from a building. They hadn't knocked it down for some reason. So what did I do but I rolled right close up to that wall. And I was on my knees, and my chin like that. And I was scraping the dirt like this, trying to make a sort of a shallow trench so I could dig myself in. Because the planes were coming closer, and I could hear the shrapnel, like rain, coming down....

So what I did, I lay there, close to that brick wall. And I just covered my hands on my head. And I dug my knees in. And I prayed. And I didn't pray, holy, quietly—I screamed from the guts, "God Almighty, don't let me die! Please, don't let me die, God! I want to see another day." And I was like that. I kept on screaming to myself. Nobody hearing me, only the Lord himself. And then the bombers went away. So I got up quick and I ran. And I ran and ran until I saw a house. I knocked there. Because we were used to it in those days. I just fell through the door and I said, "Please can I stay until the raid's over?" Well of course, they weren't going to say, "No, go home."

Well, the next day—I got to thinking about it. And the next day—I was curious, so I retraced my steps to this very place where I lay. Now there on the wall was the shrapnel pockmarks where the shrapnel had hit the wall, the brick wall, and gouged holes in it. You could almost see the shape of my body. And also you could see where I dug my knees, and put my face in it. You could see the shape of a body had been lying there. Now why wasn't I hit? Why wasn't I hit? There was no reason on earth why I shouldn't have been. And that's something that shook me. It was like God himself saying, "You're not ready. I'm not letting you go yet."

277

And then another one. There was a raid on. And I was hoping I'd get home. Because even when the raids went on, the buses would still try to run, to get people home. Whatever they could do, until the roads started getting blown up. They'd help, you know. A lot of unsung heroes in the war—people you'd never expect. So I was standing underneath an alcove kind of a place, right close to where the bus stop was—right opposite, but I was in a little sheltered place. And I heard a girl holler to me, "Come on over here, Hilda"—where there's more shelter, it's bigger—you know, more deep, depth to it. She's right across the road—it was a big road, Birmingham. And she beckoned me over. So I ran. But as I ran, I heard a bomb coming down.

Now, when you hear the whistle of a bomb, you always automatically hunch your shoulders and pull in your neck and say, "This might be for me." So I dove in the shelter where this girl was. But as I dove I looked back, to see the bomb explode right on the place where I'd been, just a minute, a few seconds, before. I tell you, that shook me. That shook me. Because it was only seconds. I would have been dead....

(*Did you tell me on the phone that it was the war that really made you believe in God, more so than before?*) Yes. I'm not an atheist, if that's what you mean. No. When I was a little girl, my mother taught me about Jesus, the baby in the manger, and Jesus died for us on the cross. I took that literally. I took God for granted. When I was a little kid, I would pray to God, "Oh please, God, let me...have enough money so I could go to the matinee"—silly things. Not emergencies. I was praying to God almost like as if he was Santa Claus.

But when I went into that war, I was barely twenty-one. I was okay. I was okay—decent, respectable person, I think. But I was sort of, little giddy—everything was "Ha, ha" fun. Well, I still have got a sense of humour, as you can see. I mean, I'd never lose that, or else I'll be dead. But I couldn't see the serious side of things. And I couldn't for the life of me understand why people were miserable and.... I was never going to get sick, and I was never going to get—without food or hungry. I was never going to get sorry. And I was never going to get old. I was never going to get gray hairs. Oh, the wisdom of youth!

So, when the war started, I just thought, well—I can always remember the day the war started. I know exactly where I was, I know my reactions, and I know what I said. Just like as if it was now. But I thought, "Well, it's going to be over in a couple of weeks, you know. I mean, the Germans— what are they? And then we'll pick up the threads where we left, and go on." But you know what? You didn't do that. Nobody. Everybody who got touched with that war was never the same again. And the world was never the same again. You know. Maybe people today, the younger ones, don't know that. But it did something—it's left scars, and it taught lessons, and it did things to people. It gave you something to think about.

And so therefore, what it did make you think about, I think, is that fact that there's a God in heaven, and he spared my life, and I'm thankful to him the rest of my life. And I will be, forever thankful, every day I live. Every day to me, when I get up, is like a little present from God. That's for me to do with whatever I wish. It's mine. I can fritter it away. I can fling it up the wall and go to sleep and forget it, and wake up the next day and say, "That's one day I didn't have to do anything with." I can do all of those things. Or else I can make it really count. And I do.

Now, I'm only a simple woman. I'm an old lady. I don't go anywhere very much—about as far as here to Sydney and back. But I never waste a day. If it's only to do this: Now, I'll be going on the street, and I'll see somebody—because we live in a very friendly area—I'll see somebody a little bit down. I don't know her. And I'll say, "Gee, that coat looks nice on you. It matches the colour of your eyes." Or, "I like your hairdo." I don't know him from a hole in the wall. That person goes off smiling. For all I know, that one person could have been contemplating suicide. Maybe they were that low they thought, "Nobody gives a damn for me—what's the use?" It didn't cost me anything to say that. And it made me feel good. Because, you know what? It came from the heart. I believe that. I really do. I give a lot of myself like that, and it doesn't cost me anything....

I know I sound gabby to you.... But I like it—I like to do those things. Because God is good to me. And I feel I owe him. Well, we all do. But I feel I owe God extra. Because I saw so much there, so many people—well, my own grandfather was blown to bits in the war. As I say, I lost a boy friend in the war. That's why I'm here. Else I'd be in England now, married over there. So many people I loved weren't spared. And yet I was. And I wasn't particularly good. In a sense, I mean—I didn't attend church regularly or pay dues to the church, I didn't pray on my knees every night. I do now, though. I do now. I go on my knees to God, and in the morning I ask him for his help. And I always ask him to forgive me, if I've said something I shouldn't say, or offended anybody. And I always tell him, "You know that anyway." You can't keep anything from God; he knows everything.

And that's what I said—from that war, there developed another Hilda, that might not have developed otherwise. Maybe I would have. Maybe I'd have gone on to maturity in peacetime, and I might have been even better than I am today. But I'm not knocking where I am, because I'm enjoying it. As long as people don't find me offensive. And I don't think they do. I know I talk a lot. But I never had anybody say, "Shut up!"

See, when you get older.... I often say this to young people. I even say it to my nephew, without meaning any offense. They love one another; it's a perfect marriage. And I said, "Yes," I said, "you love one another very much, and it's obvious. But," I said, "you don't love one another as much as you will when you get older." And he said, "That's impossible." I said, "No, it isn't." I said, "As you get older, the love deepens. It's not quite the same. You don't jump in bed every night and make love, for one thing." Pardon me for being blunt. But I mean, it's a different kind of a love. It's a different kind of a love. It's—togetherness. Now, my husband'll come along from somewhere, and he'll sit in that chair for a little while, and I'm watching television. I say, "Hi, Hon, want a cup of coffee?" "Yeah"—he'll have a cup of coffee. And he'll say, "Well, I'm going to bed." Well, he goes to bed sometimes 9:30 or 10:00. And I'll stay up and watch "The National." Now, he's gone. But he hasn't—he's upstairs, he's in the house, he's with me. So, you see, I don't need for him to continually keep saying, "I love you, Darling," and bring me flowers and stuff. We're together. And we know one another's thoughts.

(*I want to take you back to 1946. I want to know what you thought you were coming to—what you thought Glace Bay and Cape Breton were going to be like.*) Oh. Well, the first thing, when we were on the boat—this is awful. Some man had come in, and he was asking us—it was a lecture, and we were all sitting around in a great big pile. And he was asking us what parts of Canada we were going to. He said, "I've been all over Canada, so I can tell you the general area." And he was asking this one and this one. And he said to me, "And what part of Canada are you coming to?" I said, "Glace Bay." He said, "Ooo, that's the garbage dump of Canada." Well, you imagine how I felt. You imagine how I felt, in the middle of the ocean, and that's what he said to me....

And I was in a store—oh, I couldn't get used to the fact you could go in a store and buy something without [rationing] coupons. And the food— I knew I'd come to a land of plenty. And then I was in—I think it was old Shore's store—it's gone now. One of the Jews' store—Shore. I was in there, waiting my turn. I always got to kind of gingerly ask, "Could I have a pan of sausages, please?" Like as if I got to whisper, you know. And there was one woman talking to another woman. And they were displeased over the cut of a roast of beef they had. They were complaining about the colour of it or the shape.

And it took me all my energy and all my will power not to turn around and say to them—I was wanting to tell them, "How would you like, instead of that roast, to eat cat meat? Or cow's offal? And stand in line for one egg, or an ounce of cheese. How would you like that?" But I didn't say it. Because I like Cape Bretoners; they've been good to me. And they didn't know—they didn't know what was going on [in England, during the war]. But I did. I did. And that really—to hear them going on about the meat in the store—a piece of meat that I hadn't seen the size of for five or six years. It really got to me. Little things like that, you know.

It's like—something like the rationing. I heard once—and this was in the war—everything was rationed, but eggs were like gold. They were a very scarce commodity. And I remember it went around that this grocer had one box of eggs for sale, and one [to] a customer. Can you imagine? One egg a customer. So I went and stood in line, waiting my turn to get my egg. Fantasizing whether I'd have it fried or boiled or poached. I couldn't wait to lift that first delicious forkful to my mouth. Fantasizing, just like Disneyland. Well when I got my egg, it was a brown-shelled variety. And I looked at it lovingly, wishing I could even eat the shell.

So, I had a little brown paper bag at my side, and I got on the bus, had to go home. I went a bus ride to get my egg. And a very stout lady got on the bus, and went to sit down beside me. And the bus gave a lurch, and she sat right on my egg—squashed it. And there I watched this ooze out of the brown paper bag. Well, you'd never believe my feelings. You know, I grieved over that egg for months.

Now, it was only an egg. But to me it was a calamity. We could stand bombs and we could stand being kept awake at night and fighting incendiaries. But when it came to food, we were very, very vulnerable. Oh, I'm telling you—wooo! We used to have all the recipes that we could think of, to concoct our little rations, to make it a little bit more delectable, a little more tasty—putting some spice in it. I mean, they were pitiful rations, pitiful. One ounce of butter, and two ounces....

Henry said to me, during the war—he was going to take me out to go to the show or something. I was having my supper. So he said to me, "Is that your supper?" I said, "Yeah." He said, "Well, where's your meat ration, then?" And I moved a pile of mashed potatoes and a spoonful of peas, and there it was, all one ounce of it! Well, he looked, and he couldn't believe—he'd seen a real civilian's meal at last. He couldn't believe it.

Well, he worked in the kitchen. So every time he came to my house after that, he was definitely overweight. He looked it, anyway. He looked like a pregnant kangaroo. He'd got his battle dress buttoned up. And inside—he opened it onto the table, and the delectable things that fell out! Oh, the goodies we hadn't seen for years! And he used to bring them regularly. And he never got squealed on because the head cook was doing the same thing. So they didn't squeal on one another. Luckily he was never found out. Thank God, because what he did to our taste buds was marvellous. But see, we were being served by the courtesy of the Canadian army. You know, they didn't even know....

281

(Back to Glace Bay—did you know you were coming to a mining town, and did you know that Henry was a miner?) I knew—see, they promised him that when he came back from the war, that he'd have a job in the pit. So he knew he was coming back to that. So I knew that I was marrying a miner, yeah.

(Had you had any experience of mining life in the town you came from?) No, not a bit, no, no, no. And I'm telling you, the first time I heard the pit's whistle, summoning the men to work, I panicked. My hair stood on end. I thought it was a siren for the raids. I was living at my father-in-law's place then. I dived underneath the sofa. And he didn't laugh at me. He was a good man. He got me out, and very kindly and very gently he told me that there was nothing to fear. He said that it was just the pit calling the men to work. But he said they did have—sometimes they had tragedies at Caledonia pit—that was the pit down there—years ago. And he started telling me some of the stories. And of course, it sort of got stuck in my mind. Especially the song my mother used to sing when we were kids, "Don't go down in the mine, Dad." It's an old song she used to sing, and make the hair stand on our heads....

Henry's been in lots of accidents. Yes, and it's only since he's been on pension that I've heard some of them. Pretty hair-raising thing, I'm telling you. He used to cover up from me. See, he'd go to Outpatients. Or he could have something covered up. He wouldn't tell me. Like I remember he came in once—the only time he couldn't cover it up—he came to the door like a white-turbaned Indian. He had a great big bandage around his head. And I went as white as the bandages. "Not to worry," he said, "not to worry. It's only a scratch." That scratch was caused by a coupling link that flew off an air hose at full pressure, and Henry was hit between the eyes, right on the bridge of his nose. Now if it'd gone either way, he'd have had an eye knocked out. He was very lucky. So afterwards—there was no damage done to his head. He said he had hard bones.

And afterwards, he was shaving himself one day, and he was doing this and doing this. He said, "I'm going to have this dumb mark erased"— the mark from where he'd been hit. Now, all the miners, when they get cuts, when they heal they have tattoo marks on them. Because the coal dust goes in the cuts, and it seals up—it's like a tattoo. Well, I was wondering why all the fuss, because he had had those marks all over his body, more or less. So I said, "Well, why are you worried about it, Henry?" He said, "Look." He said, "I'm branded. It's two letters—an 'I' and a 'T.'" Well when I looked, there it was, a complete "I" and a "T." So he said, "I'm going back and have it opened and cleaned out."

So he went back to Dr. Green. And he opened it up and cleaned it out, and Henry went happy home. But when it healed, there was the "I-T"

282

again on his head. He said, "It's still there. I'm going back to the doctor again." Went back to Dr. Green again, and he did the same thing. Took the stitches out, and scrubbed at him real hard. And he went home. Healed again. And it was still there. So he went back to the doctor the third time. When Dr. Green saw him walking in the door he said, "Oh, no, not you!" He said, "Henry, I've done all I can. Now," he said, "you live with 'I-T.' And be thankful there's not an 'S-H' in front of it!" That's the truth—God's truth—that's what the man said.

So I mean, that was only a little thing. But his brother got buried under a pile of stone and coal. They wrapped the wires to stop the rake—that's the train—the rake—pit term for train. They knew that there had been a man trapped under coal, on the coal floor. And of course Henry ran, and he saw his brother's squashed lunch can and his pit cap, and he knew it was his brother.

So he dug and he dug and he dug. And he held most of the weight—while they were scratching their heads and saying, "How are we going to take him out?"—he sort of burrowed underneath and took the weight of a big slab of stone that was digging into him here, and took the weight on his own back. Because he said that the hardest thing he ever had to do was go and tell his sister-in-law—because he had to take Eddie's clothes home—the hardest thing he ever had to do was to tell his sister-in-law. Because she thought Henry was telling her that her husband was dead. But he wasn't, he was injured. Ooo, poor man.... But he was all right.

But anyway, that night when Henry came home, I put my arms around him in bed like I always did. And he moved away from me. I asked him if he was mad or something. He said, "No." I said, "Well, what's wrong?" "Well, I'll show you, but it's not very nice." He took his pyjama top off, and he showed me his back. And where the rocks had ground into him, it was like huge tiger claws all down his back, where he'd taken this weight of the rock off his brother. He's still got those scars today. But when they were fresh you could have played Oughts and Crosses [X's and O's] on them.

And then another time he said, a fellow worker got caught—his pants leg, or part of his clothing, was caught in the wheel, the wheel used for hoisting the cage to the top. The cage was the elevator that took the men from the deeps up to the top. And he got caught—it was working. And by the time they stopped it, it had ground into his leg and ground it to bits.

And he's screaming, "Cut it off! Cut it off!" And by the time a work-mate got the axe and severed it with one blow, it was only hanging on by a strip of flesh.

But you see—the next day they had to go to work just as if nothing had happened. They were like soldiers....

283

They had a rule, to say, "Don't ever get out of the rake"—the train—until it came to a full stop. Because sometimes it would get an extra surge in power. And if you happened to be standing in front of that rake, you'd go underneath the wheels, or on the side.

And Henry was with a young fellow—he hadn't been married very long. And he was in an all-fired hurry to get out of the rake. And he jumped out before it stopped, and it spurted up again. And Henry was holding onto his jacket saying, "No!" And he was left holding his jacket when he saw his mate's body go under the wheels until it was ground up like hamburger. And that's when he got all upset. He came home and he kept saying to me, "If only I didn't see him." He was walking the floor all night. "If only I didn't see him. If only I didn't see him." He never ate. But the next shift, he's down there again, walking over the same spot where it happened. He had to go to work.

Like I said, like in the war....

My own father-in-law, God rest his soul—he was a great man. He wouldn't let anybody talk about me. He said I was all right. And when I walked in their house, even if they could only speak a few words of English, they'd switch from Polish and talk in English so that I'd feel good. And I thought that was very nice of them....

And my father-in-law—I never knew till after he died, God love him, how much he did love me. But my mother-in-law said, "He loved you as much as his own daughter...."

Well, I'll tell you. Henry went over there one day. And I was there. And he spoke Polish to his father, and I knew he was talking about me. And I thought, "Well, why is he doing that?" Because he never used to. And Dad said something back to him in Polish, and Henry went red and swallowed, and walked out. So a long time afterwards I asked Mama. I said, "Mama, what did Henry say to Papa?" It was long after he was dead even. "When he walked in, he said something about me and you all laughed at that." She said, "Oh, I'll tell you. It wasn't nothing," she said. "He walked in and said, it's a good thing he had a cast-iron stomach because your cooking was awful. You forgot to put the yeast in the bread, and the cookies were like rocks, he had to pretend he liked them." He was going on about my cooking. And what chance did I have to learn cooking in a land that was bombarded all the time? And the rations, you weren't going to use them for experimenting with, I'm telling you. So he went on and on and on. And Papa said to him, "You shut up talking about Hilda like that to me. For a woman like that, you should go on your knees." That's the words he said. And I never knew he said it. He said it in Polish. He really liked me. He really did....

He showed me where the best cranberries were and the best mushrooms, and went blueberry picking with him. He was a great man. A miner, too, of course.

When I was getting married to Henry, we had six months waiting period—unless you happened to be very pregnant, and then of course, they wanted you to get married. Of course, I wasn't.... We had six months wait. And in that six months time, I can honestly say that it was probably the worst time of my life for decisions. Here I was, weighing my dilemma—love for the man, and love for my country. You know, even today—it's a very painful thing to go through. And to this day I'm still more or less split down the middle. I have two loyalties. I still love England. And I love this country. It's a beautiful, magnificent country. But I had this feeling, well, if I get married to Henry, I'll have to leave the country I love. And the very thought of it was tearing the heart out of me. I was very English, very English. I thought there was no place on earth like England.

So, we talked about it. And Henry even said, "Well," he said, "if I had my way, I'd like to have a chicken farm." He'd love to raise chickens and sell eggs.... But he said, "I know I won't be able to. So," he said, "I'll be in the pit, because Dad knows he can get me a job." So I knew I was marrying a coal miner. I knew.

But he said to me, "Well," he said, "I've got a piece of land all picked out, where I'd like to take you. And," he said, "I'll promise you two things"—and he kept his promise—"while I've got these two hands, you'll never go hungry. And I'll build you a house where you'll see the sea from every window." Can't get a man better than that. He kept his promise.

ALSO AVAILABLE FROM
Breton Books & Music